Diverging Approaches of Political Islamic Thought in Iran since the 1960s

Seyed Mohammad Lolaki

Diverging Approaches of Political Islamic Thought in Iran since the 1960s

palgrave
macmillan

Seyed Mohammad Lolaki
Anglican Action, Te Ara Hou Village
Centre for Social Justice
Hamilton, New Zealand

ISBN 978-981-15-0480-8   ISBN 978-981-15-0478-5   (eBook)
https://doi.org/10.1007/978-981-15-0478-5

This Palgrave Macmillan imprint is published by the registered company Springer Nature
Singapore Pte Ltd.
The registered company address is: 152 Beach Road, #21-01/04 Gateway East, Singapore
189721, Singapore

Dedicated to my beloved mother and father, who taught me everything I know.

PREFACE

Political Islam is one of the most important factors in Muslim societies. Political Islam based on Shia ideas and Iranian identity has governed Iran since the 1979 revolution. The successes and failures of this model have made a huge impact on both Iranian society and Political Islam across the Muslim world. The purpose of this book is to examine and elucidate the processes that contributed to the emergence and establishment of Political Islam in Iran and its contemporary challenges. Towards this end, I have endeavoured to study the intellectual processes of formation and the conundrums of Political Islam in Iran, and to explicate and clarify both the possibilities and limitations.

Hamilton, New Zealand   Seyed Mohammad Lolaki

ACKNOWLEDGEMENTS

I would like to express my utmost appreciation to all who supported me through this literary journey, without the presence of which this volume could not have come to fruition. This book was derived from a thesis which was written between the years 2012 and 2017 in the department of Political Science and Public Policy at the University of Waikato, New Zealand. During this time I was under the supervision of Professor Dov Bing and Professor Douglas Pratt. I would like to extend my deepest gratitude and thanks to them both. Professor Pratt especially read through every single chapter and gave me unmatchable advice and guidance for which I am profoundly grateful.

I would also like to extend my thanks to Professor Davood Feirahi from the University of Tehran for kindly reading through the book comprehensively before final publication and giving me invaluable constructive advice and abundant guidance. Many thanks to Dr. Naser Ghobadzadeh from the Australian Catholic University for also reading through the entire text with supportive publication advice.

I would like to extend my thanks to Abdullah Drury, Sajad Montazer Hojjat, Handren Delan and Ali Tavakol for giving me their invaluable support throughout this process.

Many thanks also to Professor Seyyed Sadegh Haghighat, Associate Professor Seyyed Ali Mir-Mousavi from Mofid University, Associate Professor Seyyed Mohammad Ali Hosainizadah from Shahid Beheshti University and Masoud Pedram, Iranian researcher. They all read the initial proposal and gave me their valuable constructive opinions on the various ideas articulated.

I am grateful to Dr. Ehsan Shariati, Dr. Sousan Shariati and Dr. Mohammad Navid Bazargan for their advice, friendly chats and insights into the private lives of their respective (and respected) fathers. This proved to be pivotal in constructing the clearest and most organic portrayal of their biographies and visions.

A massive thank you to the anonymous peer reviewers whose comments aided the betterment of the text itself.

Last but certainly not least, I would like to offer my endless gratitude and love to my wife and daughter for their unwavering support and kindness throughout these years. Thank you for putting up with the long days spent furiously typing away on the computer and the days in which I would be lost reading behind my colossal stacks of books. Without you two I would not be half the person I am today, and for that I am eternally grateful.

ABOUT THE BOOK

In this book, I argue that Political Islam in the Iranian context evolved into three main schools of thought during the 1960s and 1970s: jurisprudential Islam led by Ayatollah Khomeini, Leftist Islam led by Shariati and Liberal Islam led by Bazargan. Despite the fact that all schools seek an Islamic state, their chosen methods and philosophical approaches diverge considerably. The synthesis of these three contrasting sociopolitical views is structured here to provide a coherent interpretation by means of ongoing comparison. This tactic has so far not been presented within the field of academic studies in terms of Political Islam.

Furthermore, this book provides a critical analysis of the aforementioned 'Political Islam' schools in Iran, their similarities and differences, their relative success or failure, their contribution to the revolution of 1979 and how they have evolved from the pre-Revolution era to the present. It also presents the philosophical framework with regard to the politicisation of religion amongst the leading people of each school, and how this confronted the secular regime of the Shah.

CONTENTS

ABOUT THE AUTHOR

Seyed Mohammad Lolaki is a researcher who received his PhD in Political Science and Public Policy from the University of Waikato in September 2017. He obtained his Master's degree in Political Science from Mofid University of Qom in Iran in 2005. His research interests include political and social Islam, modernist discourse and democracy in the Middle East.

LIST OF TABLES

PART I

Introduction

CHAPTER 1

The Quest for Power in Iran: Principle Questions and Methodology

OF MICE AND MEN

This book provides a critical analysis of three major Iranian thinkers of the mid-twentieth century, namely Ayatollah Sayyid Ruhollah Musavi Khomeini, Ali Shariati and Mehdi Bazargan.[1] Each one was a leading proponent of what is known as 'Political Islam' during the 1960s and 1970s, in the critical lead-up to the Iranian Revolution (1979). This study sheds light on the implications for Iranian society of their thought, and in terms of the evolution of their ideas from post-revolutionary Iran to the present day. Their key texts and conceptualisations of Political Islam will be examined in this study and compared in order to demonstrate the core arguments advanced in relation to normative objectives.

The term 'Political Islam' in Iran refers to the political groups and associations which sought the establishment and continuity of an Islamic government in Iran. The main theme of the discourse around Political Islam is its emphasis on the continuing central relevance of Islam and its holy texts to the way modern societies operate and how they should operate. Arguments, theory and methodology are premised on the notion that the best, most moral/ethical society and polity is one in which politics and political discourse are inextricably intertwined with elements of religion.

---

[1] Full names are used here, thereafter only last names will be referred to throughout this book.

© The Author(s) 2020
S. M. Lolaki, *Diverging Approaches of Political Islamic Thought in Iran since the 1960s*,
https://doi.org/10.1007/978-981-15-0478-5_1

Advocates for Political Islam all share a belief that divine revelation is enshrined in the Qur'an and the Hadith, and that these provide an essential directive on how to live one's life and organise society. Intellectuals and politicians of this particular tradition have therefore advanced and utilised concepts which are closely indexed to the Islamic religion and its holy texts. The revival and the relevance of religious texts and their applicability to the needs and problems of modern or contemporary societies have been central themes in debates about contemporary Political Islam in Iran and indeed, throughout the Islamic world.

The ultimate goal of Political Islam is the creation of a community governed according to the principles of Islam. To achieve its goals, Political Islam seeks power to reorient society on a religious basis. Proponents view Islam as a comprehensive ideology that encompasses temporal and spiritual ends. Political Islamic discourse strongly critiques those who draw a line between religion and politics—'secularists' in its own terminology. One of the pillars of Western liberal democracy—the division between 'church and state'—is therefore rejected outright. Religion and politics are said to be intimately and irreducibly intertwined.

Nonetheless, Political Islam, as a relatively recent phenomenon, has also been perceived as a product of Western modernity, something that has had a pervasive influence on many Muslim countries. This is because Political Islam attempts to combine, selectively, positive elements of Western modernity with certain traditions present in Islamic or Muslim societies (Hosainizadeh 2007, p. 18). Much of the mainstream discourse in Political Islam does not reject modernity as such, but rather seeks to fuse aspects of it with traditions mainly originating in religious texts. However, the philosophical approach of Political Islam does reject certain dimensions of Western secular modernity. Some thinkers within Political Islam consider Western modernity to be a decayed version of a true or healthy society. To save society from such moral decline, Political Islam seeks to reinterpret religious traditions in order to reinfuse society with a moral bearing and thereby reinvigorate normative traditions.

The politicisation of religion has, over the course of time, evolved into different schools of thought. Despite the fact that all schools seek an Islamic state, their chosen methods and philosophical approaches diverge. Over the 1960s and 1970s, Political Islam evolved into three main schools of thought in Iran: Liberal Islam led by Bazargan, Leftist Islam led by Shariati and Jurisprudential Islam led by Khomeini (Hosainizadeh 2007, p. 195). Opponents of the royal Pahlavi regime made an attempt to politicise religion and came up with an alternative project which reflected certain unique characteristics of Shia Islam. These opponents of the secular Shah were of the view that secular ideologies had failed Iranian society and their own project was seen as a viable, indeed essential, alternative that would take into account these unique Iranian cultural characteristics. The peculiar social and political conditions enabled Political Islam to come to the forefront of the struggle against the secular vision of the Pahlavi regime (1925–1979).

Religion was promoted as being able to play a more effective and influential role given Iranian cultural characteristics. As a consequence, elements of the cultural milieu of Iran and religious undercurrents were able to gain a dominant voice in critiques of the social crisis and economic transformation which engulfed the country during the 1960s and 1970s. This politicisation of religion manifested itself in popular discourse in a variety of ways. Differences emerged with respect to the interpretation and use of Islam in addressing the chronic issues that beset Iranian society. More specifically, the differences in emphasis of the participants in this discourse can be summarised broadly within the tripartite typology of the legalistic Islam championed by Khomeini, the politically left-wing interpretation of Islam predicated on the scholarship of Shariati, and the reform-orientated Islam based on the ideas of Bazargan and those around him.

This book provides an analysis of these three broad schools of thought. Its own contribution to scholarship on contemporary Iran lies in its analytical approach contrasting the ideas of the main exponents of the three schools, identifying their similarities and differences, investigating their relative success or failure, and their influence or relevance, to the present. The importance of this analysis is that it offers a coherent textual treatment of the ideological and ideational bases of the Islamic revolution in the 1960s and 1970s, not yet satisfactorily achieved in other scholarly works. The Islamist discourse and political agenda has been the subject of much debate in various Islamic countries, but the peculiarity of this package in the Iranian case lies in how it was filtered through Iran's particular version of Shia Islam, and how this affected its ultimate manifestation. Furthermore, the enduring importance of this topic can be seen every day in the Middle East as the region goes through astonishing changes in which the Islamist discourse in all countries remains, in some cases, a salient overriding variable. The revolutions of the 'Arab Spring'[2]

---

[2] The Arab Spring consisted of revolutionary protests, civil wars and uprising. It began in late 2010 with Tunisian Revolution and continued in some Arab countries.

reflect the return of religion to a central role in the politics of many states. For example, some strands of the Islamist discourse now posit Iran (jurisprudential Islam) and Turkey (liberal Islam) as two models for postrevolutionary societies in Egypt, Tunisia and to an extent in Libya. In the case of the Iranian political spectrum there has been a change of leanings over time: Throughout the 1960s and 1970s, Shariati and his followers were ideologically closer to the ideas of Khomeini, however this gradually shifted in the post-revolutionary era towards the ideas of Bazargan.

SIGNIFICANCE

The significance of this topic lies in the uniqueness of the Iranian version of Islam, namely Twelver Shi'ism. Shia Islam is quintessential to contemporary Iranian national identity, and remains a central pillar of Iranian society. Furthermore, this identity is a mix of Shia Islam coupled with an evolving, if primordial, nationalism amalgamated in the crucible of modernity. During the time of the Pahlavi dynasty's reign there was a concerted attempt to marginalise religion not only in political institutions, but also in the wider public sphere. This was done without taking account of the central role of religion for many individuals as a component of Iranian identity. The Shah's social and political programme was underpinned by a desire to fuse modernity and secular nationalism. But many believe the Shah's programme did not reflect the Iranian cultural context, rather it was seen as an import from the West. In other words, the Shah's programme had two conflicting pillars. On the one hand, it advanced the notion that Iranian nationalism should be based on the symbols and glories of the pre-Islamic era, and on the other, that modernity should be strictly secular (Hosainizadeh 2007, pp. 112–117). This was not a small problem. This was a serious structural flaw that would not disappear with time. Political Islam, by contrast attempted to strike a balance between three interconnected dimensions of Iran's national identity: Religion, nationalism and modernity. In doing so, thinkers of Political Islam attempted to give religion more space to play a role and run its course in society and state institutions. Following the revolution, an unforeseen outcome occurred with religion gaining ascendance over both nationalism and modernity. Iranian thinkers were originally of the view that aspects of tradition deeply rooted in Iranian culture and modernity could be combined and reconciled. These factors brought to the fore the paradoxical nature of political thought which survived in pre and post-revolutionary Iran.

Three fundamental dimensions underpin the significance of this topic. The first is the fact that in Iran, during the constitutional era (1905–1911), and in its aftermath, there developed an intense interest in Political Islam. The sanctification of the political realm further intensified in the 1960s and 1970s. Political groups and associations, emerged within the relative shelter of the religious realm, wanted to apply an Islamic agenda to address the issues which engaged the Iranian masses. These political factions, by utilising an Islamic platform, wanted to stand against the Pahlavi dynasty which promoted a secular ideology and which was said by its critics to emanate from the West. The religiously oriented factions were able to mobilise and galvanise a broad section of Iranian society around Islamic discourses and energise them with religious slogans. Furthermore, the vacuum which the political system created in the 1960s and 1970s paved the way for Political Islam to step in and fill the space following the imprisonment of secular and liberal intellectuals by the Shah. They presented an Islamic agenda in a new form and this appealed to many marginalised Iranians.

The second dimension underpinning the significance of the topic lies in the fact that Political Islam took power, in practical terms, in three countries in the twentieth century: Iran, Afghanistan and Sudan. In the case of Iran, Political Islam came to power through mass protests by the Iranian people which manifested itself in the Islamic revolution of 1979. In the context of Afghanistan, Political Islam seized political power in the aftermath of the civil war (1992) which dominated the political scene in the post-Soviet communist-backed government led by Mohammad Najibuallah. In the context of Sudan, Political Islam took power after a military coup (Fuller 2003, p. 97). The proponents of Political Islam in Iran were able to form a government because they capitalised on Iranian Shia tenets which form a part of modern Iranian national identity.

Political Islam in Iran became a blueprint or role model for other Islamic-oriented movements in the region. The basic reason for this development was the fact that for the first time Political Islam transformed both the structure of the government and its underlying administrative principles. The ideals behind the Iranian-Islamic revolution played an influential role within other countries in the region. Some Western observers believe that because of the accumulated problems, which remain unresolved in Iran, Political Islam has failed to achieve its goals (Gilles 2002, p. 365). According to Roy, a prominent expert on Political Islam, the approach has been unsuccessful. He asserts failure is related to Islamist involvement with terrorism and the acquisition of power by force (Roy 1994). However, Political Islam still defines the identity of large numbers of Iranian people. According to a 2006 survey conducted by the Ministry of Culture, 80% of the people are not content with the prevailing situation in Iran, although less than 30% of Iranians are in favour of fundamental change (Hosainizadeh 2007, p. 506). It seems that in the contemporary era, and despite the existence of many pressing political issues, Political Islam is not a spent force. This enquiry has its foundation in that assumption, in relation to the ideological implications and prevailing discursive practices.

The third dimension which underlies the importance of the topic is the quality of the Islamic discourse and its different manifestations. In spite of the differences between discourses, all use the tenets of Shi'a Islam, Iranian nationalism and Western ideas in a combined package (Milani 1994, p. 154). All the tenets which cut across the Iranian national or regional loyalties attracted a large number of followers among Iranians nationwide. Differences in Political Islamic discourse played tactically into the hands of those religious-inspired factions which were active in the 1960s and 1970s. Political Islam, because of its close affiliation with religious society, is a force to be reckoned with both within the Iranian state and regionally. The strength of Political Islam in Iran lies in the religious traditions within the society and its expansion globally. In the absence of strong opposition to the Islamic government, Political Islam still enjoys the largest audience in the country (Hosainizadeh 2007, p. 507).

METHODOLOGY

A critical analysis of primary sources related to the writings of Khomeini, Shariati and Bazargan provides a conceptual framework for this book. The synthesis of these three socio-political views is structured to provide a coherent interpretation which to date has not been presented within the field of academic studies in terms of Political Islam. In this regard, the socio-political dimensions of the ideas of each of these political thinkers will be closely investigated. In addition, to summarise their ideas, ideological comparisons will be made between their ideas covering the five key aspects below. These comparisons seek to demonstrate and enquire into how these thinkers managed to invoke regime change and introduce into the political structure of the new government the Islamic ideologies they had created. The aforementioned aspects include: Firstly, an explanation of the situation with reference to the subjective and objective views these intellectuals held concerning the historical reality of Iranian society over the various decades. Secondly, the system of knowledge indicative of reference points in the ideas of these three intellectuals. It should be noted that knowledge differs from epochs and countries. For example, in ancient Greece intuitionism, empiricism and philosophy underpinned political thought in that age; however, philosophies of knowledge governed according to political, cultural, social and religious norms. As another example, in present-day Iran the religious Shia ideas presented by these thinkers have generally overridden other ideas. Thirdly, the system of norms which, in every country, defines a limited list of values and principles including democracy, independence, equality and peace existed. What is important is how these entities are prioritised in a society, especially by its thinkers. Fourthly, the Iranian system of power that forms the strategies and structure of government is analysed. Fifthly, the public policy is explored in relation to the policies a government makes with regard to domestic and foreign affairs. Furthermore, this study uses secondary sources to conceptualise the political thought of the three thinkers. In the course of the examination an analysis is made in terms of differences and similarities between the three schools of Political Islam in Iran. The main ideas underpinning Political Islam from the 1960s is found in the following primary and secondary sources.

This book investigates Political Islam in Iran from the 1960s to the present. It examines how contemporary Islamic thought was transformed into a revolutionary ideology by Khomeini, Shariati and Bazargan. There are a number of assumptions underpinning the issues which need to be taken into account. Firstly, the period was politically represented by a variety of conflicting ideologies such as liberalism, nationalism, socialism and communism. Secondly, promoters of the competing schools of thought that emerged all maintained that Islam as an Ideology has the potential to construct a political order and provide solution to human problems. Thirdly, the two decades of the 1960s and 1970s heightened the significance of Western notions of the political right and left ideologies in Iran. The significance of ideologies is to be found in the national movement's struggle against imperialism. This period was marked by an independence movement and return to cultural Shiism. Fourthly, this period was highly revolutionary, and driven by ideologies. The period saw the rise of the political notion that in the cultural realm Iran was in opposition to the West, in particular the United States (US), the United Kingdom (UK) and also the Union of Soviet Socialist Republics (USSR).

REFERENCES

Fuller, G. E. (2003). *The future of political Islam*. New York, NY: Palgrave.

Gilles, K. (2002). *Jihad: The trail of political Islam*. Cambridge, MA: Harvard University Press.

Hosainizadeh, S. M. A. (2007). *Islam siasi dar Iran* [Political Islam in Iran]. Qom, Iran: Mofid University.

Milani, M. M. (1994). *The making of Iran's Islamic revolution: From monarchy to Islamic republic*. Boulder, CO: Westview Press.

Roy, O. (1994). *The failure of political Islam*. Cambridge, MA: Harvard University Press.

CHAPTER 2

Concepts and Context

This chapter examines Political Islam in the Iranian context and starts by providing a definition with particular reference to an application of ideological thought. It analyses the key ideas associated with Khomeini, Shariati and Bazargan. This chapter forms the theoretical foundation for the following chapters.

POLITICAL ISLAM: CONCEPT

Mohammad Abed Al-Jaberi defines Islamic civilisation as a collection of societies governed by religious *fiqh* (Islamic jurisprudence based on Sharia law) (Ayubi 1991, p. 11). By contrast, Greek civilisation (specifically Athenian civilisation), which was an important source of epistemic models and scientific knowledge for early Islamic societies, was premised on philosophical imperatives that sought negotiation of interests and values by an informed and politically engaged polis or citizenry. Modern European civilisation revived many of the main elements of Greek speculative philosophy (Ayubi 1991, p. 11). While reason and scientific rationalism became a central pillar for political life in Western states in the post-Kantian era, *fiqh* came to be perceived as a pillar of indigenous legitimacy and an orienting political principle in a number of Islamic countries.

Modern Islamic movements and revolutions such as occurred in Iran were in some respects a reaction to European colonialism. Proponents of Political Islam such as Khomeini, Shariati and Bazargan therefore sought

© The Author(s) 2020
S. M. Lolaki, *Diverging Approaches of Political Islamic Thought in Iran since the 1960s,*
https://doi.org/10.1007/978-981-15-0478-5_2

11

to frame political responses that rejected both colonial oppression and what they believed to be the inextricably linked philosophies underpinning the social and political disruptions and transformations their societies were experiencing. They reacted to what they saw as the ideational core of modernity—autonomous reason, and individualism. Their defensive response was to argue that the values and traditions understood to be under threat from an externally imposed modernity were based on an indigenous *fiqh* (jurisprudence) tradition, which constituted both a normative values system and a functioning rule of law, and had to be reasserted for the sake of the moral and cultural integrity of Muslim society.

For Islam, traditional notions derive from divine revelation (enshrined in the Qur'an and Hadiths). Its judicial function is applied through the body of Sharia law which is the product of scholarly interpretive process that is *fiqh*/Islamic jurisprudence. While philosophy, mysticism and conventional religious theology (kalam) are important fields of intellectual endeavour in Islamic scholarship, *fiqh* came to occupy a hegemonic position of pre-eminence as Islam evolved (Feirahi 2010, p. 239). Islamic scholars see themselves as the orthodox guardians of the scripture and doctrines. From this position it was natural that these thinkers and their movements would come to view modernism as a near existential threat to religion as they understood it, and to the verities and truth-claims they made on its behalf. Viewed through the lens of a *fiqh* scholar, modernity was a supreme threat to traditional cultural fabric and its associated values system.

The Renaissance and the Reformation from the fourteenth to the seventeenth century in the West (Johnson 2013, pp. 4–6), from which arose the hallmarks of modernity, both material and existential, have often been regarded in the Islamic world as constituting, in effect, an implied attack on Islam. For these hallmarks—secularity, the autonomy of reason, universality of education and, most importantly, the advocacy and expansion of individual rights and civil institutions—are themselves the product of a mentality that is opposed to theocracy. Hence, when juxtaposed with colonial imperialism and xenophobic ideas, and especially when deployed to de-legitimise Islam, and paint it as an atavistic static religion without the capacity to adapt and evolve, the attack is much more than implicit. Inevitably and understandably Muslims reacted.

Islamic thinkers such as Khomeini, Shariati and Bazargan responded by trying to restore religious concepts to a central position in the intellectual and political life of their societies, making them relevant and practical again. They saw Islam as assailed by colonialism, neo-colonialism and imperialism and under constant cultural attack from the West (Heywood 2012, p. 283). Political Islamic tendencies largely emerged as a reactionary movement to the perceived political, economic and cultural dominance of the West. Societies in Muslim countries became more observant and a politicised religion became a popular mobilising force and orienting principle for activists wanting to defend what they viewed as threatened traditional values systems (Rajaee 2007, p. 12). In this way Political Islam became variously a liberation theology, a trenchant intellectual defence of tradition and a mobilising clarion call. Of course, within Islamic countries not all facets of modernity were rejected. Islamic movements and almost all the theoreticians behind them accepted that some aspects of Western modernity were compatible with scripture and religious law, especially technological progress and industrialisation. Islamic activists parsed this seeming inconsistency by arguing that "we have modernities rather than modernity" (Possamai 2009, pp. 153–154). They looked for and found lines in Islamic texts that appeared to offer support for selected elements of modernity. In this way, the schools of Islamic *fiqh* came to accept the material gains of modernity, particularly those concerned with technological advances, while rejecting the intellectual principles that had laid the ground for these gains to come about.

Some groups and thinkers did accept some of the more fundamental philosophical aspects of modernity, quite beyond the material technology and scientific gains (Gellner 1992, p. 2). In the context of Iran in the 1960s and 1970s, this is reflected in the writings of a number of prominent thinkers including Bazargan and Shariati, who respected the principle of independent individual reason. They came to view Islam and modernity's intellectual project as inherently compatible. They argued that a tradition of applying autonomous reason can be found in Islamic jurisprudence which is consistent with intellectual modernity, and which they believed was based solely on reason (Pedram 2004, pp. 2–10).

Essentially, *fiqh* contains three basic elements: (1) Devotional *fiqh*—for example fasting, praying and pilgrimage; (2) Transactional *fiqh*—for instance the rule of inheritance and economy and (3) Political *fiqh*—for example government, Islamic administration and its regulations. Islamist thinkers amenable to coming to a modus operandi with modernity argued that transactional and political *fiqh* are mainly concerned with issues related to autonomous individual reason. The concept of autonomous reason has not been subject to total acceptance in Islamic discourse. This is because mainstream Islamic discourses are still dominated by a heavy emphasis on the 'completeness' of divine revelation and a strong conservative aversion to 'innovation'—a word which carries the taint of heresy in its implication. This is one of the main reasons why the Islamic world has been able to resist secularisation in the past century (Rajaee 2007, pp. 13–14).

POLITICAL ISLAM: IRANIAN CONTEXT

Out of the 1979 Iranian revolution, Khomeini, Bazargan and Shariati emerged as particularly influential. Before and during the revolution, numerous political groups consciously adopted and adapted the theories and intellectual justifications of these thinkers. Individuals from these groups, in turn, played an important role in writing the constitution of the Islamic Republic of Iran. The constitution clearly attempts to negotiate a middle road between elements of modernity and elements of tradition. It was accepted by a large majority of Iranians by referendum in March 1979. The constitution accepted popular sovereignty, a fundamental principle of modern democratic governance and a legal system based on the Islamic principle of the *Velayat-e Faqih* (the guardianship of jurisconsult), a theory developed by Khomeini. The subsequent Iranian system gained its legitimacy from two different sources—the sovereignty of the people based on modern principles of government (democratically elected executive presidency and parliament) and the sovereignty of God, applied through the *Velayat-e Faqih* system. The *Velayat-e Faqih* involves parallel institutions in addition to the Supreme Leader who must be a cleric of high standing, it vets government actions for their conformity to Islamic scripture and law, ensuring in theory, that governance outcomes are truly 'Islamic' (Beinin and Stork 1997, p. 103).

IDEOLOGY

The term 'ideology' gained political currency following the 1790 French revolution (Heywood 2012, p. 5). It refers to a (usually) socio-political structuralist body of thought that makes truth-claims about itself which explicitly or implicitly rejects the truth-claims of other, often competing ideologies. Pratt suggests an 'ideology' is a coherent set of ideas and values by which an individual, group or society may order their identity and worldview. Thus, for example, it is extremist ideologies of both religious and political kinds which have a totalitarian and impositional dimension as an expression of their worldview and identity (Pratt 2006). While the concept of ideology emerged out of political philosophy in the last quarter of the eighteenth century and early nineteenth century, the roots of the term date back to the Greek words 'eidos' and 'logos' which typically referred to the science of ideas by ideologues who wanted to shape society in terms of ideas and doctrines (Vincent 2010, pp. 1–2). To clear the confusion over the meaning of the term 'ideology' Heywood regards the term as meaning a political belief system, an action-oriented set of political ideas encompassing the ideas of the ruling class or the world views of a particular social class or social group inclusive of political ideas that embody or articulate class or social interests. Reference is made to ideas that propagate false consciousness among the exploited or oppressed, and which situate the individual within a social context while generating a sense of collective belonging, coupled with an officially sanctioned set of ideas that legitimise a political system or regime. In turn this becomes an all-embracing political doctrine that claims a monopoly on truth; an abstract and highly systematic set of political ideas (Heywood 2012, p. 5). According to Vincent, the term 'ideology' is represented by four phases: Firstly, it must be acknowledged according to the original 1796 designation of Destutt de Tracey, tying it to a new empirical science of ideas. Secondly, the term came to denote an affiliation to a form of secular liberal republicanism. Thirdly, it took on a pejorative connotation implying intellectual and practical sterility as well as dangerous radicalism. Finally, and most tenuously, it evolved to denote a political doctrine in general (Vincent 2010, p. 1).

Political Thought (Doctrine) and Ideology

According to Vincent, ideologies contain two dimensions: Descriptive and prescriptive. In other words, ideologies contain dual functions. On the one hand, they describe complexities of human nature and human society. On the other hand, ideologies bindingly prescribe solutions to those complexities which arise in any given society. Ideologies are more complex and sophisticated structures than popular perceptions which strictly confine ideologies to empirical world views. Aspects of ideologies can be empirical or non-empirical. For example, ideology which emanates from religion has elements beyond the empirical societal facts (Vincent 2010, pp. 18–21).

In addition, ideologies, which are by and large the product of modern enlightenment, cannot be seen as distinct from philosophy. Nonetheless ideologies have been subject to sharp criticism in the sense that unlike philosophy, which undertakes its self-reviewing and self-critiquing, they (ideologies) do not have the luxury of self-critiquing. Despite this common distinction, on an empirical level political thought and ideologies overlap. Ideologies contain elements of political thought and vice versa (Vincent 2010, pp. 18–21). Contrary to their conceptualisation, ideologies can undertake a change while shaping empirical facts and the same can be said of ideologies being subjected to modification by the magnitude of social facts. This can be true of all ideologies whether religious or non-religious.

Hossien Bashiriyeh posits that between political thought and political ideology there exists similarities and differences. He maintained that political ideologies encourage followers to be committed to them and also obey them. Political ideologies create propagandists to promote fluctuating ideological agendas. Meanwhile, political thought, in some cases, is ideological in the context of epistemology. Political ideologies are closer to religious ideologies than to philosophy or political theory. It is hard to distinguish between political ideology and political thought as sometimes they often amalgamate and overlap (Bashiriyeh 2012, pp. 18–19).

Religion as an Ideology: The Perspective of Plamenatz

Plamenatz presents a concise overview of the history of ideologies as follows. Religion represents five different things: Firstly, as a social construction; secondly, as a consolation in a harsh uncaring world; thirdly, as a sacred thing helping to mediate social integrations and prevent disintegration; fourthly, in terms of religion as an incentive to live a moral life and do as little harm as possible; fifthly, by thinkers who viewed religion as a vehicle through which individuals may reflect on their place in the world and think about self and their mortality (Plamenatz 1970, pp. 91–92).

Before the eighteenth century, philosophers generally did not focus on why people chose religious ideas instead viewing religion as an essential pillar of public and private life that guided morality There were those who saw religion as prone to becoming hostage to prejudicial and extremist elements. For Machiavelli religion was positive in society, as it formalised and legitimised various forms of social relations. He argued that the foundations of religion were better than the foundations of governments. Hobbes did not give a mandate to religion but neither did he explicitly express hostility to its practice. He disagreed with the idea of religious diversity and believed government or a ruler should have the right to decree a state religion. Hobbes' primary focus was on order and security, which was, he believed, in some manner to be had in social conformity and religious uniformity. The French philosopher, Montesquieu, later focused on the social function of religion claiming religion is not primarily about legitimising power; rather it plays an important role in creating social cohesion. Pascal advanced the theory that religion offers identity to humans because they are conscious and self-reflective which makes them different to other animals. For Rousseau religion provides a consolation to human beings—something science cannot offer. Kant argued that if human beings want to live a life based on morality, they should believe in three things—God, freedom of choice and the survival of the soul. According to Kant, like some of his contemporaries, humans are naturally moral beings. For Hegel religion provided society with a universal language that is functional at the particular stage of social evolution, although he was reluctant to concede a significant role for religion in the age of reason. Marx was enormously influenced by Hegel and believed that religion was an imaginary construction of use to existing power structures and elites who employ it to maintain the status quo; this kept the masses superstitious and subservient—the famous opium of the people (Plamenatz 1970, pp. 87–88).

Unlike classical Marxists, neo-Marxists approached religion in a more reciprocal way. While classic Marxism regarded religion as irrelevant in modern era, the neo-Marxists accord religion a significant role in society in terms of mobilisation. According to neo-Marxists and humanists, religion is more than an entity based on economic structure. They believe that religion is a cultural entity which accords the human beings with a collective outlook of the world (Plamenatz 1970, pp. 110–111). For instance, Gramsci distinguished between arbitrary and organic ideology. He believed that an organic ideology helps to mobilise the masses and give them a common identity. Religion, to him, encourages individuals to conform, and thus underpins social cohesion. A religious person deals with society according to his or her spiritual belief system and values. Gramsci also drew a distinction between traditional and organic intellectuals. The traditional intellectual separates themselves from the social class they came from and attempts to raise themselves to a higher level than people who are more directly politically and socially engaged such as artists, philosophers and priests. By contrast, the organic intellectual maintains solidarity with the social class they belong to (McLellan 1986, p. 29).

In the context of Iran, during the 1960s and 1970s, religious orientated thinkers sought to create a counter-hegemonic discourse based on faith against the dominant secular nationalist ideology of the government, drawing similar conclusions to the ideas of Gramsci on hegemony.

The Iranian Context

The majority of Iranians in the 1920s consented to Reza Shah Pahlavi's absolute monarchy during which modernisation began in earnest. Rather than permitting mass political participation and peaceful democratic political competition, Reza Shah wanted top-down modernisation with a strong authoritarian orientation. Modernisation thus became something largely perceived by the masses as an unwelcome external political project. Its rationale did not Establish deep roots across Iranian society and important sections were alienated by the processes and paradigms (Bashiriyeh 2002, pp. 68–69).

In contemporary Iran, the ideology of the Islamic Republic's Islamic revolution offers a hegemonic political narrative that tries to neutralise other important identity markers such as ethnicity and social class, while emphasising the Islamic dimension of an individual's identity. The motive of the new revolutionary elite was to develop a cohesive discourse for the masses, mobilised and united with a single purpose, irrespective of social class or ethnicity. The Iran-Iraq War (1980–1988) was in some ways a fortuitous event for the infant Islamic Republic system. The war helped consolidate the idea of mobilised, ideologically homogeneous populace. Throughout the war, the concept was developed in slicker, more coherent ways. Interestingly, the new revolutionary political elite were ideologically flexible enough to combine Islam with Iran's pre-existing nationalist tradition, which proved to be an effective recipe for mobilising the country against the existential external threat represented by Saddam Hussein in the war with Iraq. Emphasising the idea of an oppressed Shiism confronting a well-armed, secular, Western-backed Iraq, dominated by a Sunni Arab elite, clearly fitted the emerging hegemonic discourse very well. Religion became the core of the new ideological hegemony, just as Gramsci had postulated in his work, on the nature of hegemony and ruling elites.

Hegemonic Islamic-oriented discourse revealed itself in the 1979 constitution and politically marginalised other singular ideologies such as nationalism, liberalism and socialism in the aftermath of the revolution. Similarly, the Islamisation of government had a significant impact in law, education and other spheres of public and private in Iranian society (Amirahmadi and Parvin 1988, pp. 252–253).

Heywood points to four late twentieth-century factors related to religious fundamentalism: (1) Secularisation; (2) The era of post colonisation; (3) The defeat of socialist revolution; and (4) Globalisation. In terms of secularisation in the Iranian context, he firstly argued that fundamentalism was a reaction to the decline of morality in society during the reign of the Shah in the 1960s and 1970s. Secondly, he maintains that under the impact of postcolonial discourse, which resulted in the revolution of Iran in 1979, Political Islam showed nativist character and 'otherness' by distinguishing itself from Western models of national reconstruction. This revolutionary discourse manifested itself in the construction of a logo of Great Satan for the US. Thirdly, the public repudiation of socialism was a major cause for people to return Political Islam. Fourthly, during the height of globalisation, in the absence of civic nationalism, Political Islam emerged as a robust discourse to fill an ideological vacuum (Heywood 1998, pp. 275–285).

POLITICAL ISLAMIC SCHOOLS OF THOUGHT: IRANIAN CONTEXT

The Jurisprudential Islamic Perspective: Khomeini

The main proponent of Jurisprudential Islam was Khomeini, the supreme leader of the 1979 Islamic Revolution in Iran. Khomeini (1902–1989) was born into a religious family in the small town called Khomein. He entered the theological world early in life, travelling first to Qom and then on to the holy city of Najaf in Iraq where he continued his seminary studies. He rose to prominence as a dissident cleric in the wake of Mohammad Reza Shah's 1962 attempt at comprehensive modernising land reform, known as the 'White Revolution'. Following this he became an irreconcilable critic of the Pahlavi dynasty and was imprisoned, then exiled to Iraq, and finally, to France. His return to Tehran in January 1979 marked the success of the revolution, after which he was swiftly made leader. He remained Supreme Leader of the Islamic Republic of Iran until his death in 1989, shortly after the end of the Iran-Iraq War.

Khomeini's political Islamic vision was based almost exclusively on *fiqh* injunctions. His main aim was the repudiation of Western secularism and the revival of the traditional power of the Shi'a Clergy. His discourse was aimed at defending the traditional institutions and organisations of Iranian society. His version of Political Islam was concerned with the antithesis of imported secular ideologies such as nationalism, communism and liberalism. According to Kadivar, the Islamic discourse, which was promoted by Khomeini, reflects four consecutive phases: The Qom period, Najaf and Turkey, Paris, Qom, and Tehran. The political discourse of Khomeini is categorised into four stages (Kadivar 2001, p. 141).

In the first stage, circa 1954, Khomeini began developing his ideas on Islam whilst still in Qom, Iran, where a centre of Shia emulation and learning gave rise to his theory contained in a book entitled *Kashf al-Asrar* (*Discovering the Secrets*). Here, he first postulated the concept of 'Jurisconsult Supervision', arguing that "government should not be run by the Jurisconsult, but rather should be run along the lines of Allah's sacred law, as enshrined in the scriptures of the Qur'an and Hadiths" (Khomeini 1942, p. 221). According to Khomeini, a government without the sanction of sacred law will decay into political and cultural stagnation. He found support for this view in the philosophy of the Constitutional Revolution (Khomeini 1942, p. 222). Khomeini seems to have borrowed this idea from the literature of the Constitutional Revolution.[1] He further asserted that, "the government run by the jurisconsult does not mean that the king or ministers or military chiefs cannot be sovereign. According to Khomeini, the essence of Jurisprudential government was that qualified members of the clergy must officially supervise the decisions of the legislative and executive branches of an Islamic state" (Khomeini 1942, pp. 232–233).

The second phase emerged in Qom and was further elaborated when Khomeini was in exile in Najaf, Iraq. His main theory was elucidated in three books: *Al-Rasel* (*Messages*), *Tahrir Al-Vasileh* (*Commentary on the Means*) and *Kitab Baea* (*Book of Social Dealings*). These books fleshed out the theory of Jurisconsult guardianship in some detail. For the first time Khomeini was advocating that the just Jurisconsult should involve himself in the public political sphere. In other words, Islamic government should mean a government run *and* supervised by the guardianship of the Jurisconsult (*Velayat-e Faqhih*).[2]

---

[1] The Constitutional Revolution in Iran in 1906 was a turning point which transferred the absolute power wielded by King to limitation by constitution.

[2] The guardianship of the Jurisconsult is an expression in Sharia law which, according to contemporary Iranian context, grants power to the supreme leader.

The third phase of Khomeini's notion of Islamic discourse was developed in a series of speeches he made in Paris and Qom, between 1978 and 1980. He presented the notion of Jurisprudential supervision to a public audience. In the speeches of this period he did not focus heavily on the precise details of the office of the guardianship of the Jurisconsult. For instance, in one of his interviews, conducted in Paris, he outlined his vision as follows:

In the future, after the victory of Islamic revolution, I will play the same role as I do now. My chief role is to inspire and guide. Whenever the situation of the country requires my assistance, I will play a necessary role. And whenever something goes wrong, I will elaborate on it. But I will not play any role whatsoever in the policy of the state. (Khomeini 1996a, p. 215).

Answering a question about his duty as state leader, the Ayatollah maintained that "I will personally not accept such a role" (Khomeini 1996b, p. 107). He went further asserting that the duty of a spiritual figure is only to advise the government (Khomeini 1996b, p. 128). At this stage, the Ayatollah's thinking was focused on the theme of Jurisconsult supervision.

The fourth phase of Khomeini's Islamic discourse emerged in Tehran in 1988 his final year of life. The Ayatollah proposed the idea of an absolute guardianship of the Jurisconsult. Here, 'Islamic government' meant 'simply Jurisconsult guardianship'. He asserted that it should be devised by the sacred law of God for the people. The Prophets and Imams appointed by God had the authority of a just Jurist. In this realm, in order to protect the interests of the state, the Jurisconsult was permitted to nullify Sharia law in extremis.

On several occasions Khomeini revisited his theory of Jurisconsult supervision. In 1983 he commented further on his theory in the Islamic revolution. In his encounters with visitors in Paris and Najaf, Khomeini made it clear that he considered spiritual leaders superior to those who are preoccupied with the day-to-day execution of the government. Khomeini argued when it came back to the realities on the ground in Iran, the situation was completely different (Khomeini 1996c, pp. 211–212). It was evident, according to Khomeini in 1983, that most temporal political leaders wanted to push the country into the arms of the superpowers with whom Khomeini was not on good terms. The Ayatollah made it clear that because Iran did not appear to have people of a calibre who could lead the country in a neutral and independent direction, Iran had to choose a President for the country from among the clergy. It was evident, according to him, that politicians, even if religiously oriented, would make the country dependent on foreign power. Thus, Khomeini argued that a cleric was needed in the position of President, because lay politicians lacked the scholarly foundations and intellectual autonomy to hold genuinely independent points of view. If, at some hypothetical point in the future, Iran arrived at a stage where the country could be run independently of the clergy and in the way that God wanted, then Khomeini would decree that the clergy should prioritise their spiritual duties in the non-governmental sector, which he claimed where superior to the temporal functions of governance (Khomeini 1996c, pp. 211–212).

The reasons behind Khomeini's change of view were closely related to political exigencies which had emerged in post-revolutionary Iran including his change of position on Jurisprudential grounds. His arguments contained three main elements between 1954 and 1978:

(a) Islam suggests that in order to implement its injunctions, a Muslim government becomes a matter of necessity. In Islam the temporal government is clearly charged with bringing justice to earthly human affairs (Khomeini 1965a, pp. 461–472).

(b) It becomes obligatory for the just Jurisconsult to interfere in the affairs of the Islamic state to bring about justice and make a clear stand against oppressors. The Islamic government should follow the injunctions of *Nahi Anil Munkar* (Forbidding Evil) and *Amr Bil Mahroof* (Enjoining good) (Khomeini 1965c, pp. 472–483). *Munkar* and *Mahruf* are terms which deal with social activity in an Islamic setting. According to Islamic Sharia, it is argued for or against something on religious matters.

(c) The Islamic government is based on the Just Jurisconsult guardianship. The Jurisconsult is appointed by God to guard and serve the interest of the masses. The Prophet and Imams are appointed by God to guard the public interest (Khomeini 1965b, p. 465).

Khomeini was not unique in promoting this kind of discourse in the 1960s and the 1970s. Other political groups followed Khomeini's thinking. The most significant were *Mo'talefe* (Islamic Coalition) and *Rohaniyat-e-Mobarez* (Combatant Clerics Association) (Rajaee 2007, p. 123). However, in order to refute Western-oriented ideological discourses, Khomeini borrowed and adapted elements of nationalism, communism and liberalism to reinforce his own personal idea and articulation of an ideal Islamic state. His political Islamic discourse placed emphasis on the supremacy of religion over politics. In this sense, he stressed Islamic democracy, Islamic human rights and the guardianship of the 'jurisconsult' simultaneously. Despite the philosophical differences and conclusions between himself and Western philosophical concepts, his jurisprudential discourse is in fact based on a modern conception of nationhood, republicanism, democracy, rule of law, freedom, equity and human rights. He incorporated all these modern concepts into his jurisprudential discourse, claiming all had respectable precedents in Islamic scripture and law. From his perspective, all social and political institutions of government should reflect jurisprudential discourse which contain all modern notions as mentioned. Arguably his discourse produced a paradoxical system, one that encompasses popularly elected institutions such as parliament and presidency, and theocratic supervisory institutions appointed and responsible to the *Velayat-e Faqih*.

The Left-Wing Interpretation of Islam: Shariati

The left-wing Islamic perspective was enunciated foremost by Shariati, a prominent intellectual. Shariati (1933–1977) was a sociologist and social theorist. He gained a PhD in history at the Sorbonne, Paris, at a time when Marxism was highly influential, popular and widespread. Shariati became one of Iran's most authoritative left-wing Islamic thinkers across the entire Islamic world. His father, Mohammad Taghi Shariati, was a religious scholar of note. Shariati thus grew up in an intellectual family where religious ideas were the subject of much rigorous discussion within family circles. Shariati's main theme was to develop a counter-discourse which refuted traditional religious practices and ideas (some pure superstition), and also some elements of modernity that he believed were incompatible with certain aspects of Iranian culture. He was a serious critic of both unthinking traditionalist religion and modernity, and he attempted to meld elements of religion and modernity into a uniquely Islamic-Iranian combination. Shariati stressed positive aspects of religion and modernity which were in tune with each other. In particular, he opened up new insights into the meanings of Islamic concepts like Imamate, Shura (council), *shirk* (associations), *kufr* (blasphemy), *erfan* (mysticism) and *Tawhed* (theism) and concepts related to modernity such as freedom, intellectualism, alienation, imperialism, justice, social rights and democracy.

Shariati critiqued both modernity and tradition. His efforts aimed at finding a third way—an accommodation between modernity and tradition. He criticised modernist intellectuals in Iran as Western clones. These intellectuals, according to Shariati, were not familiar with the epistemological foundations of their own societies (Pedram 2004, p. 140). Instead, they simply tried to import ideas from the West and apply them to their society which, from a cultural point of view, was vastly different in context and history to that of the West. His critique embodied one main assumption, that the traditionalist intellectuals did not have the knowledge or dynamism to suggest a viable way forward for their society, because they could only draw from tradition, scripture and Islamic law (Pedram 2004, p. 140). Shariati was well aware of the importance of tradition for many Iranians, but also the effectiveness and attractiveness of modernity for some sections of society. His third way was a conscious attempt to negotiate a synthesis between elements of tradition and modernity. He tried to sustain elements of culture he believed were important for human identity while at the same time eliminating pathological elements which could arrest the pace of progress in the society. In this connection, he confronted both the orthodox traditionalists and orthodox modernists (Pedram 2004, p. 142).

Ideology
Shariati sought to transform and invigorate Islamic discourse, particularly the Shia version of Islam,[3] into a comprehensive revolutionary ideology, cross-fertilised with the philosophical ideas of Marxism and Liberalism. Ideology, according to Shariati, defined all aspects of human life (Shariati 1981b, p. 29). According to him the concept of nation, literally 'Milleyat' in Arabic, is an ideological reference and Islam is a comprehensive ideology which encompasses the entirety of human experience. Ideology, despite its multifaceted dimension, pays particular attention to politics as a human activity (Shariati 1995, p. 91). Shariati describes two kinds of Islam: Ideological and cultural. Ideological Islam employs religion to define all human material and moral dimensions of life. Cultural Islam

---

[3] The sources of *fiqh* in Shia Islam are based on The Qur'an, Hadith (sayings of prophet and the 12 Imams), rationality based on revelation, consensus of community. The sources of Sunni *fiqh* are based on Qur'an, Sunnah of the Prophet, consensus of community, and analogy. The differences lie in *fiqh* sources but in the political realm Sunnis and Shia political Islam is divided along liberal, left and jurisprudential Islam line of thinking.

encompasses science, jurisprudence, dialectics, philosophy, mysticism and the science of Hadith interpretation (اجتهاد). The ideology of Islam is shaped by the *Mujtahed* (someone who strives—an interpreter of the faith), whereas a *Mujahed* (fighter) is an expression of cultural Islam. The Ideology of Islam forms the intellectual, while the Culture of Islam shapes the scientist (Shariati 1981a, p. 274).

According to Shariati, Islam as a matter of ideology is in complete harmony with a religion based on a divine revelation. His characterisation of Islam as an ideology emerged in the 1960s and 1970s, as a tool to mobilise and raise the consciousness of the Iranian masses. He utilised Islamic terminology and ideology to foment a movement for liberating the people (Shariati 1995, p. 105). Shariati's reading of religion is based on Shia literature and utilised concepts in Shia texts to give them new meaning and contemporary significance. It is here that the difference lies between Shia ideology and traditions. By reviving traditions, Shariati tried to undercut the traditionalist clergy, who he believed had in one way or another become an obstacle to the progress of Iranian society (Hosainizadeh 2007, p. 209).

The Shia: A Complete Political Party

Shariati was firmly of the view that a complete Shia Party, if properly constructed, would be capable of mobilising the masses to achieve a particular political purpose (Dabashi 2006, p. 110). For him, Shi'ism delivers a revolutionary message of struggle against three pillars: Power, wealth and political manipulation. He believed the Shia could constitute a political party of global reach, with a coherent ideology and aims that encompassed the philosophy of history, anthropology, social class and political views, along with the fundamentals of economy, symbolism, strategy and tactics (Shariati 1995, pp. 114–115). According to Shariati, being Shia means one has responsibility to engage in jihad and propagate one's beliefs. Any Shia Muslim must understand these pillars as fundamental to the philosophical outlook of Shiism. Shariati argued that the programme of such a hypothetical political party should be synonymous with Shiism.

Democracy: Ummah and Imamate

Shariati examined what he saw as the distinction between liberal democracy and 'gifted democracy' as sanctioned by God (Jahanbakhsh 2001, p. 121). The leader, he theorised, was a person with extraordinary characteristics and talents not possessed by ordinary people (Shariati 1981c,

p. 95). The system of gifted democracy addressed political and intellectual freedoms. His view of liberal democracy prevailing in the West was negative. According to Shariati, Western democracy based on individual choice, destroyed the foundations of morality and eventually leads to moral decadence in society. His version of democracy revolved around the careful creation of a society predicated on informed moral virtues.

Shariati's central argument emerged after the Bandung conference (1954), the first held by the group of Non-Aligned countries during the Cold War (Shariati 1989, p. 599). He was of the opinion that liberal democracy is a modern Western creed, ever hostage to shifting and malleable public opinion. He felt this was manipulated in the West by self-interested political elites who mislead the masses for their own greedy ends (Shariati 1980b, p. 47). In sum, Western elites do not necessarily promote the public good. An ideal leader, according to Shariati, should lead the nation in the right direction morally without resorting to political demagoguery under the guise of promoting the public interest. He believed a leader can be elected, but cannot be dismissed by the people. This genuine democracy has two foundations: (a) the public representative should be elected by the people; (b) the duration of the elected term must be extensive. For Shariati political leadership is synonymous with the Imamate[4](Shariati 1980a, p. 232).

The ideas of Shariati need further comment and analysis. By referring to the Imamate, he does not necessarily mean spiritual emulation or clerical rule. The reason for which he rejects the traditional concept of Imamate is that the institution which regards itself as a Viceroy to God on earth interferes in all aspects of human life. In other words, the people cannot have any say whatsoever in the realm of governance in a society ruled by the clergy. According to Shariati, it is a recipe for the entrenchment of an absolute dictatorship (Shariati 2002, pp. 197–198). An Islamic government means a government legitimised by ideology rather than a government ruled by Jurisconsults and Jurisprudentialists (Yosefi Ashkevari 1997, p. 277).

---

[4]The Imamate is a tradition in Shia Islam with reference to the household of Prophet Mohammad as the only source of true successors to the leadership of the Prophet. It started with Ali, son-in-law of the Prophet, and ended with the disappearance (occultation) of Imam Mahdi who was the 12th in the series of Imams.

Shariati: The Middle Way

Shariati developed his fully fledged version of Islamic discourse in 1956. He posited that his Islamic thought represented a *Maktab-e Vaseteh-e Islam* (Islam is a median school), which is a synthesis of idealism and materialism. According to Iranian scholar Ali Rahnema, Islam mandates a socio-economic system that sits midway on a continuum between Marxism and Capitalism (Rahnema 1998, pp. 61–62). Shariati chose examples and role models with modern quasi-socialist interpretations drawn from Islam history. For example, Shariati believed that Abu Zar[5] represented a strong socialist strand within Islam. Shariati related socialism to religion, regarding it as a philosophy of life rejecting a socialism based purely on temporal or materialistic things while employing Marxist-related concepts and combining them with similar concepts in Islam. For example, class conflict, which is a central theme in Marxism, was attributed the connotation in Islam. According to Shariati, Qabel (Cain) represents the class which is related to power and ownership of wealth, while Habel (Abel) represents the proletariat class controlled by the wealthy, powerful elite. Shariati insisted that throughout the course of human history there had always existed two classes: The rulers and the ruled (Rahnema 1998, p. 292). In a stricter sense, Shariati reconstructs the Left in Shia religious garb. Shariati argued that concepts prevalent in Marxism, such as dialectics, ideology, bourgeoisie, classless society, super-structure, infrastructure and revolutionary ideas, can be found also in the roots of Islam. The influence of Marxism on Shariati's Islamic left is clearly a factor which inspired him to seek Marxist equivalents in Islamic scripture and law (Mirsepassi 2000, p. 115). As a result, Shariati's philosophical Islamic left runs radically contrary to capitalism and liberalism.

The political groups which followed Shariati's philosophical outlook in the 1960s and 1970s were *Khodaparastan-e-Socialist* (Socialist God-worshippers) and *Jonbesh-e-Mosalmanan-e Mobarez* (Movement of Militant Muslims). These groups operationalised Shariati's thought in the 1960s and 1970s (Hosainizadeh 2007, p. 277).

---

[5] Abu Zar was one of the closest companions of Prophet Mohammad. He was the closest companion to the household of the Prophet. He and others who were close to Ali are known as the Party of the Shia's. Abu Zar was known as a campaigner against the corruption of the Umayyad family which ruled over Damascus, because of his opposition to the accumulation of wealth by certain Islamic Emperors.

Shariati's intellectual standpoint influenced and mobilised a young generation, especially the university-educated class, to rise against the Shah during the 1970s. Despite the fact that he left Iran, and died in mysterious circumstances in 1976. Shariati was regarded as the intellectual architect and ideologue of the Islamic Left during the 1979 Revolution by the educated youth and the intelligentsia of Iran. Shariati's political speeches and publications worked effectively to motivate and mobilise a wide spectrum of Iranian society across social and ideological lines during the revolution. His works inspired moderate secular people as well as moderate religious people in the pre-revolutionary phase. It must, however, be noted that his ideas were also effective in contributing to revolutionary zeal post-revolution.

Reform-Orientated Islam: Bazargan

Bazargan (1907–1995) was born in Tehran into a religious and well-to-do family. He was educated in France and became an engineer and Islamist thinker, but stood outside the ratified atmosphere of a clerical seminary. As a political activist he spent his life promoting democracy in Iran before becoming the first Prime Minister of the Islamic Republic of Iran, for a period of nine months after the revolution. The main thrust of his corpus was to emphasise the compatibility of Islam and liberal democracy. Although he tried to draw a line between Islam and democracy, his key interest was in reconciling Islamic spirituality with what he perceived to be the positive achievements of Western civilisation.

Bazargan viewed religion and the state as two separate entities, although in his writings he repeatedly indicated that religion and politics overlap in many ways. His interpretation of liberal Islam stressed freedom, democracy, political rights and toleration of difference. He did not view the implementation of Sharia law in society as necessary, but emphasised democracy and conciliatory consultation with the guardianship of the jurisconsult and the supervision of jurisconsults. He wanted to improve Iranian relations with the West by indexing closely foreign policy guidelines to what he saw as the pragmatic national interests of the country. In post-revolutionary Iran, Bazargan seriously re-evaluated his discourse and argued for minimising the participation of Islamic institutions and clergy in state affairs. He was of the view that clerics should restrain themselves from interfering in government affairs, positing that religion is essentially about something between God and the individual in the context of eschatological belief in the 'last day'. In other words, Bazargan tried to reduce the power of the religious voices in state affairs. He firmly believed that the institutions of modern society cannot be derived solely from religious texts. Nevertheless, Bazargan's interpretation of democracy remained firmly rooted and justified by reference to the texts of Shia Islam. He argued for government based on democratic standards, in tune with Islamic culture and ethos. Emphasis was placed on the harmony between science and faith. Bazargan believed that the spirit of modernity and certain religious traditions were essentially compatible (Hosainizadeh 2007, p. 195).

Islam as an Ideology

Bazargan held from the traditional Muslim view that Islam is a religion of society as a whole and, like other religions, has a social function. However, it extended beyond other religions in terms of providing a comprehensive formula for temporal and spiritual matters concerning human life. It acknowledged all aspects and functions of the state such as war, peace and marriage which for Bazargan made Islam a divine ideology—this comprised a body of beliefs, including those of the schools of philosophical speculation (Bazargan 1963, p. 31). Ideology, identity, aims, education, methodology, tactics and programmes were all things related to the social realm of society (Bazargan 1999, p. 239). Accordingly, the only ideology which is sustainable and lasting is the one which is premised on religion, and specifically Islam.

Negative Secularism

Bazargan believed that Islam, unlike Judaism and Christianity, is political to the core. In Islam, there is no separation between spiritual, political and temporal matters. His views are best summarised in the following quote:

> In Islam religion and the functions of the Government can be in league with each other. Islam synthesises the matters which are related to Government and the matters which are related to the spiritual realm. The Quran and Sunna reflect the Islamic concern about the government and the affairs of the state. Shiism is dual in the sense that one part is about spiritual things whereas another part strictly tackles the issues related to the state. (Bazargan 1999, p. 282)

Bazargan acknowledged however, that despite the fact that Islam is closely intertwined with politics, there is also a fine line separating temporal and spiritual matters. While religion is superior to politics, politics should not be subservient to religion. In politics, unintentionally or otherwise, blunders take place. In religion there is a single dimension moving forward (Bazargan 1999, p. 382). Religion should guide only the broad framework or strategy without getting into the precise details of governance—the tactics belong to the realm of politics. Religion, in a stricter sense, does not, or should not involve itself with the detail of fluctuating political issues (Bazargan 1998, p. 287). In sum, Government must not be led by clerical institutions.

Freedom, the Rights of the People and the Struggle Against Despotism
Islamic Government, in Bazargan's view, must be free and liberal in all its aspects. From a broad Islamic philosophical perspective, freedom is concerned with and related to the promotion of the rights which are sanctioned by God. To take a stand against such freedoms is to abrogate God's command (Bazargan 1998, p. 317). All aspects of democratic governance such as freedom of expression and press, elections, opposition parties and individual rights should all be upheld and respected under an Islamic Government. All these principles are God-given and so must be included (Bazargan 1985, p. 90). Freedom involves limitations; however, it is not the place of the Government to undermine natural rights (Bazargan 1998, p. 322). Bazargan was of the view that undermining natural rights renders the human being from being a unique creature to an irrational one. According to Bazargan this is a grave violation of God's decrees (Bazargan 1998, p. 47). Thus, the struggle against despotism, and upholding freedom, are central themes in his ideal Islamic argument. Further, a government, under no circumstances, has the right to interfere, without due consultation, with individual freedoms. Accordingly, proper checks and balances are central elements in the functioning of a democratic system. His thought upheld the harmony between religious principles and democracy. In other words, Bazargan was of the opinion that religion's main mission is aimed at securing human freedom and dignity.

Democracy: People's Right to Rule
For Bazargan democracy is based on the value of the human as an independent individual. This is also stated in the Qur'an where the right to self-determination is enshrined in a democratic constitutional order in many surahs of the Qur'an. Bazargan's belief in democracy rests on the concept of Islamic government according to the Shia version of Islam,

with particular reference to Imam Ali (Bazargan 1998, pp. 306–326). Bazargan went a step further by arguing that the Qur'an and Hadiths only offer general outlines; neither give details about the specific form of government. The reason for this lies in the fact that any form of government should reflect the cultural context and prevailing social mores (عرف). The administration of government must be based on consensus among the people and political actors whether in power or in opposition. A government without the consent of the majority is not legitimate (Bazargan 1998, p. 335). In short, liberal Islamic discourse is based on consensus, concealed contract, Shura and election which is deemed compatible with democracy. The political groups which broadly followed this conceptualisation of Islam in Iran during the 1960s and 1970s were *Nahzat-e Azad-e Iran* (Movement for Freedom Iran) and the *Hezb-e Jomhurikhah-e Khalq-e Musulman* (The Muslim Republican People's Party) (Hosainizadeh 2007, p. 277).

REFERENCES

Amirahmadi, H., & Parvin, M. (1988). *Post-Revolutionary Iran*. Boulder, CO: Westview Press.

Ayubi, N. N. (1991). *Political Islam: Religion and politics in the Arab world*. London, England: Routledge.

Bashiriyeh, H. (2002). *An introduction to the political sociology of Iran: The era of the Islamic republic*. Tehran, Iran: Negah-e Moaser Press.

Bashiriyeh, H. (2012). *Tarikh Andishehai Sisasi dar Gharn Bistom* [History of political thought in the twentieth century] (Vol. 1). Tehran, Iran: Nashr Nay.

Bazargan, M. (1963). *Marz bin din va siasat* [The frontier between religion and policy]. Tehran, Iran: Bina.

Bazargan, M. (1985). *Bazyabi arzeshha* [Regaining values]. Tehran, Iran: Enteshrate Nehzate Azadi.

Bazargan, M. (1998). *Besat* [Prophetic mission] (Vol. 1–22). Tehran, Iran: Bonyad Bazargan.

Bazargan, M. (1999). *Mabahes elmi ejtemae Islami* [Scientific, social, Islamic controversy] (Vol. 8). Tehran, Iran: Sherkat Sahami Enteshar.

Beinin, J., & Stork, J. (1997). *Political Islam: Essays from Middle East report*. Berkeley, CA: University of California Press.

Dabashi, H. (2006). *Theology of discontent: The ideological foundation of the Islamic revolution in Iran*. New Brunswick, NJ: Transaction Publishers.

Feirahi, D. (2010). *Din va Dolat dar Asr Modern (2)* [Religion and State in Modern Age (2)] (Vol. 2). Tehran, Iran: Rokhdad No.

Gellner, E. (1992). *Postmodernism, reason and religion*. London, England: Routledge.

Heywood, A. (1998). *Political ideologies: An introduction* (2nd ed.). New York, NY: Palgrave.

Heywood, A. (2012). *Political ideologies: An introduction* (5th ed.). New York, NY: Palgrave Macmillan.

Hosainizadeh, S. M. A. (2007). *Islam siasi dar Iran* [Political Islam in Iran]. Qom, Iran: Mofid University.

Jahanbakhsh, F. (2001). *Islam, democracy and religious modernism in Iran, 1953–2000: From Bāzargān to Soroush*. Leiden, The Netherlands: Brill.

Johnson, P. (2013). *The Renaissance: A short history*. London, England: Phoenix.

Kadivar, M. (2001). *Hokomat Velaei* [Theocratic State]. Tehran, Iran: Nashr Nay.

Khomeini, S. R. M. M. (1942). *Kashf al asrar* [Key to the secrets]. Qom, Iran: Bita.

Khomeini, S. R. M. M. (1965a). *Ketab baie* [Book of social dealings] (Vol. 2). Qom, Iran: Bita.

Khomeini, S. R. M. M. (1965b). *Ketab baie* [Book of social dealings] (Vol. 1). Qom, Iran: Bita.

Khomeini, S. R. M. M. (1965c). *Tahrir al-vasileh* [Commentary on the vehicle] (Vol. 1). Qom, Iran: Bita.

Khomeini, S. R. M. M. (1996a). *Sahife- ye- Noor* [The lighting page] (Vol. 4). Tehran, Iran: Ministry of Culture and Islamic Guidance.

Khomeini, S. R. M. M. (1996b). *Sahife- ye- Noor* [The lighting page] (Vol. 3). Tehran, Iran: Ministry of Culture and Islamic Guidance.

Khomeini, S. R. M. M. (1996c). *Sahife- ye- Noor* [The lighting page] (Vol. 16). Tehran, Iran: Ministry of Culture and Islamic Guidance.

McLellan, D. (1986). *Ideology*. Milton Keynes: Open University Press.

Mirsepassi, A. (2000). *Intellectual discourse and the politics of modernization: Negotiating modernity in Iran*. Cambridge, MA: Cambridge University Press.

Pedram, M. (2004). *Theologians and modern intellectuals in post-Iranian revolution*. Tehran, Iran: Gaam-e Naw Press.

Plamenatz, J. (1970). *Ideology*. New York, NY: Praeger.

Possamai, A. (2009). *Sociology of religion for generations X and Y*. London, England: Equinox.

Pratt, D. (2006). Terrorism and religious fundamentalism: Prospects for a predictive paradigm. *Marburg Journal of Religion, 11* (1), 1–15. Retrieved from http://www.uni-marburg.de/fb03/ivk/mjr/pdfs/2006/articles/pratt2006.pdf

Rahnema, A. (1998). *An Islamic utopian: A political biography of Ali Shariati*. London, England: I.B. Tauris.

Rajaee, F. (2007). *Islamism and modernism: The changing discourse in Iran*. Austin, TX: University of Texas Press.

Shariati, A. (1980a). *Tarikh tamadon* [History of civilization] (Vol. 12). Tehran, Iran: Daftare Tanzim va Nashre Asar Shariati.

Shariati, A. (1980b). *Tarikh va shenakht adiyan* [History and knowledge of religion] (Vol. 15). Tehran, Iran: Bina.

Shariati, A. (1981a). *Hosein varese Adam* [Hosein Adam's heir] (Vol. 19). Tehran, Iran: Ghalam.

Shariati, A. (1981b). *Islam shenasi* [Islamology] (Vol. 16). Tehran, Iran: Ghalam.

Shariati, A. (1981c). *Omat va Imamat* [Nation and Imamate] (Vol. 26). Tehran, Iran: Ghalam.

Shariati, A. (1989). *Islam shenasi* [Islamology] (Vol. 30). Tehran, Iran: Chapakhsh.

Shariati, A. (1995). *Shie* [Shiite] (Vol. 7). Qom, Iran: Bita.

Shariati, A. (2002). *Mazhab alihe mazhab* [Religion versus religion] (Vol. 22). Tehran, Iran: Chapakhsh.

Vincent, A. (2010). *Modern political ideologies* (3rd ed.). Chichester, England: Wiley-Blackwell.

Yosefi Ashkevari, H. (1997). *Shariati va naghd sonnat* [Shariati and criticism of tradition]. Tehran, Iran: Yad Avaran.

PART II

A Duality of Radicalism and Reform: Analyses of the Ideas of Khomeini, Shariati and Bazargan

CHAPTER 3

Key Ideological Elements

As mentioned in Chap. 2, the term 'ideology' (from its etymological inception by Destutt de Tracy in 1796) took on a new contextual meaning and connotation in Iran shaped by significant political experiences. Ideology thus became powerful force behind social and political arrangements in the contemporary era. Culturally it is notable that ideology originates from the heart of a society and has implications for the contextual development of that society. The ideological tendencies in the twentieth century are distinguished in two manifestations: Indigenous ideology, which emerges from the core social fabric of a society, and imported ideology, which is influenced by forces outside the cultural context of the society.

Political Islamic groups follow an ideology which is premised on religious texts because religious-inspired thinkers and groups believe in God's revelation as a programme for social reconstruction. They reject all non-religious ideologies as lacking in religious-oriented morality (Heywood 2012, p. 264). This chapter examines the viewpoints of Khomeini, Shariati and Bazargan, and makes critical comparisons between them, with regard to Islamic ideology. Further, this chapter elaborates on ideology through five aspects: An explanation of the situation, the system of knowledge, the system of norms, the system of government and public policy. This part of the study illuminates the ideological similarities and differences between Khomeini, Shariati and Bazargan.

© The Author(s) 2020   37
S. M. Lolaki, *Diverging Approaches of Political Islamic Thought in
Iran since the 1960s*,
https://doi.org/10.1007/978-981-15-0478-5_3

IDEOLOGY DEFINED

Khomeini

In an interview with the UK *Times* newspaper in *Nofel Loshato* in Paris in 1978 (Khomeini 2010b, pp. 387–388), Khomeini was questioned about his beliefs: What are his beliefs? Where and how does he manifest these beliefs? And how does he act on these beliefs? His answer was that the root of his beliefs, like those of all other Muslims, came from the Holy Qur'an, Prophet Mohammad and other leaders, following the guiding principles of monotheism centred on a belief in God as the Creator of this world, who is knowledgeable of everything and omnipotent with respect to everything. These principles underpin human obedience to God alone, and function in accordance with the Islamic perspective that individuals are not submissive to another one. From this principle arises liberty (freedom) whereby nobody can make laws unilaterally because only God determines law in this world along with human happiness and perfections. Obedience to God and instruction comes from following the message of the prophets. Therefore all people must be servants of God and not of other people such as autocratic or colonial powers (Khomeini 2010b, pp. 387–388).

This stance was clarified, in an interview with a Japanese journalist which took place in the city of Qom in 1980 (Khomeini 2010c, pp. 125–126), where Khomeini made it clear that Shia Islam is a political Islamic ideology which has resonance in the traditional Iranian context. He stated in forceful terms that the distinctive Shia identity, from the inception of the Imamate, was contiguous with the Islamic principles of Shia Islam and is thus a socio-political religion which notably faced extensive struggles with the Sunni Umayyad and Abbasid Caliphates. As a consequence of these struggles, the Shia people were under pressure and Shia ideas spread into other lands. This led to Shia lending support to other oppressed people. From the viewpoint of Khomeini it is the Shias who represent the oppressed and who continue the war against all oppressors (Khomeini 2010c, pp. 125–126). In effect, Khomeini advocated a form of liberationist interpretation of Shia Islam: Its raison d'être as to struggle against oppression not only as directly encountered by Shia people, but also against all oppressors everywhere.

In another 1978 interview in Paris (Khomeini 2010b, pp. 407–408), Khomeini maintained that the religious-minded people in Iran played a pivotal role in the politics of protest in successive movements such as the Constitutional Revolution and the Tobacco movement (1891), the establishment of a seminary at Qom (1920s) and the uprising on 15th of Khordad (5 June 1963). From his standpoint, the Shia religion supports modernisation in terms of the growth of scientific research while rejecting aspects of modernisation when it comes to morality and consumerism. He pointed out that clerics (mullahs) have always been pioneers of such ideas and movements (Khomeini 2010b, pp. 407–408).

Shariati

For Shariati ideology exists as a special sphere of knowledge helping people to realise their social position in a world determined by historical and global conditions. Thus, ideology assigns responsibilities and upholds specific ideals and judgements (Shariati 2011a, p. 42). As a belief-system ideology guides people in their social orientation, nationality, class, system of values, and plays a part in the interactions between individuals and society (Shariati 2011a, p. 43). Ideologues and ideologies in Islam are given recognition by Shariati.

For Shariati an ideologue is somebody who holds and advocates a distinct ideological worldview (Shariati 2010b, p. 625). The role of an ideologue is a theoretical one which, in Islamic terms, is attuned to the figurehead of Prophet Mohammad and, politically, is tantamount to the role of prophet. Seen from this prism, the role of an ideologue is not the same as that of a person who leads a political party in a democratic society. This is because a theoretician (ideologue) is different from that of a secretary general of a political party, for example. In Islam some groups make a distinction between Imamate and Caliphate. In this regard, Prophet Mohammad enjoys a position with dual functions: Imamate (spiritual) and leadership (political). Imam Ali was appointed, primarily in the spiritual role, as the first Imam. Politically, the people at the time established a Shura (council) to deal with temporal issues of the society (Shariati 2010b, p. 625). By doing so a clear separation line was drawn between the institutions of temporality, which is peculiar to the consensus reached by the community, and the Imamate which is strictly an arena of the spiritual world.

Furthermore, Shariati held that the term ideology has a direct relation with another word, namely, 'intellectual'. An intellectual is one who has a special ideology, one which is appropriate for the time and age in which they live. Today we live in an era of a self-awareness. Shariati argued that somebody who does not have an ideology might live as a 'normal' person but cannot have an informed view about any aspect of social life beyond his/her subjective sphere and responsibility (Shariati 2010c, p. 60).

Bazargan

Bazargan asserted that (Muslim) ideology is something that emanates from the nature of God and God's prophets. Subjective prejudices marginalised in favour of a 'good' ideology represented through God. For Bazargan, a principled ideology stems from the Holy Qur'an and the Sunnah of Prophet Mohammad (Bazargan 2009b, p. 293). From a scientific and temporal perspective, the prophets alone can teach humans about life. The prophets' teachings and their struggles against oppressive obstacles and hardships have had a far-reaching impact on the people and helped to shape their evolving social life (Bazargan 2005, pp. 168–169). In addition, it is of paramount importance that the door for Ijtihad (interpretation) should be an open one, in order that people are able to update their ideologies to meet the changing demands of their time and contemporary social conditions. Additionally, such Ijtihad, from Bazargan's point of view, is the driver for scientific activity, research and fertile intellectual engagement (Bazargan 2009a, p. 29).

ISLAMIC IDEOLOGY IN THE THOUGHT OF KHOMEINI, SHARIATI AND BAZARGAN

Khomeini

This section will analyse the significance of the ideas of Khomeini, which can be summarised as follows.

1. Khomeini held that Islam is comprehensive as a 'school of thought' (Khomeini 2010b, p. 218). Despite Islam's cultural richness and capacity to embrace all aspects of human life, some thinkers have singularly focused on selective dimensions of Islam (Khomeini 2010b, p. 218). Khomeini believed that Prophet Mohammad was a 'comprehensive man' and is thus a role model (Khomeini 2010d, pp. 420–421). The mission of Prophet Mohammad was to represent all aspects of life (Khomeini 2010d, pp. 420–421). With

regard to *fiqh*, Khomeini followed the school of Jafari jurisprudence that emerged in the sixth Imam in the series of the Shia
Imamate. He asserted in a speech for seminary council of Qom in
1983 that Jafari jurisprudence should be studied in seminaries and
should be strengthened (Khomeini 2010e, p. 72). Jafari jurisprudence is essentially based on the Qur'an, the Sunnah of the prophet
and the Twelver Imam, together with the application of reason and
the consensus of a community of scholars. Khomeini himself
belonged to the Osoliyon (Principalists) school. His jurisprudential approach was influenced mainly by the principalists who historically follow the four key principles of Qur'an, Sunnah, consensus
of community and reason—and in that order of priority.
Furthermore, Khomeini placed the primacy of Islam over nationalism (Khomeini 2010f, pp. 167–168). He maintained that the
notion of fatherland has been respected by Islam, but nevertheless
for Islam the belief in God which fosters brotherhood among
Muslims is more important than the notion of nationalism
which has influenced the Islamic world in the modern era. Further,
the notion of government in Islam is based on just government
(Khomeini 2010f, pp. 167–168).

2. The important role of clergy. Khomeini noted in a 1978 speech
   that some people held the view that he is an exceptional person
   within the rank and file of the clergy (Khomeini 2010b, pp. 279–
   280). However, from his perspective, it would be a grave error to
   separate clergy from the masses. He himself is therefore 'one of the
   people', not separate from them. Nonetheless, as a group, the Shia
   clergy in Iran have historically been a symbol of Islam. The masses
   have followed the guidance of the clergy and the 12 imams. The
   predominant argument by some intellectuals was that no reform
   could be achieved without guidance from the clergy. For Khomeini,
   unity between clergy and the masses had a position of priority in
   his thinking. Thus, the role which the masses play reinforces the
   role played by Islamic academics and clergy (Khomeini 2010b,
   pp. 279–280).

   Khomeini maintained that some groups had attempted to
   remove the clergy from the political scene, along the pattern followed in the West where a separation was made between the
   authority of the church and the state from the nineteenth century
   onwards. Khomeini did not endorse the demarcation between the

religious and state institutions. Indeed, quite the contrary. He argued that unlike Christianity for which its founder was crucified before having the time and opportunity to establish a temporal institution (Church) as such, let alone a Christian state, Prophet Mohammad by contrast founded a government in Medina (622 CE/1AH) as an integral part of the second phase of the early development of Islam. In line with the Medina government, Imam Ali, the first Imam in Shia Islam, established a temporal Muslim state as the last of the Rashidun (the four 'Rightly Guided Caliphs' who followed Prophet Mohammad in leading the Muslim community). According to Khomeini, politics like any other social affair of human life is a duty which Muslims must practise within the public sphere. Thus, he held that in the absence of the Muslims' active participation in the international sphere, the US and the USSR, being the two superpowers of the time, had come to manage Iranian society in keeping with their national interests, rather than the best interests of Iran (Khomeini 2010g, pp. 10–11).

3. The maturity of culture. Khomeini noted in a speech in 1987 that the contemporary world had changed (Khomeini 2010h, pp. 241–242). He claimed that the common people in Europe, Asia and Africa were knowledgeable with regard to their past. By contrast, the cultural maturity of Iranians was by no means similar to the times of Pahlavi and Qajar dynasties when Iranian political affairs were directed by foreign ambassadors. He asserted unequivocally that contemporary Iranians were driven by the spirit of revolution which aimed at returning Iran to its authentic Islamic roots. Thus, political progress and awareness lay at the heart of the cultural renaissance of Iranians and Iran (Khomeini 2010h, pp. 241–242).

    To achieve the ideals of the revolution, Khomeini was a staunch proponent of public education. For him, literacy empowered Iranians and prevented foreign exploitation which had historically weakened Iran equating education and knowledge with power (Khomeini 2010f, pp. 451–452).

4. Fighting against despotism. Khomeini believed in fighting the Pahlavi dynasty in order to resist despotism and a regime which was supported by foreign powers (Khomeini 2010i, pp. 368–369).

    Khomeini maintained that Reza Khan took power in Iran through a coup engineered by the British applying coercive state power to detach Islam from public life. The coercive nature of the dictatorship of the Shah was reflected in the laws prohibiting the Hijab, the traditional veil of Muslim women, and efforts to restrict or marginalise popular Islamic religious events and festivities from public life. State power was employed with force. For instance, Mohammad Reza Pahlavi ordered the killing of people in the uprising 15th of Khordad in 5 June 1963. The 'white revolution' in 1963 enacted land reforms and opened the Iranian economy and market to US. The irony of the 'white revolution' lay in the fact that Iran's market would be open to US commercial benefits. Khomeini's reservation was not only confined to the Reza Shah dynasty, for the army and all state institutions were dominated and directed by the US as far as he was concerned (Khomeini 2010j, pp. 298–309). In other words, he believed that Mohammed Reza Shah had undermined the freedom of the Iranian people by imposing censorship of the media, and impeding democratic progress (Khomeini 2010k, pp. 73–74).

As far as Khomeini was concerned, Mohammad Reza Shah represented the mindset of a stagnant culture. This mindset caused a great deal of harm to the country in terms of both its spiritual and temporal values. Because of this mindset Khomeini and others could not stay in Iran to help manage the country (Khomeini 2010b, p. 15). For Khomeini, Mohammad Reza Shah was a corrupt personality who failed to promote issues associated with human rights. Indeed, the monarchical system was not based on equality. People did not even enjoy basic political rights in respect to electing their own representatives. Khomeini held that in the wake of the Iranian revolution, people would enjoy human rights and be able to manage their own affairs (Khomeini 2010l, pp. 197–198).

Furthermore, he argued that Mohammad Reza Shah was the cause of poverty in Iran. The Shah had bought weapons from the US and USSR while the average citizens of Iran did not have basic essentials such as food and water. Also, he added that political activists and intellectuals were imprisoned and subject to torture. To sustain a repressive regime, the Shah had created Savak, an intelligence organisation which fundamentally aimed at monitoring, spying and controlling all political activist groups (Khomeini 2010m, pp. 147–148).

5. The role of colonialism. Khomeini asserted that Islamic governments are under pressure from colonial powers (Khomeini 2010a,

pp. 373–375). According to him, the cross-sectarian war between Sunni and the Shia Islam was intentionally created and intensified by colonial powers in the wake of the crumbling of the Ottoman Empire. In the post-Ottoman period, the main thrust of colonial policy was aimed at creating a schism between the Shias and the Sunnis. Following the collapse of the Ottoman Caliphate this policy, typically known as divide and rule, was devised to exploit the Muslim countries (Khomeini 2010a, pp. 373–375). Khomeini categorically criticised the colonial world for not according respect and prestige to the Third World. He believed the colonial powers also devised policies which left the Islamic countries undeveloped. For instance, he argued that technological prowess was denied to Third World states, and their universities imposed restrictions that effectively negated efforts by students from Muslim or Third World societies and also negated an opportunity to study certain subjects. These policies were aimed at sustaining the status quo which emerged in the post-Ottoman Empire era and later during the decolonisation phase following the Second World War (Khomeini 2010n, pp. 434–435). Khomeini posited the theory that, following the 1979 revolution, several overseas governments regularly treated Iran as inferior and imposed economic sanctions. On occasions, the colonial policy extended to military action upon the country (Khomeini 2010c, p. 514).

6. The independence of Iran. Khomeini cited national trauma within the country arising from a lack of independence in terms of culture, economy and the military. The economy was dependent on imported goods, and rather than creating an independent national economic system, the 1970s saw Iran in a precarious position with regard to running its domestic and foreign policy. As a consequence of these policies, Iran was reduced to being little more than a consumer economy (Khomeini 2010b, p. 54). By 1978 he stated that if the Iranian people wanted stability they needed to establish a government based on popular sovereignty and remove the US and other colonial powers from the country in order to make Iran and the rest of the Muslim world powerful and autonomous (Khomeini 2010b, p. 98). In a speech to the Minster of Oil and some mangers of that ministry in 1981 he argued economic sanctions provided an opportunity for national self-sufficiency to begin predicting that, despite the pressure applied by the hegemonic powers against Iran, in a decade or two Iran would be in a position

to run its varying economic sectors such as agriculture and oil without receiving any technical or other advisory input from other countries (Khomeini 2010o, pp. 114–115).

7. Freedom of Iran. In a speech after the 1979 Islamic revolution Khomeini declared that liberty was the greatest gift denied to the Iranian people during Pahlavi dynasty. It is worth mentioning here that he related liberties to an arena of God's sanctioning to be employed or exercised in the right way (Khomeini 2010p, p. 491). In a speech in 1983 Khomeini argued that some political parties such as *Tudeh* party and associates belonging to the USSR should not be allowed to engage in political activities in Iran, for they pose a threat to Iranian liberty, understood from a Shia Islamic perspective. Such groups or parties, whether belonging to the East or the West, act according to foreign edicts. From Khomeini's standpoint, these groups were not genuine political groups since their main aim was engagement in espionage in the country (Khomeini 2010q, pp. 675–676).

8. The fight between oppressed and oppressor. Khomeini maintained that all Abrahamic religions were for the masses. In Islam, Prophet Mohammad stood up for oppressed people and finally defeated the oppressors (Khomeini 2010m, p. 327). Khomeini did not hold back on his ideas for the establishment of a party which could represent the oppressed people in the Islamic world. This party should stand up against any in the West or the East that seek to plunder oppressed peoples. This party is the party of God and it would fulfil the message of God on earth (Khomeini 2010r, pp. 280–281). Indeed, he mentioned in a speech in 1983 that it was a blessing of God that the government of Iran was the government of oppressed people. Today, the president and ministers recognise the pain of these people and serve them better because they were oppressed people (Khomeini 2010e, pp. 28–29).

9. The role of women in society. Khomeini claims that in two historical periods women suffered injustices. The first was during the time of ignorance (the pre-Islamic period of *al-jahaliyyah*) which was a time when women were treated poorly and degraded. But with the emergence of Islam women gained their rightful position in society. The second time was during the Pahlavi period when women were treated like acquisitions and part of material consumption. For Khomeini Islamic women are accorded equal status with himself. He reiterated the view that the kernel of happiness of

a society related to the position of women (Khomeini 2010m, pp. 338–339). In a speech to women academic university members in 1985 Khomeini elaborated on the fact that women in Iran played a significant role in the 1906 Constitutional Revolution, the 1979 Islamic Revolution and the in war between Iran and Iraq (1980–1988). Also, in the contemporary era, they had enjoyed good growth in education statistics. He endorsed the attendance of women in the public sphere and decried the instrumental use of women which had become a common practice in the era of modernity (Khomeini 2010h, pp. 7–8).

10. The role of martyrdom in Islam. Khomeini asserted that for Iranian martyrdom self-sacrifice is an important subject. In Islam Prophet Mohammad and the Imams accepted martyrdom, with some of the latter even becoming martyrs for Islam themselves. All Muslims from the dawn of Islam welcomed this concept based on the spiritual dimensions of human existence. For Khomeini, the notion of martyrdom would lead to the eternal world (Khomeini 2010m, pp. 276–277).

11. Neither West nor East. Khomeini argued in 1978 that China, the USSR and US all supported the Shah but that the Iranian people should not lean on either the West or the East since these powers supported the killing of people in the country. It is duty of revolutionaries to remove the influence of these international powers from Iran (Khomeini 2010j, p. 484).

12. Revolutionary nation—revolutionary Iran. Khomeini believed that Iranians brought about the revolution because they wanted the country to be managed by the Iranian people, not foreign powers. The removal of the superpowers from Iran would lay the ground for Iranians to manage their own country (Khomeini 2010k, pp. 115–116). Khomeini pointed to other serious revolutions, such as those of France and the 1917 Russian revolution. However, he held that the purpose of these revolutions resulted in the grabbing of temporal power, in contrast to the Iranian revolution which was oriented by divine inspiration and hence aimed at delivering justice for all (Khomeini 2010h, pp. 202–203).

13. The Islamic Republic. Responding to a question concerning the content or substance of an Islamic Republic, Khomeini answered this was a matter for government based on the foundations of Islam and respect for the system of voting, which in a new Iran, translated to freedom of the press. In sum, communities and parties are free

so long as they do not jeopardise the ideals of the Islamic revolution and the national interest (Khomeini 2010k, p. 266). The protection of the Islamic republic was a divine duty. In his view, the agendas of the various superpowers were deceptive and included the instigation of war between Iran and Iraq, the support of certain opposition and terrorist groups intent on political assassinations and sabotage. Khomeini claimed these were all efforts to destabilise the Islamic Republic. It was necessary therefore to protect the divine blessing of the Republic with a unity of people and purpose, and so put aside interfering differences (Khomeini 2010g, pp. 364–365).

14. Export of Revolution. Khomeini, in a post-revolution speech, asserted that the Iranian-Islamic republic is a good role model for other countries to follow, not only because it is an autonomous country, but also to break the hegemonic agendas of the superpowers (Khomeini 2010c, p. 336). He asserted that Iran needed to export its revolution not with weapons but with cultural resources, and had a duty to enlighten other Muslim countries. From his perspective, the export of the revolution required a solid unity among Muslims against the imperialistic powers, especially in terms of Israel in the region (Khomeini 2010f, pp. 90–91).

15. The cultural revolution with focus on universities. Khomeini supported the Cultural Revolution between 1980 and 1983 which involved the closing of universities and the removal of academics and students who supported ideas and trends from either the East or the West. He asserted that Iran agreed with the progress and development of universities and knowledge, but would not support those academics who followed or espoused non-Islamic values as he and the ulema chose to define them. For him, Islamic universities must be based on Islamic culture. If universities are genuinely autonomous, meaning free from external influence, Iran can be an autonomous country (Khomeini 2010o, pp. 427–428).

Shariati

This section will review and discuss the significance of the socio-political ideas of Shariati. It is important to provide a broad overview of his evolving conceptualisations in order to understand their contribution to political thought of the era. His understanding can be summarised as follows.

1. The genesis of ideological Islam. Shariati asserted that in the contemporary era the transformation of Islam from culture to ideology was to be applauded (Shariati 2008a, pp. 202–203). The transformation brought contemporary Islam in line with the original form of Islam that emerged in the seventh century. He held that while Islam in its original form was inspired by Prophet Mohammad, in the contemporary era intellectuals could play a role similar to that of the original founders of Islam. In the absence of the prophet, Muslim intellectuals could similarly be inspired by the Qur'an directly inherited from Prophet Mohammad (Shariati 2008a, pp. 202–203). Shariati held that Islam was a pure ideology in its original form: The personalities, and movements which they led, had an ideological face, but in the subsequent centuries Islam was transformed into a complex cultural phenomenon which eventually developed social capacities such as philosophy, jurisprudence, mysticism and Sufism. Given the successive periods which Islamic emperors ruled, differences appeared in contrast to the Medina phase (622–632 CE) which was predominantly reflected in ideology and represented through culture and civilisation, while the Abbasid Caliphate (750–1258 CE) was culturally based. In other words, religious ideology was transformed into culture (Shariati 2009a, pp. 192–193).

2. Monotheism. Shariati believed that monotheism is not just a matter of believing in one God, but also means unity and equality among people regardless of race and class (Shariati 2010d, pp. 12–16). He viewed monotheism as a comprehensive social movement without class implying the negation of inequality. The invitation to monotheism and the service of God thus represents the kernel of monotheistic revolutionary religion which demands from its followers that they follow the only Being that is God. Monotheism thus asserts itself in terms of a permanent revolutionary form which is directed against all kinds of oppression. Monotheism is premised on a system which has potential to offer justice, equality, brotherhood and public ownership of wealth. The prophecy of Mohammad was against all social ills (Shariati 2010d, pp. 12–16).

3. The role of Martyrdom. Martyrdom is another ideological aspect of Shariati's revolutionary thinking (Shariati 2010a, pp. 176–181). According to standard Shia interpretation, Imam Hussein was the

third Imam of Shiism who stood up to the Umayyad Caliphate which was based on a myriad injustices. He and some followers were martyred at Karbala by order of the Caliph Yazid bin Muawiyah. Some scholars believe that this was the start of the eventual failure of the Umayyad dynasty. Shariati examined the concept of Martyrdom in two speeches in the wake of the martyrdom of the founders of the Mujahidin party in 1972. He asserted that whilst Imam Hussein could have remained silent, he instead chose an informed martyrdom. Shariati presented the martyrdom of Imam Hussein as a revolutionary role model which had a great impact on young people both before and after the revolution (Shariati 2010a, pp. 176–181).

4. The role of *Entezar* (expectation). The concept of *Entezar* (expectation) is related to the belief in the eventual return of the last Imam as the Mahdi. Shia interpretation holds that the final leader in the line of Imams did not die, but is alive and has vanished from the sight of believers and will reappear and deliver justice to the world. Shariati (Shariati 2010a, p. 264) wrote that there were two expectations: Negative and positive. The negative was shaped by stagnation and silence represented by the status quo in society. The positive sanctions emancipation by way of revolution encompassing justice and equality. Moreover, an expectant human is ready for revolutionary jihad which is imminent. In the absence of the Imam Mahdi, the responsibility for justice lies with the people. This, therefore, puts a heavy responsibility on the people (Shariati 2010a, p. 264).

5. Revolution. Shariati created the concept of revolution in subscribing to a revolutionary rather than reformist Islam. For him, reformist Islam is a recipe for maintaining the status quo (Shariati 2010c, p. 108). He believed that Islam entails three dimensions of permanent revolution. Firstly, Islam is an interpretation which is aimed at creating a scientific society. Secondly *Nahi Anil Munkar* (Forbidding Evil) and *Amr Bil Mahroof* (Enjoining good) are duties which prompt people to engage in political and social activities in the public sphere. Thirdly, immigration manifests itself in two ways: Inner and outer (spiritual and temporal) (Shariati 2011b, pp. 81–83). He asserted that today's Munkar (Evil) reflected itself in global imperialism, global Zionism, immature cultural, norms, old and new colonialism, racism, Westernisation and cultural colonialism (Shariati 2009b, p. 77).

6. Taqiyeh (reservation). This is another traditional concept to which Shariati ascribed a new meaning. In the old, or usual, meaning it refers to the act of dissimulation when one's life and property are in danger. But Shariati asserted that Taqiyeh is a type of counsel which, during revolutionary struggles, brings safety and security for the revolutionary organisation (Shariati 2009b, pp. 201–202). Here dissimulation becomes rather a form of secrecy or hiddenness. In this sense, Taqiyeh was undertaken by the Mujahidin to support a hidden organisation in order to fight the oppressive regime (Shariati 2009b, pp. 201–202).

7. Alawi and Safavid Shi'ism. The contrast of the Alawites and the Safavid Shias is another challenging idea of Shariati. He identified himself as an Alawi Shia rather than Safavid Shia. He asserted that Shia ideas emerged in a revolutionary form before the Safavid Empire. But with the settlement of Shia Islam in Iran, Shi'ism became a tool in the hands of the Safavid emperor to serve the government and family dynasty. Shi'ism therefore became a stagnant religion with negative Taqiyeh (reservation) and *Entezar* (expectation). People were invited to be silent about evils and deviations. But Alawi Shia is a positive *Entezar* (expectation), and Taqiyeh (reservation) is a notion by which people should stand up against the unjust governments (Shariati 2011c, pp. 8–15).

8. Exploitation, colonisation and despotism versus mysticism, equality and liberty. Shariati believed in two natural human impulses which first manifested themselves in the dialectical battle between the two sons of Adam—Abel and Cain (Shariati 2007, pp. 47–53). Cain has three faces Zar (gold), Zor (force) and Tazvir (deception). These are manifested throughout history in exploitation, colonisation and despotism. Shariati believed that people are the victims of these impulses. He wanted to replace these with mysticism, equality and liberty (Shariati 2007, pp. 47–53).

Bazargan

Bazargan, in a speech in 1985, pointed to three different categories concerning the genesis of Islamic ideology in Iran: The pre-Islamic revolution, the post-Islamic revolution and the future Islamic ideology (Bazargan 2012, p. 313).

The Genesis of Islamic Ideology Pre-1979 Revolution
Bazargan asserted that the Iranian people, in light of their successive social and political experiences, supported a long-standing devotion to the Constitutional Revolution, the military coup conducted by Reza Khan, the struggle against British hegemony, communism in the region and the campaign to nationalise oil. All this showed that with the removal of authoritarianism, monarchical power and foreign domination, cultural and intellectual stagnation could be eliminated (Bazargan 2012, p. 313). Under prosecution in a 1963 military court (which sentenced Bazargan to ten years imprisonment), he defended himself and members of his party (Freedom of Movement of Iran) by saying that the happiness of the Iranian people in this world, and the hereafter, lies in the dismissal and abolishment of political despotism practised by Iranian kings in the last two and half millennia (Bazargan 2012, p. 314).

In reference to past ideologies and governments, he claimed that the best government was a state based on the Islamic experience of Prophet Mohammad in Medina (622–32 CE). The period of five years of Imam Ali's governance worked as an effective supplement to the administration of Medina by Prophet Mohammad. Both governments were based on sound notions of justice, equality, humanity and liberty. Bazargan was in tune with Khomeini and while in Paris in 1978 he reiterated in his speeches and interviews that a future Iranian government would be based on democracy in accordance with the principles of Islam. Aside from a few Marxists, secular nationalists and monarchists, who formed no more than 10% of the population, the Iranian masses and intellectuals assented to these themes associated with freedom, independence and the Islamic republic (Bazargan 2012, p. 316).

The Genesis of Islamic Ideology Post-1979 Revolution
In the wake of the Islamic revolution in 1979, Bazargan maintained that removing the monarchy from the political landscape would lay the ground for loosening the grip of despotism which had been in place for the last two and half thousand years. Nonetheless, contrary to general public optimism, he was cautious in his prediction since he profoundly believed profoundly that a political regime which had functioned for a long period of time would leave its legacy in the mindset of the people. He held that the Islamic government which emerged in the post-1979 period deviated from the pre-Islamic revolution in respect to the following points.

1. The slogan of the 'permanence of revolution'. He asserted that at first all revolutionaries have the same ideology, but some revolutionaries seek to continue the revolution through a mentality of revenge, which resulted in the ruling party removing some of its followers (Bazargan 2012, p. 319).

2. Bazargan asserted there was no mention or intimation of the full scope and powers of the office of *Velayat-e Faqih* by Khomeini in Paris before the revolution, or during the establishment of a care-taker government and the revolutionary councils (Bazargan 2012, p. 320).

3. The ruling theocracy. He believed that theocracy was more powerful than national governance and democracy. Furthermore, he added that the Islamic government became a state Islam (Bazargan 2012, p. 321).

4. The polarisation of the country. He maintained that some people had tendencies towards jurisprudential Islam, however, others did not subscribe to the same ideas (Bazargan 2012, p. 322).

5. With profound insight, he accurately spotted Marxist philosophy and rhetoric within revolutionary discourse, and asserted that Marxist individuals and groups impacted on some revolutionaries and thinkers such as Shariati and Khomeini. From his point of view, the ideas of Shariati and Khomeini, which were related to the defence of marginalised and oppressed people in Iran, led the fight against international capitalism and imperialism. He related this Marxist influence to the occupation of the American embassy in Tehran in 1981 which occurred under the influence of Marxist-inspired literature. He was of the view that the Marxist-oriented groups and the Islamic-inspired associations, which were in tune with regard to monarchy and international imperialism, emerged in the post-constitutional phase and competed with one another until the Islamic revolution. In the wake of the Islamic revolution, juris-prudential Islam prevailed and thus gradually removed the varying Marxist groups (Bazargan 2012, pp. 325–326).

6. The continuation of Iran-Iraq War provided another distortion of the ideology of the Islamic revolution because the continuation of the war aimed at exporting the ideals of revolution beyond the boundary of the national state. He added that after liberating the city of Khorramshahr from Iraqi occupation, it wasn't necessary to

continue this war because Iran would lose out with respect to both finance capital and people (Bazargan 2012, p. 327).

7. The bitter experience of revolution. He asserted all social classes including intellectuals, middle classes as well as deprived people were worried about the ideology of Islamic revolution. He added that some people believed all the problems were related to clerical government or the relationship between politics and religion (Bazargan 2012, p. 327).

8. Cultural and moral bankruptcy. Bazargan added that some people were disappointed and the government related all problems to foreign enemies and imperialism, especially the US, rather than acknowledge their own failings. In the wake of the removal of Marxists and monarchists from the political scene, the government became increasingly intolerant of any vocal opposition groups (Bazargan 2012, p. 328).

Islamic Ideology Present and Future
Bazargan posed the question: In this stage of history, what kind of ideology do we need? He answered as follows.

1. The first step was to reject the present ideology and review it again (Bazargan 2012, p. 331).

2. Bazargan maintained that the context of ideology, and the revolutionary slogans, required realignment or reconsideration as the current Islamic ideology created problems which had implications for the entire project surrounding the Islamic revolution. Compromises of pre-revolutionary Islamic ideals reflected inadequate governance by the caretaker government led by Bazargan in the post-revolutionary period. Faced with disagreements and pressure by different groups the government of Bazargan failed to implement the main ideological aspects of the Islamic revolution due to mounting pressure from all political groups, including secular and non-secular ones[1] (Bazargan 2012, p. 332). The resignation of Bazargan saw a caretaker government tasked to control law and order, prepare

---

[1] It is necessary to mention that after the victory of the revolution in 1979 Khomeini, in consultation with the Revolutionary Council, appointed Bazargan as the prime minister (between 11 February and 4 November 1979).

arrangements for a national referendum to change the country's political system to that of an Islamic Republic, and to hold an election for a national assembly.

3. Bazargan had argued that Islamic ideology be based on public consent, national sovereignty and the observance of God, although it was not the duty of government to impose religion and interfere in the private sphere the lives of individuals and their moral consciences. From his perspective, the notion of guardianship by the clerics (mullahs) to claim sovereignty over the people was unnecessary (Bazargan 2012, p. 337).

4. Bazargan maintained that the ethos of nationalism be based on patriotism in accordance with Islamic ideology. In this vein, the ideology would result in friendship among Iranians from different ethic, social and political groups. He added that support for this ideology of patriotism, without any monopolistic tendency by particular groups, was a nationalism that was not in contradiction to God (Bazargan 2012, p. 340).

'OTHERNESS' AND THE WEST

This section will examine some ideological elements of 'otherness' with respect to the West as expressed through the ideas of Khomeini, Shariati and Bazargan. Khomeini argued that Westernisation was a great tragedy for countries of the East (Khomeini 2010r, pp. 75–76). Here, the Islamic world's sense of identity is more valuable than the oil they supplied to Western countries that depended upon it. His perspective is reflected in the idea that Muslim countries should be self-sufficient in managing their interests and be politically and economically detached from the West (Khomeini 2010r, pp. 75–76). Furthermore, Khomeini held that Western foreigners have undertaken numerous studies about Eastern countries and this knowledge allows them to exploit the people. According to Khomeini, Iran was a country studied very closely by the West; its human and material sources were debased so as to curtail Iranian independence for the imperialistic benefit of the Western powers involved (Khomeini 2010n, pp. 118–119).

Khomeini asserted that the West lacked spiritual development (Khomeini 2010p, p. 108). In terms of material wealth Western countries had made considerable progress while they had stagnated in terms of normative values. Islam as a monotheistic school seeks to create moral individuals that reflect, in their thinking and actions, societal values. Khomeini believed Western enlightenment was rigidly based on reason and the will to dominate nature which is a realist perspective. In his view, the Western countries developed only in respect to war techniques while at the same time rejecting moral fortitude. He asserted categorically that promoting human morality, is consistent with Islamic culture (Khomeini 2010p, p. 108). Elsewhere he is on record as having stated that if Iran fails it is the failure of the East, and therefore it is the failure of the oppressed people. So the rank and file of the Muslim nations should be united against the enemy of oppression, expressed in terms of "don't allow America to dominate us" (Khomeini 2010c, p. 108).

By contrast, Shariati believed that the end of an era, that of the dominance of Western civilisation and the ideology of Communism, was at hand. Neither system had guided human beings to redemption, and both had ended up in a catastrophic human tragedy. Therefore, today Islam is an important force with a strong spiritual dimension: The future belonged to Islam as capitalism and Marxism had failed to realise or raise the ideal of humanity. However, he held that for Islam to become an effective and widely embraced guiding ideology, it must get rid of its attendant superstitions (Shariati 2012b, pp. 142–143). Further, he came up with an explanation about the tensions and struggles between the East and the West today (Shariati 2010e, pp. 145–146). He stated that there were various types of knowledge, including philosophical, technical, and literary and art based, mystical or religious, political, social, scientific, and belief-based knowledge, which is referred to as ideology. He believed that the West had all of the aforementioned types of knowledge except the last one, namely ideology. Regarding the above-mentioned struggle, he maintained that the West has the capacity to fight, but it lacked knowledge or motivation about fighting. On the contrary, the East lacked all of the types of knowledge mentioned above but had ideology. For this reason, he thought that the East had no means for fighting but knew what it was fighting for.

He argued that ideology was the winner of the above-mentioned struggle, in that under difficulties where other types of knowledge decline, ideology gains power. In sum, ideological-based movements always emerge victorious in declining societies. In this regard, he enumerated the movements led by people including Abraham, Mohammad, Buddha and Christ. Shariati continued that ideology-based knowledge, characteristic of which is the creation of faith, is responsible for building new societies, new nations and new movements as shown throughout history. He claimed that other types of knowledge cannot create faith. For example, an artist or philosopher may exchange his/her knowledge for money, whereas this is not the case for ideology. In fact, one never relinquishes ideology even at the cost of sacrificing life let alone exchanging it for capital gain. He believes this is because ideology generates faith while other types of knowledge produce political power (Shariati 2010e, pp. 145–146).

Bazargan, in a 1981 interview with *Mizan* newspaper,[2] stated both superpowers the US and the USSR under capitalism and communism, faced rejection. Bazargan argued that the Western superpowers would like Iran to be under their domination which would impinge on the autonomy of Iran. He agreed that Western scientific and technological advances would benefit development in the Islamic world and that the West enjoyed an advantage compared to Marxist views because the latter repudiated religion (Bazargan 2010, p. 73). Bazargan also added that the 1979 Islamic revolution and Constitutional reform in Iran, and all Eastern movements, were the result of a collision with Western civilisation. This is a good point if it can lead to the reform of our own system in a moderate way (Bazargan 2010, p. 124).

Returning to Shia Islamic Culture

This section will examine key ideological elements associated with a return to Shia Islamic culture in relation to the ideas of Khomeini, Shariati and Bazargan. In 1980, Khomeini asserted in a speech that Iranians should study the beginning of Islam with great care and attention (Khomeini 2010r, pp. 38–39). Both the Iranian (Sassanian) and the Eastern Roman (Byzantine) empires were overrun after a short period of time, and this was largely due to the strength and solidity of the Islamic faith, despite more advanced military equipment held in the hands of the Roman and Persian empires. It was essentially the power of faith which led to the Islamic success. The decline of the first Islamic empires unfolded only when the Muslims focused on worldly material things and hence lost the power of faith. Therefore, from the Imam's point of view, the solution to the social and political ills of Muslim societies lay only in returning to the tenets of the early Islamic faith (Khomeini 2010r, pp. 38–39). Additionally

[2] It was the publication organ of the Freedom Movement of Iran (Nehzat-e Azadi-e Iran) after the 1979 Iranian Revolution between 1979 and 1981.

Khomeini stressed in another speech, also in 1980 (Khomeini 2010m, pp. 240–241), when speaking of the martyrdom of Mortaza Motahari (who had been assassinated by an opposition group in 1979), that the Muslim's true guideline for action is the path of the prophets. He went on to advocate a return to the Qur'an and the teachings of Islam. According to Khomeini, the prophets stood with the oppressed peoples and fought against the oppressors, for people marginalised at the hands of oppressors and powerful patronages networks (Khomeini 2010m, pp. 240–241).

Khomeini believed that everything required for both the spiritual and temporal realms could be found in the holy book, the Qur'an (Khomeini 2010p, p. 64). The Qur'an is a resourceful text which covers issues associated with war, peace and morality. In other words, the Qur'an is a dual text which covers two human dimensions: spirit and materialism. A balance must be struck between the spiritual and temporal dimensions of life without going to an extreme on either (Khomeini 2010k, pp. 33–34). He also spoke of an Iranian tendency that seeks to establish an Islamic state based on the Qur'an. For the Imam, it was important that the state be structured in such a way that it corresponded to the Islamic culture as reflected in the Holy Qur'an, rather than duplicating a secular political model based on the notion of human autonomous freedom. He emphasised that any notion of autonomy and freedom must be attuned to the Qur'an. For Khomeini, the importance of reforming the political and social structures lay in the formation of balance between the spiritual and temporal worlds. Seen from this perspective, the Western model is strictly premised on material dimensions. In contrast, a return to the model of early Islam, which represented an age of self-sacrifices in the path of happiness, is the proper path to follow (Khomeini 2010p, p. 64).

Shariati held that within Iran in the contemporary era there is a movement of return to the teachings of the Qur'an. From Shariati's perspective, the tenets of the Qur'an cannot be reduced to the Fatwa or jurisprudence or social rules of morality such as apply to marriage or death, for example. According to Shariati's understanding, the Qur'an is a text which can be employed for fostering human political consciousness and progression. It provides a blueprint for political and social orientation (Shariati 2006, pp. 82–83). Shariati maintained that the aim and philosophy of Shiism is represented by a return to the early Shia phase (Shariati 2008b, pp. 112–113). However, the return to the initial Shia period must be fashioned in a way which corresponds to contemporary conditions and needs. For him, the return to the early stage of Shia Islam would necessitate an ideology which is different from that of ordinary Muslim beliefs. Therefore, a new interpretation of Islamic intellectual sources would be needed (Shariati 2008b, pp. 112–113).

Shariati argued that Prophet Mohammad was the only one who could fashion a new society during his lifetime of faith (Shariati 2012a, pp. 417–418). Moses and Christ during their lifetimes could only restructure their immediate communities. The distinctness of the Prophet rested with the fact that he dealt with a real society rather than a virtual city or utopia. According to Shariati, Prophet Mohammad's version of community reflected itself in the realistic understanding of society as such, and hence could serve as a viable blueprint for Iranian society. This model would have the potential to serve and guarantee the rights of individuals, classes, and groups and thus function effectively at the social, political, economic and moral levels. In the view of Shariati, the Muslim polity in Medina, which lasted ten years, was a period that represented a distinct school of thought with regard to the governance of the Islamic nation based on the Islamic faith (Shariati 2012a, pp. 417–418).

Bazargan also believed that, for an Islamic society, there is no other way than a return to the foundations of the Islamic faith (Bazargan 2010, pp. 74–75). By returning to the Qur'an and the Sunnah of Prophet Mohammad, the spiritual and temporal affairs of people as subjective and objective beings can be properly dealt with; any question of ideology can be referred to the Qur'an. However, in pursuing this tactic the model Islamic society must make proper use of science and technology. From his standpoint, the Qur'an is a text which retains its relevance in line with changing social conditions. He suggested that the interpretations of the Qur'an and the Sunnah are to be based on the notions of Imamate, reason and the consensus of the Muslim community. Thus, the social and political needs of the contemporary era would be met (Bazargan 2010, pp. 74–75).

COMPARATIVE DISCUSSION

This chapter elucidates the ideas of three political Islamic thinkers and their respective Islamic ideological views. A comparative examination revealed five dimensions pertinent to understanding how Islamic ideology was formed and applied.

1. An explanation of the situation. Over three decades, from the 1960s to the 1980s, there was a flourishing enunciation of Shia Islamic

ideological tenets among Iranians. Some Shia terms were redefined by these three Iranian thinkers in particular within and during this period. They critiqued common ideas especially in respect of the Pahlavi monarchy, which symbolised a triangle of despotism, exploitation and colonisation. These three imported elements simultaneously resulted in corrupt morality, economic and social stagnation, and political despotism in Iran. While they sought to transform the monarchy into a constitutional monarchy, in the end they advocated for the outright removal of the entire dynasty from Iran.

2. The system of knowledge. Political Islamic ideas sought to employ three different dimensions: Islamism, nationalism and modernity. These embodied religious ideas demonstrated they had become more important than other political ideologies. Also, these thinkers believed that a *Maktab-e Vaseteh-e Islam* (Islam is a median school) system would take the middle path on a continuum between Marxism and Capitalism. Arguably, there is a delicate difference between these three Iranian thinkers in their comprehension and referencing of Islam. Khomeini opted for jurisprudentialism; Bazargan selected the Qur'an; while Shariati chose the history of Islam, consequently their ideas were common in relation to religion but differed in terms of methods, references and conclusions.

3. A system of norms. It is important to note that the 1979 Islamic revolution gave rise to several ideas and slogans popularised and inspired by these thinkers and the Iranian people. Two were more important than the others, the first was the slogan: 'Neither East nor West, the Republic of Islam', while the second related to independence, freedom and the Islamic Republic. It is clear that these thinkers all focused on freedom, justice, independence and egalitarian ideals for contemporary Iran with all three suggesting these be expanded upon within the society.

4. The system of government. All three thinkers suggested different models. Shariati suggested two theories: Firstly a revolutionary government based on the Ummah and the Imamate and secondly, 'Mysticism, Equality and Liberty'. However, his untimely death meant he could not follow through on his ideas. Nevertheless, his ideas had a significant impact on the formation of events in 1979. For Khomeini an Islamic Republic system based upon *Velayat-e Faqhih* (the guardianship of jurisconsult) was chosen. Bazargan, on the other hand, proposed an Islamic Democratic Republic. Unlike

Bazargan, Khomeini did not use the term 'democratic' since he
believed that an Islamic system is a self-contained one not needing
any addition.
5. Public policy. The Iranian revolution employed both tradition and
modernity-related ideas. This duality shows itself in the Iranian constitution, some parts of which obtain their legislation from Sharia
law while other parts derive legislation from autonomous reason.
This dualism in domestic policies has generally resulted in some
clashes between these schools which revealed itself during political
events including respective elections. Moreover, in terms of foreign
policy, Khomeini and Shariati tended towards a global Islamic civilisation, whereas Bazargan leaned towards Islamic liberal nationalism.

REFERENCES

Bazargan, M. (2005). *Mabahes Eteghadi va Ejtemaei* [Theological and Social issues] (Vol. 11). Tehran, Iran: Sherkat Sahami Enteshar.
Bazargan, M. (2009a). *Bazgast be Quran (1)* [Returning to the Quran (1)] (Vol. 18). Tehran, Iran: Sherkat Sahami Enteshar.
Bazargan, M. (2009b). *Besat* [Prophetic mission] (Vol. 2). Tehran, Iran: Glam.
Bazargan, M. (2010). *Bazyabi Arzesha (1)* [Recovery values (1)] (Vol. 25). Tehran, Iran: Sherkat Shami Enteshar.
Bazargan, M. (2012). *Enghelab Eslami Iran (3)* [Islamic Revolution in Iran (3)] (Vol. 24). Tehran, Iran: Sherkat Shami Enteshar.
Heywood, A. (2012). *Political ideologies: An introduction* (5th ed.). New York, NY: Palgrave Macmillan.
Khomeini, S. R. (2010a). *Sahifeh Imam: Majmoe asar Imam Khomeini bayanat, payamha, mosahebeha, ahkam, ejazat sharei va nameha* [Sahifeh-Ye Imam: An anthology of Imam Khomeini's speeches, messages, interviews, decrees, reli-gious permissions, and letters] (Vol. 1). Tehran, Iran: The Institute for Compilation and Publication of Imam Khomeini's Works.
Khomeini, S. R. (2010b). *Sahifeh Imam: Majmoe asar Imam Khomeini bayanat, payamha, mosahebeha, ahkam, ejazat sharei va nameha* [Sahifeh-Ye Imam: An anthology of Imam Khomeini's speeches, messages, interviews, decrees, reli-gious permissions, and letters] (Vol. 5). Tehran, Iran: Institute for Compilation and Publication of Imam Khomeini's Works.
Khomeini, S. R. (2010c). *Sahifeh Imam: Majmoe asar Imam Khomeini bayanat, payamha, mosahebeha, ahkam, ejazat sharei va nameha* [Sahifeh-Ye Imam: An anthology of Imam Khomeini's speeches, messages, interviews, decrees, reli-

gious permissions, and letters] (Vol. 11). Tehran: Institute for Compilation and Publication of Imam Khomeini's Works.

Khomeini, S. R. (2010d). *Sahifeh Imam: Majmoe asar Imam Khomeini bayanat, payamha, mosahebeha, ahkam, ejazat sharei va nameha* [Sahifeh-Ye Imam: An anthology of Imam Khomeini's speeches, messages, interviews, decrees, religious permissions, and letters] (Vol. 12). Tehran, Iran: The Institute for Compilation and Publication of Imam Khomeini's Works.

Khomeini, S. R. (2010e). *Sahifeh Imam: Majmoe asar Imam Khomeini bayanat, payamha, mosahebeha, ahkam, ejazat sharei va nameha* [Sahifeh-Ye Imam: An anthology of Imam Khomeini's speeches, messages, interviews, decrees, religious permissions, and letters] (Vol. 18). Tehran, Iran: The Institute for Compilation and Publication of Imam Khomeini's Works.

Khomeini, S. R. (2010f). *Sahifeh Imam: Majmoe asar imam Khomeini bayanat, payamha, mosahebeha, ahkam, ejazat sharei va nameha* [Sahifeh-Ye Imam: An anthology of Imam Khomeini's speeches, messages, interviews, decrees, religious permissions, and letters] (Vol. 13). Tehran, Iran: The Institute for Compilation and Publication of Imam Khomeini's Works.

Khomeini, S. R. (2010g). *Sahifeh Imam: Majmoe asar Imam Khomeini bayanat, payamha, mosahebeha, ahkam, ejazat sharei va nameha* [Sahifeh-Ye Imam: An anthology of Imam Khomeini's speeches, messages, interviews, decrees, religious permissions, and letters] (Vol. 15). Tehran, Iran: The Institute for Compilation and Publication of Imam Khomeini's Works.

Khomeini, S. R. (2010h). *Sahifeh Imam: Majmoe asar Imam Khomeini bayanat, payamha, mosahebeha, ahkam, ejazat sharei va nameha* [Sahifeh-Ye Imam: An anthology of Imam Khomeini's speeches, messages, interviews, decrees, religious permissions, and letters] (Vol. 20). Tehran, Iran: The Institute for Compilation and Publication of Imam Khomeini's Works.

Khomeini, S. R. (2010i). *Sahifeh Imam: Majmoe asar Imam Khomeini bayanat, payamha, mosahebeha, ahkam, ejazat sharei va nameha* [Sahifeh-Ye Imam: An anthology of Imam Khomeini's speeches, messages, interviews, decrees, religious permissions, and letters] (Vol. 2). Tehran, Iran: The Institute for Compilation and Publication of Imam Khomeini's Works.

Khomeini, S. R. (2010j). *Sahifeh Imam: Majmoe asar Imam Khomeini bayanat, payamha, mosahebeha, ahkam, ejazat sharei va nameha* [Sahifeh-Ye Imam: An anthology of Imam Khomeini's speeches, messages, interviews, decrees, religious permissions, and letters] (Vol. 3). Tehran, Iran: The Institute for Compilation and Publication of Imam Khomeini's Works.

Khomeini, S. R. (2010k). *Sahifeh Imam: Majmoe asar Imam Khomeini bayanat, payamha, mosahebeha, ahkam, ejazat sharei va nameha* [Sahifeh-Ye Imam: An anthology of Imam Khomeini's speeches, messages, interviews, decrees, religious permissions, and letters] (Vol. 4). Tehran, Iran: The Institute for Compilation and Publication of Imam Khomeini's Works.

Khomeini, S. R. (2010l). *Sahifeh Imam: Majmoe asar Imam Khomeini bayanat, payamha, mosahebeha, ahkam, ejazat sharei va nameha* [Sahifeh-Ye Imam: An anthology of Imam Khomeini's speeches, messages, interviews, decrees, religious permissions, and letters] (Vol. 6). Tehran, Iran: The Institute for Compilation and Publication of Imam Khomeini's Works.

Khomeini, S. R. (2010m). *Sahifeh Imam: Majmoe asar Imam Khomeini bayanat, payamha, mosahebeha, ahkam, ejazat sharei va nameha* [Sahifeh-Ye Imam: An anthology of Imam Khomeini's speeches, messages, interviews, decrees, religious permissions, and letters] (Vol. 7). Tehran, Iran: Institute for Compilation and Publication of Imam Khomeini's Works.

Khomeini, S. R. (2010n). *Sahifeh Imam: Majmoe asar imam Khomeini bayanat, payamha, mosahebeha, ahkam, ejazat sharei va nameha* [Sahifeh-Ye Imam: An anthology of Imam Khomeini's speeches, messages, interviews, decrees, religious permissions, and letters] (Vol. 10). Tehran, Iran: The Institute for Compilation and Publication of Imam Khomeini's Works.

Khomeini, S. R. (2010o). *Sahifeh Imam: Majmoe asar Imam Khomeini bayanat, payamha, mosahebeha, ahkam, ejazat sharei va nameha* [Sahifeh-Ye Imam: An anthology of Imam Khomeini's speeches, messages, interviews, decrees, religious permissions, and letters] (Vol. 14). Tehran, Iran: The Institute for Compilation and Publication of Imam Khomeini's Works.

Khomeini, S. R. (2010p). *Sahifeh Imam: Majmoe asar Imam Khomeini bayanat, payamha, mosahebeha, ahkam, ejazat sharei va nameha* [Sahifeh-Ye Imam: An anthology of Imam Khomeini's speeches, messages, interviews, decrees, religious permissions, and letters] (Vol. 8). Tehran, Iran: The Institute for Compilation and Publication of Imam Khomeini's Works.

Khomeini, S. R. (2010q). *Sahifeh Imam: Majmoe asar Imam Khomeini bayanat, payamha, mosahebeha, ahkam, ejazat sharei va nameha* [Sahifeh-Ye Imam: An anthology of Imam Khomeini's speeches, messages, interviews, decrees, religious permissions, and letters] (Vol. 21). Tehran, Iran: The Institute for Compilation and Publication of Imam Khomeini's Works.

Khomeini, S. R. (2010r). *Sahifeh Imam: Majmoe asar imam Khomeini bayanat, payamha, mosahebeha, ahkam, ejazat sharei va nameha* [Sahifeh-Ye Imam: An anthology of Imam Khomeini's speeches, messages, interviews, decrees, religious permissions, and letters] (Vol. 9). Tehran, Iran: The Institute for Compilation and Publication of Imam Khomeini's Works.

Shariati, A. (2006). *Ma va Iqbal* [We and Iqbal] (Vol. 5). Tehran, Iran: Entesharat Elham.

Shariati, A. (2007). *Khodsazi Enghelabi* [Revolutionary Self monitoring] (Vol. 2). Tehran, Iran: Enteshrat Elham.

Shariati, A. (2008a). *Ba Mokhatabhai Ashena* [With Familiar Audiences] (Vol. 1). Tehran, Iran: Enteshrat Chappakhsh va Bonyad Farhangi Doctor Ali Shariati.

Shariati, A. (2008b). *Islamshenasi (3)* [Islamology (3)] (Vol. 18). Tehran, Iran: Entesharat Elham.

Shariati, A. (2009a). *Bazshenasi Hoviyat Irani Islami* [Recognition of Iranian and Islamic identity.] (Vol. 27). Tehran, Iran: Entesharat Elham.

Shariati, A. (2009b). *Shie* [Shiite] (Vol. 7). Tehran, Iran: Entesharat Elham.

Shariati, A. (2010a). *Hosein Varese Adam* [Hosein Adam's heir] (Vol. 19). Tehran, Iran: Entesharat Ghalam.

Shariati, A. (2010b). *Islamshenasi Mashhad* [Mashhad Islamology] (Vol. 30). Tehran: Chappakhsh.

Shariati, A. (2010c). *Jahanbini va Ideology* [Worldview and ideology] (Vol. 23). Tehran, Iran: Sherkat Shami Enteshar.

Shariati, A. (2010d). *Mazhab Alihe Mazhab* [Religion versus religion] (Vol. 22). Tehran, Iran Entesharat Chappakhsh.

Shariati, A. (2010e). *Tarikh Tamadon (1)* [History of Civilization (1)] (Vol. 11). Tehran, Iran: Entesharat Ghalam.

Shariati, A. (2011a). *Islamshenasi (1)* [Islamology (1)] (Vol. 16). Tehran, Iran: Glam.

Shariati, A. (2011b). *Islamshenasi (2)* [Islamology (2)] (Vol. 17). Tehran, Iran: Entesharat Ghalam.

Shariati, A. (2011c). *Tashyoe Alawi va Tashyoe Safavi* [Alawi Shiite and Safavid Shiite] (Vol. 9). Tehran, Iran: Entesharat Chappakhsh.

Shariati, A. (2012a). *Che Bayad Kard?* [What Must Do?] (Vol. 20). Tehran, Iran: Enteshrat Ghlam.

Shariati, A. (2012b). *Ensan* [Man] (Vol. 24). Tehran, Iran: Entesharat Elham.

CHAPTER 4

The West and 'Otherness': The Question of Modernity

This chapter critically examines and compares the views of Khomeini, Shariati and Bazargan towards the West and the idea of otherness. It extends the understanding of ideology with regard to five aspects: An explanation of the situation, the system of knowledge, the system of norms, the system of government and public policy. These five elements and its application to ideology illuminates the similarities and differences between Khomeini, Shariati and Bazargan.

Khomeini

For Khomeini, Western countries had some degree of internal emancipation but their domination of the Iranian people in particular, and the Third World more generally, was distinguished by secularisation and colonisation. His ideas about the main elements of secularisation are addressed first.

Khomeini argued that the West sought to deny the East its own identity in order to control the political direction (Gebleh) of Iran. Thus, they came to the Eastern countries and studied everything about the society, in order to dominate it. They preferred that Iranian people be dependent on them in thought, philosophy, industry, medicine and indeed everything (Khomeini 2010o, pp. 390–391). Also, he maintained the West attempted to eliminate Islam, the Qur'an and clerics. Indeed, he stated that a former prime minster of Great Britain stated that they should remove the Qur'an

© The Author(s) 2020
S. M. Lolaki, *Diverging Approaches of Political Islamic Thought in Iran since the 1960s*,
https://doi.org/10.1007/978-981-15-0478-5_4

from Muslim people in order to manage them and so achieve domination (Khomeini 2010g, p. 396).

Moreover, Khomeini asserted that the West did not treat morality with respect. The West supported freedom, but only in the libertarian sense of allowing immoral activities such as gambling, alcohol and drug addiction. His view was that the West wanted to influence Iran's young people. But, says Khomeini, we want our people, the young in particular, to be religious and moral (Khomeini 2010o, pp. 342–343). The above statements show that Khomeini was concerned about secularisation in terms of identity, the elimination of Islam, the Qur'an and the clergy from the public sphere, and also the decline in morality in Iran and other Islamic societies. Khomeini believed that his era would end superpower hegemony and therefore no longer dictate terms to Iranian society. People all over the world were also rejecting hegemonic ideas (Khomeini 2010c, p. 38).

It was Khomeini's opinion that the US exerted hegemony in several ways. First, by way of 'capitulation', which was diplomatic immunity granted by the Shah to American military personnel in Iran. This 'capitulation' allowed members of the US armed forces in Iran to be tried in their own military courts if they committed a crime in Iran. Khomeini, in a speech in Qom in November 1964, denounced the Shah and the US for this capitulation. He believed the US wanted to effectively subjugate Iran as a colony by implementing this law. Khomeini called upon all Iranian people to stand up against this law (Khomeini 2010a, pp. 415–422).

Second, Khomeini asserted Iran was like a state within a state formed by virtue of the people's vote, but that in reality the US controlled that state through the Shah (Khomeini 2010j, pp. 16–17). By contrast, Khomeini believed that Iran needed just one autonomous state.

He believed that the imperialism of the US and the USSR led to subservience, whereas Iran should be an independent country under Islamic precepts (Khomeini 2010j, pp. 190–191). Khomeini believed that a key aim of the superpowers was to gain control over the resources in the region, especially gas and oil and to exploit them at low cost (Khomeini 2010b, pp. 273–274).

Khomeini was clearly focused on three main hegemonic areas with respect to the superpowers: Imperialism, colonialism and racial discrimination. As a consequence of these he was exiled by the Shah in 1964. This exile lasted until the Islamic revolution in 1979.

Khomeini maintained that two internal factors supported his colonisation and secularisation thesis in Iran: First, the Pahlavi dynasty, which lasted around 54 years until the Islamic revolution in 1979; second, some parties and groups that were followers of the superpowers after the revolution. He believed that in the era of the Pahlavi dynasty, Reza Khan sought to limit Muslim seminaries and remove the clergy from the public arena. He also banned the wearing of the veil (Hijab) for women and prohibited the practice of mourning of Ahl al-Bayt (for Prophet Mohammad and the Imams). His son, Mohammad Reza Shah Pahlavi, continued to Westernise Iran (Khomeini 2010h, pp. 298–310).

Khomeini constantly expressed the view that the US was the primary problem, and the Shah was the secondary one. He believed everything was dictated to the Shah by the US and, in turn, the Shah was a good servant of US. He said that all the problems of Iran were related to American influence (Khomeini 2010h, pp. 405–406). He asserted several times that, during the Shah's reign, Iran faced more poverty creating a greater gap between the poor and rich. Iranian industries functioned as an assembly line for goods and the Iranian army became dependent on the West with resources such as oil and gas plundered by both the West and the East. This situation and despotism made the Pahlavi dynasty a corrupt agent of the superpowers and also promoted the secularisation and Westernisation of Iran as a kind of colony.

According to Khomeini, the second internal factor had to do with some parties and groups, such as *Fdaeiyan Khakgh* and *Komole* parties which took their ideas from the superpowers. Khomeini believed that they had the following goals: Firstly, they disagreed with Islamic directives (Khomeini 2010l, pp. 408–409); secondly, they sought to disrupt peace by separating out some parts of Iran such as Kurdistan and Baluchistan (Khomeini 2010k, pp. 81–82); finally, propaganda and misinformation was distributed about Iran by them (Khomeini 2010b, pp. 478–479).

Khomeini was highly sensitive to external geopolitical factors and apart from the US and the USSR, his focus was, in particular, on China, Britain and Israel. The first category of countries that drew Khomeini's attention were the USSR and China, two communist countries. In some interviews around the time of the Islamic revolution in 1979 concerning the future of Iran, Khomeini alleged that Iran would not be a communist country because the Iranian people are Muslim people (Khomeini 2010h, p. 495). Also, communist beliefs, according to which religion plays the negative role of an 'opium for masses' (Marx), was repudiated in Iran as it was an unsuitable theory and since it was religion which motivated the masses instead (Khomeini 2010i, pp. 316–318). Furthermore, he believed that the USSR and China supported the Shah when people were killed during demonstrations around the Islamic revolution in 1979 (Khomeini 2010d, pp. 305–306). Finally, he believed that the USSR made superficial gestures for supporting poor people, but in fact it was a dictatorship and supporter of capitalism.

The second category consisted of the US, Britain and Israel. Khomeini claimed repeatedly that the US was the primary guilty party in Iran because of its direct support of the Shah (Khomeini 2010h, p. 407). According to him, the US had lots of interests in Iran and held a number of illegal contracts to plunder Iranian oil. Also, the army was a dependent army that bought weapons from the West at a high price, and the parliament of Iran was a parliament that advocated for America (Khomeini 2010h, p. 79). In general, Iran had become captive to American interests (Khomeini 2010h, pp. 300–302). Khomeini supported capturing the US embassy upon the Islamic revolution as he believed it was a spying nest (Khomeini 2010e, pp. 90–95). He also denounced Britain multiple times because of its interference in Iran over a long period in pursuit of its own interests. Also, he believed that the superpowers created Israel in order to occupy all the Arabic and Islamic countries, given the opportunity; Israel occupied and oppressed Islamic lands, and the US supported. Khomeini distinguished between Judaism and Zionism, and repudiated the latter.

Another important standpoint in relation to Khomeini's thought concerned human rights. He maintained that, according to the US and the USSR, human rights unequivocally meant their own rights (Khomeini 2010m, p. 56). He believed that in fact the superpowers followed their interests rather than human rights (Khomeini 2010f, p. 428) believing in human rights for their own citizens but not all human beings (Khomeini 2010c, pp. 117–118). He believed the US military waged both real wars (such as in Vietnam) (Khomeini 2010l, p. 360) and supported proxy wars (such as in Palestine) (Khomeini 2010h, pp. 345–346). The US regularly interfered in other countries' affairs, especially those of Iran. Khomeini defended human rights based on a religious reliance on God. Imam Ali stated that if a Jewish woman faced discrimination in an Islamic territory and Muslims died from the distress thereof, they should not be blamed. According to Khomeini this is the true depiction of human rights (Khomeini 2010i, pp. 401–405).

Frequently, Khomeini declared that the superpowers were afraid of the Iranian clergy because they prevented Iran from becoming their colony (Khomeini 2010i, p. 15). Clerical power manifested itself in many situations including the tobacco fatwa by Mirzai Shraziai (Khomeini 2010m, p. 451). According to Khomeini, the superpowers, directly or indirectly through the Pahlavi dynasty and some other political parties, sought to destroy Islam but failed while in the era of Reza Shah, they tried to ruin the seminary of Qom unsuccessfully (Khomeini 2010a, pp. 207–208).

In many cases, Khomeini concentrated on freedom and the independence of Iran. He held the belief that as long as the superpowers did not respect the Iranian nation, these kinds of struggles would continue. Hence, he believed that the Iranian people should support relationships with all countries based on moral codes (Khomeini 2010l, p. 449). He also believed and supported the national interests of Iran (Khomeini 2010d, p. 383).

Khomeini and Modernity

Khomeini employed both modernity and tradition. On the one hand, he advocated duty, guardianship and expediency; on the other hand, he paid attention to rights, freedom and the law. These concepts formed a political order expressed through *fiqh*, Islamic jurisprudence. There are three basic elements: (1) Devotional *fiqh*—for example, fasting, praying and pilgrimage; (2) Transactional *fiqh*—for instance, the laws of inheritance and economy and (3) Political *fiqh*—for example, Islamic government and administration. Khomeini also supported both traditional (*Jvaheri*) and dynamic (*Poya*) jurisprudence. Traditional (*Jvaheri*) jurisprudence is based on resources of Shia jurisprudence, namely Qur'an, Hadith, Reason and Consensus. However, in addition to the foundations of traditional jurisprudence, dynamic jurisprudence considers two important elements, namely time and place, when issuing new Fatwas in the modern era in all aspects of life (Khomeini 2010n, pp. 289–290).

Khomeini's model for government in the Islamic Republic of Iran is based on *Velayat-e Faqih* (the guardianship of jurisconsult). He devised this as something between collectivism and individualism, based on duties and rights. He believed that a *Maktab-e Vaseteh-e Islam* (Islam is a median school) system would take the middle way on a continuum between Marxism and Capitalism. Also, he recognised the modern sciences, including engineering and medical sciences, as universal.

In summary, Khomeini resented colonisation and secularisation based on both internal and external factors.

SHARIATI

Shariati believed that the spirit of the West centred on three dimensions: The Greek and Roman civilisation, and Christianity (Shariati 2009b, pp. 138–139). He asserted that the West has experienced both emancipation and domination. According to him, the West (Europe) is not holistic, indeed it is atomistic (Shariati 2011c, p. 180) and thus a fractured society (Shariati 2008, p. 248).

Shariati believed that Iranians fall between the West and East; however, as far as geographical location is concerned, they belong to the East. In terms of history and culture they are somewhere between the East and the West and have always oscillated between them. In fact, he believed that the building blocks of Iran's body of culture and civilisation were taken from the East, namely China and India, and also from the West, namely Greece and Rome. In Shariati's view, some aspects of Iran's Islamic civilisation had been developed with reference to the both the East and the West. For instance, Sufism and theosophy were inspired by the Eastern culture, whereas philosophy was inspired by the Western culture (Shariati 2009b, pp. 139–140).

Shariati's View on the Spirit of the West

According to Shariati, power informs Western culture. Ancient Greece, Rome and subsequent civilisations of the West had sought power over others. He presumed that during the Middle Ages Europe was dominated by the spirit of Eastern culture due to the fact that Christianity effectively went from the East to the West. After the Renaissance, however, the West sought power, which is a characteristic of the Western spirit. He believed this power was a materialistic one which sought to dominate nature as well as the social, economic and political spheres. According to thinkers and philosophers in the East, science was anathema to power. Rather, science and scientists are sacred and follow spiritual values (Shariati 2009b, pp. 141–142).

Further, Shariati claims the West has a materialistic view of nature while the East takes more account of the mystery of creation (Shariati 2009b, pp. 142–143). And in regard to the dominant perspective on life itself, Shariati believed that the Western individual is motivated to fulfil temporal and natural instincts. In other words, the West seeks the 'best' life. On the other hand, the East follows passion and love (Shariati 2009b, pp. 143–

146). However, the West tends to uphold order and discipline in order to attain security both in work and the structure of society (Shariati 2009b, p. 147).

Further distinctions are identified by Shariati including a penchant consumerism: Economically, the West seeks to consume more and more (Shariati 2009b, p. 147). It also follows a rational path based on the application of analytical reason: The West attempts to analyse everything based on reason and logic (Shariati 2009b, pp. 148–149). According to Shariati, in the East, the archetypal city is constructed around a temple, whereas, in the West, the temple is built beside the city to safeguard it. In other words, Shariati thinks that, contrary to the East, in the West what primarily matters, are city and society; the temple is of secondary interest. He argues that, in the East, the city has a spiritual not a mundane origin. In support of this claim, Shariati gives examples of cities constructed around the graves of the prophets Adam and Solomon (Shariati 2009b, pp. 150–151). In the West, the individual is regarded, in effect, as being at the centre of the world, and other people who live in other parts of the world are marginalised. In other words, the Western belief in Occidentalism means that the only valid civilisation in the world is that of the West; others must either choose it or go through degeneration. (Shariati 2009b, pp. 152–158). And finally, for Shariati, the secular value and normative focus of the West is humanism, which places individuals ahead of divinity (Shariati 2009b, pp. 158–167).

Shariati also maintained that it is the duty of intellectuals to understand the new era in which they live. He suggested that intellectuals must realise both the emancipation and domination dimensions of the West and select emancipation while rejecting domination. In this regard, Shariati explained some characteristics of the present century. He identified this century as one of global colonialism which he believed showed itself in different aspects of political, cultural and economic areas of life (Shariati 2010, p. 5). This is the case especially in Latin America, Africa and Asia. This century is also one of capitalist exploitation on the one hand and the unreliability of liberal democracy on the other. He posed the question of what form of democracy had predominated in this era? In reply he sees a surface phenomenon named democracy but, in reality its substance is dictatorship (Shariati 2010, p. 6). He maintained that colonialism, capitalism, liberal democracy, and also European communist and socialism were silent when millions of people all over the world were plundered. Hence, in the view of the West, people living in Latin America, Asia and Africa were a second class citizens of the world (Shariati 2011a, p. 425).

In the past century the mechanisation of life has occurred in the West where machines have replaced thought, feeling and will. In fact, the so-called 'free' human had become a tool for machines. In the past, humans could make free choices; however, nowadays it is not the case (Shariati 2010, pp. 7–8). Another dominant motif of the West is individualism. Shariati maintained that individualism became more powerful and individuals prefer to keep clear of other people. Therefore, people would like to be more isolated from their societies (Shariati 2010, pp. 8–9). Perhaps this is seen with respect to bureaucracy. Shariati believed that bureaucracy has become more and more dominant in the West. He declared that bureaucracy had grown in two steps: First, it became managerial meaning humans had to do everything based on bureaucratic decisions; second, bureaucracy has captured policy in relation to human beings. As he stated, today, administrative order has replaced human needs (Shariati 2010, pp. 13–14).

In other ways, the West has been responsible for the spread of fear and philosophical nihilism. Shariati believed that some philosophers in the West had emphasised the absurdness of the divine creation of humankind. Thus, as there was no creation by God, they promote the autonomy of the human individual. He also believed that today theism has been superseded by the worship of heroes (Shariati 2010, pp. 17–18). Religion has also been challenged in the West by the decline of spirituality. He argued that, today, autonomous reason, especially instrumental reason, has become more powerful whereas human values have become weaker. This application of reason in the West has created a special human who is clever and powerful but who lacks spirit and is relentless in the pursuit of capital. Accordingly, love and devotion have become more superficial, and lust and mundane benefits have become important (Shariati 2010, pp. 19–20). This contributes to the decline and disintegration of the family. Shariati maintained that to have a family has become less and less desirable and people preferred new models of living with each other. In his view, a lack of love for mother and father could lead to serious problems and even crises. He believed that the family is the cornerstone of the society and it faces many problems nowadays (Shariati 2010, pp. 21–22).

The West in the past century has, according to Shariati, witnessed the death of various cultures and civilisations and the genesis of a single global civilisation. He asserted that today the West tries to victimise and remove all other civilisations by imposing a harsh machine-like modernity. Shariati stated that the West sought to replace all civilisations with its own. This way, all cities, buildings, clothing and relations between men and women must be harmonised throughout the world (Shariati 2010, p. 25). But this, he thinks, breeds isolation and despair. He believed that, today, everything has focused on individuals and that, in the West, the young generally leave their families and do not have proper relationships with them. Moreover, he believed that the rate of physiological and psychological problems had increased (Shariati 2009a, pp. 58–62). Finally, he touches on the West's instrumental use of women. Shariati believed that in the West a woman is not viewed as a human with a strong moral base—a beloved person, a mother, a companion—but just a piece of merchandise. Since Western societies are based on production and consumerism, everything is based on instrumental reason and women are regarded as, in effect, sexual goods. He denounced capitalism for supporting these ideas (Shariati 2011d, pp. 93–94).

Shariati and Modernity

Shariati sought to transform and invigorate Islamic discourse, particularly the Shia version of Islam, into a comprehensive revolutionary ideology, cross-fertilised with the philosophical ideas of Marxism and Liberalism. As previously mentioned, Political Islam in the modern era is formed from the encounter between autonomous reason (which is the core of modernity) and recourse to what is understood as inspiration by God (which is the core of traditional Islamic ideas). The result of this encounter is that it produced a broad spectrum of Political Islam. As was stated previously, *fiqh* contains three basic elements: Devotional, Transactional and Political *fiqh*. Shariati maintained that devotional jurisprudence would remain a universal dimension forever. With regard to political and transactional jurisprudence, he referred to autonomous reason based on the Islamic and Iranian contexts (Shariati 2011b, p. 126). This type of reason is value based. It is necessary to mention that the core of modernity is based on autonomous reason and its derivatives which, in the modern era, are individualism and science. Shariati refers to something between individualism and collectivism. He advocated a *Maktab-e Vaseteh-e Islam* (Islam is a median school) system. For the relevant type of government model, he proposed two of his theoretical frames, namely 'The Theory of Ummah and Imamate' and 'Mysticism, Equality and Liberty'. Also, he recognised the modern sciences, including engineering and medical sciences, as universal.

It seems that Shariati, at the same time, criticised both modernity and traditional ideas in order to open a third way for religious intellectuals. In this chapter I have examined the idea of 'Otherness' along with Western modernity-related ideas, focusing on Shariati's critical viewpoints with regard to Western modernity. He believed that it was the duty of Muslim intellectuals to stand against these ideas by returning to a sense of self-centred on the new ideology derived from Iranian-Islamic culture and identity. He also denounced Western modernity for colonialism and secularist features, as well as both capitalism and communism.

BAZARGAN

Bazargan spent some seven years studying in France where, apart from engineering, he studied his own civilisation and those of Greece and Rome, as well as the Middle Ages and the new era of Western modernity. He became familiar with many Western thinkers including Freud, Marx and Sartre. He developed the view that for decades after the Iranian Constitutional revolution, European countries and the US had provided Iran with an inspiration for hope, but also a source of fear; the West was not only the origin of positives but also evils, that affected Iran. He asserted it was the duty of Iranian people to judge the good and bad points of American, German, French and Russian people; it was necessary for Iranians to acknowledge their part in humanity and, therefore, the people should study and learn the good points from the West while rejecting the bad (Bazargan 2011, pp. 406–407).

In this regard, he maintained that there were many good features to come from Western countries. European art, music and painting enabled individuals to be better human beings and to develop humanity-related values. Likewise, for European people wealth is for further production, activity and work, and this provides a job with dignity and a love of industry (Bazargan 2009a, pp. 28–29).

Bazargan believed that, in the West, individuals have devotion to, and serve, their compatriots based on a sense of duty, altruism and patriotism (Bazargan 2009a, p. 30). Furthermore, they seek to gain more knowledge because they enjoy what they are able to gain from truth and wisdom. Also, these kinds of efforts promote morality (Bazargan 2009a, p. 30). Thus, they have three dimensions: A sense of beauty, a sense of service and a sense of curiosity (Bazargan 2009a, p. 31). All people had a role in shaping the new Western civilisation, according to Bazargan, and made an effort towards that goal (Bazargan 2006, p. 187). Thereby, the success of European life in the new modern era is based on a complex social system not just individualism. He believed that in the West people have trust in each other and are able to work collectively and democratically to manage systems (Bazargan 2006, pp. 187–188).

However, he disagreed with colonisation and the secularisation of Western countries. He asserted that for two or three centuries hegemonic relationships expanded in all aspects, especially with regard to new ideologies such as nationalism, liberalism, socialism and communism. He maintained that Muslim intellectuals should seek to create a new ideology and worldview in contrast to Western ideas. He added that Muslims had appropriate relevant experience at the beginning of Islam based on public faith and knowledge. At the same time, they had devotion and acted positively to develop Islam in all aspects of life. Between 1962 and 1964, when he was held in prison by the Pahlavi dynasty, Bazargan tried to use the principles of Islam to form a school of thought to stand against despotism inside the country and resist foreign hegemony from abroad. He sought to form a programme for producing an Islamic state (Bazargan 2009b, pp. 273–274).

Below are Bazargan's points concerning colonisation. He believed that Iran was not directly a colony in modern times. He maintained that there was a competition between the USSR and Britain, and after that the US, to have cultural, economic and political hegemony over Iran (Bazargan 2008, pp. 353–354).

Bazargan asserted that, in the past, ideas came to Iran from the West, and also the East. For instance, Sufic ideas came from India, and philosophical wisdom from Greece. This had both advantages and disadvantages. These kinds of ideas caused damage to both Islam and Christianity and led to some new ideas such as idealism, isolation from life and existentialism. Iran paid less attention to the real nature and originality of Islam. However, with regard to mysticism and wisdom, these ideas remained relevant to Iran (Bazargan 2005, p. 393).

Bazargan was of the view that some terms and concepts, such as colonialism or imperialism, were in fact invented by Lenin based on an interpretation of Marx's ideas; therefore, we should be cautious about them. In fact, so far as Bazargan was concerned, colonialism and human rights had become tools of the USSR, the US and Europe. So, by contrast, Iran should take an alternative path based on definitions and understandings of Islamic and Iranian values. The Superpowers were engaged in a struggle to gain hegemony over the other as far as Bazargan was concerned, so Iran should steer a path between them (Bazargan 2005, p. 394).

Bazargan noted that at the time of the national oil movement in 1953, the Iranian people saw how Britain encouraged the US to mount a coup against Mohammad Mosaddegh, the Prime Minster of Iran. This was because they believed that Iran had become a foothold for the USSR in the region. However, the main problem for Iran had been despotism—and this had been around for 2500 years. (Bazargan 2005, p. 395). So far as Bazargan was concerned, Iran had adopted good points from the West, such as independence, national bias, freedom, egalitarianism, being progressive and revolutionary. Also, it had learned from them how to fight against superstition and so return to a genuine religious revival and thus a pure Islam. Furthermore, he believed that some occidental thinkers were good and fair people; however some ideas were bad and should be rejected (Bazargan 2008, pp. 349–350).

Bazargan believed that Iran had confronted three different influences during its history. Sometimes Iran was faced with absolute despotism, for example in the eras of the Great Cyrus, Shah Abbas and Nader Shah, and this was without any foreign hegemony. Across history, however, Iran had been confronted by foreign hegemonic power, for instance, with the invasion by Alexander the Great, the Umayyad Caliphate and the invasion by Genghis Khan. Similarly, Iran faced hegemony during the Pahlavi dynasty when both despotism and foreign influence coexisted (Bazargan 2008, p. 355). Moreover, he maintained that, in the era of new colonialism some international powers tried to form a hegemony by utilising internal factors such as, in the case of Iran, the Pahlavi dynasty. These countries pursued their hegemonic aims with respect to their own national interest. Here he referred to the constitutional revolution and the coup backed by the superpowers. They brought the Pahlavi dynasty into power to help them achieve what they wanted in the country (Bazargan 2005, p. 54).

Bazargan's second point is the criticism of, and otherness with respect to, the modern trend to secularise the public sphere. He believed that Western modernity was based on autonomous reason and this dominated both talk of God and of nature. So the West, as a public entity, abandoned God and focussed solely on the temporal life. The crisis of Western modernity was brought about by replacing religion and spirituality with science and autonomous reason. A lack of spirituality and religion had caused lots of problems for them, and also meant the West inclined towards nihilism (Bazargan 2009a, pp. 25–26). Further, he asserted, as noted above, that the West was good with respect to the sense of beauty, the sense of service and the sense of inquiry and curiosity. However, the West lacked the fourth dimension which was an innate sense of religion and spirituality. He mentioned that some thinkers and philosophers tried to open again a way for religious beliefs however these efforts were subjected to the hegemony of temporal beliefs (Bazargan 2009a, pp. 33–34). He stated that when he was in the US, he noticed that people were viewed as merchandise. The US looked at a human being in terms of the dollar. It was a really rich country where people generally live very well in terms of health, education, nutrition and housing, but he believed the population were losing spirituality more and more every day (Bazargan 2009a, pp. 83–85).

Bazargan and Modernity

Bazargan believed that making a distinction between the East and the West was a mistake. In fact, there is no real difference between Britain, the US, China and the USSR since all of them want to make Iranians their slaves (Bazargan 2007, p. 32). He asserted that there is nothing to liberalism, nationalism, socialism and Marxism that has a counterpart in Islam. He asserted that all things including justice, equality, friendship and freedom exist in Islam. In this regard, he claimed that he could cite verses of Qur'an, and also Hadith and jurisprudence to support his claims. Hence, it seems that Bazargan believed that the content of these terms and concepts should be determined by our indigenous Islamic interpretations (Bazargan 2007, pp. 32–33).

As mentioned, Political Islam in the modern era is formed from the encounter between autonomous reason and religious inspiration. The result of this encounter is a broad spectrum of political Islam. From the 1960s to the Islamic revolution in 1979, Bazargan enunciated Islamic ideology as a method to stand up to modern Western intellectual frameworks and paradigms. However, after Iran's revolution and the triumph of the hegemony of jurisprudence of Islam in Iran, he changed his mind and argued that the aim of the prophets was to promote a belief in God and the eternal world (Bazargan 2009b, pp. 284–288). In respect to the three basic elements of *fiqh*, Bazargan believed in devotional jurisprudence and with regard to political and transactional jurisprudence he referred to autonomous reason based on an Islamic and Iranian mandate. He cited normative reason over instrumental reason.

With regard to autonomous reason and its derivatives of individualism and science in the modern era, Bazargan referred to notions of individualism and collectivism predicated on Islam and the Iranian context. He believed, rather like Shariati, that a *Maktab-e Vaseteh-e Islam* (Islam is a median school) system would follow the middle way on a continuum between Marxism and capitalism. His model government was that of an Islamic Democratic Republic of Iran (Bazargan 2010, pp. 445–452). Also, he recognised the modern sciences, including engineering and medical sciences, as universal.

In a similar fashion to Shariati, Bazargan analysed emancipation and domination. He explained that the emancipation of the West had been encouraged among the Iranian people. However, he was opposed to the domination of West with respect to issues of colonisation and secularisation. He argued that Iranians should indeed pay more attention to the external influences affecting the country. He believed that Iran should renegotiate these terms, based on Islamic and Iranian precepts. From his point of view, defeating domestic despotism was more significant than foreign hegemony; recognising that in the era of the Pahlavi dynasty, despotism and foreign hegemony went hand in hand. As far as secularisation was concerned, Bazargan disagreed with philosophical and social secularism. Nonetheless, he supported political secularisation, especially in his later life.

CONCLUDING ANALYSIS

This chapter has outlined and discussed the ideas of three political thinkers, Khomeini, Shariati and Bazargan with regard to their views about the West and about Iranian otherness from the West. Five salient concluding points can be made.

First, with regard to the explanation of the situation it is clear that all three thinkers were opposed to interference by the West and East in Iran through colonisation and secularisation believing that these elements would damage the Iranian people and diminish spirituality and morality within the Iranian society. Also, they believed that the Shah's Pahlavi dynasty had plundered Iran in cultural, political and economic aspects supported by Western and Eastern states. However, after the 1979 Islamic revolution, the otherness with regard to the West became more important than ideas about the East from an historical point of view, and the fact that the Iranian people had felt humiliated by the 1953 coup against Mosaddegh. Arguably, communist and Marxist secular groups were rivals and secular liberal groups were the enemy of jurisprudential Islamic and left Islamic groups around and after the Islamic revolution of 1979. Also, jurisprudential Islamic and left Islamic groups accused Bazargan and advocates of liberal Islam of supporting the West and its ideas.

Second, in connection with the system of knowledge, and focusing on the Iranian context it is clear they all sought to form an amalgamation of Islam, nationalism and modernity to create an ideology against the imported ideologies of nationalism, communism, socialism and liberalism while rejecting imported modernity. Further, they believed in an Islamic school that offered a balanced approach between communism and capitalism. In sum, Khomeini believed it the duty of jurists to utilise traditional and dynamic jurisprudence to subordinate imported ideologies. Shariati believed that it is the duty of Muslim intellectuals to reject imported ideologies with reference to the early Iranian-Islamic history. Bazargan argued Muslim intellectuals ought to withstand pressure from imported ideologies by referring to the Qur'an. Although using Islam as the basis of their arguments, these three thinkers adopted differing approaches to follow otherness with Western and Eastern ideas.

Third, with regard to the system of norms, these thinkers had somewhat different views about the West and the East. Two slogans became important in the course of the Iranian revolution in 1979: One was 'no West no East' rather just the Islamic Republic of Iran; the other was independence, freedom and the Islamic Republic of Iran. All of these thinkers disagreed with the West and East hegemony and thus supported the Non-Aligned Movement. They supported freedom, justice and independence from inside, and the breaking of any hegemonic ties with either the West or the East. Also, Khomeini focused on the independence of Iran because from his standpoint, foreign hegemony of the West and East was more catastrophic than internal despotism. However, to Bazargan despotism was more disastrous than foreign hegemony. Hence, from his perspective freedom was more important than an abstract notion of the independence of the country.

Furthermore, with respect to the system of government, they sought to combine modern and traditional beliefs to make Iran a modern country shifting from Western ideas. However, different models were proposed. Shariati proposed his two theories, namely 'The Theory of Ummah and Imamate' and 'Mysticism, Equality and Liberty'. Shariati supported the establishment of a government which was an alternative of Eastern and Western thoughts since communist and Marxist secular groups were his main rival, in particular those who were from academia. He also considered liberal secular groups as his enemies. Khomeini's model was Islamic Republic based on *Velayat-e Faqih* (the guardianship of jurisconsult). Borrowing its modernistic and traditional parts from the 'Republic' and 'Islamic' parts of the 'Islamic Republic' this model leaves it to a jurist to govern society to protect Islam. Bazargan's model was an Islamic Democratic Republic which found credibility in Islam, especially the Qur'anic thoughts of Bazargan as opposed to imported thoughts from West or East. However, in his later life he relied mostly on normative autonomous reason to prove his validity of the model because he believed that the aim of the prophets was just to promote belief in God and the eternal world.

Finally, with regard to Public policy, the three thinkers synthesised teachings from their ancestors, while acknowledging contemporary democratic values. While Khomeini had a tendency towards religion based on jurisprudence, he was averse to secularism. Indeed, he disagreed with all the three types of secularism: Philosophical secularism which denies God and the other world, social secularism which denies attendance of religious people in the public sphere, and political secularism that proposes separation between state and religion. Khomeini believed in a maximised Islam based on jurisprudence, which includes all aspects, namely devotional, transactional and political. In contrast, Bazargan, especially in his later life, believed in political secularism but disagreed with philosophical and social secularism. For him a minimised Islam meant that he recognised devotional jurisprudence as a universal value. He, however, believed in political and transactional/economic jurisprudence based on value-based (normative) reason in terms of time. Bazargan did not believe in philosophical and social secularism, but he did believe in political secularism. Also in terms of foreign policy, Khomeini and Shariati tended to focus on Islamic civilisation to defend against Western civilisation, whereas Bazargan had more tendency towards liberal nationalism.

References

Bazargan, M. (2005). *Mabahes Eteghadi va Ejtemaei* [Theological and Social issues] (Vol. 11). Tehran, Iran: Sherkat Sahami Enteshar.

Bazargan, M. (2006). *Modafeat* [Court Defenses] (Vol. 6). Tehran, Iran: Sherkat Shami Enteshar.

Bazargan, M. (2007). *Mghalat Eteghdi va Ejtemaei* [Articles Believe and Social] (Vol. 16). Tehran, Iran: Sherkat Shami Enteshar.

Bazargan, M. (2008). *Koba, Hendostan, Iran* [Cuba, India, Iran] (Vol. 15). Tehran, Iran: Sherkat Shami Enteshar.

Bazargan, M. (2009a). *Besat* [Prophetic mission] (Vol. 2). Tehran, Iran: Glam.

Bazargan, M. (2009b). *Besat (2)* [Prophetic mission (2)] (Vol. 17). Tehran, Iran: Sherkat Shami Enteshar.

Bazargan, M. (2010). *Bazyabi Arzesha (1)* [Recovery values (1)] (Vol. 25). Tehran, Iran: Sherkat Shami Enteshar.

Bazargan, M. (2011). *Maghalat Ejtemaei va Fani* [Social and Technical Articles] (Vol. 4). Tehran, Iran: Sherkat Shami Enteshar.

Khomeini, S. R. (2010a). *Sahifeh Imam: Majmoe asar Imam Khomeini bayanat, payamha, mosahebeha, ahkam, ejazat sharei va nameha* [Sahifeh-Ye Imam: An anthology of Imam Khomeini's speeches, messages, interviews, decrees, religious permissions, and letters] (Vol. 1). Tehran, Iran: The Institute for Compilation and Publication of Imam Khomeini's Works.

Khomeini, S. R. (2010b). *Sahifeh Imam: Majmoe asar Imam Khomeini bayanat, payamha, mosahebeha, ahkam, ejazat sharei va nameha* [Sahifeh-Ye Imam: An anthology of Imam Khomeini's speeches, messages, interviews, decrees, religious permissions, and letters] (Vol. 16). Tehran, Iran: The Institute for Compilation and Publication of Imam Khomeini's Works.

Khomeini, S. R. (2010c). *Sahifeh Imam: Majmoe asar Imam Khomeini bayanat, payamha, mosahebeha, ahkam, ejazat sharei va nameha* [Sahifeh-Ye Imam: An anthology of Imam Khomeini's speeches, messages, interviews, decrees, religious permissions, and letters] (Vol. 19). Tehran, Iran: The Institute for Compilation and Publication of Imam Khomeini's Works.

Khomeini, S. R. (2010d). *Sahifeh Imam: Majmoe asar Imam Khomeini bayanat, payamha, mosahebeha, ahkam, ejazat sharei va nameha* [Sahifeh-Ye Imam: An anthology of Imam Khomeini's speeches, messages, interviews, decrees, religious permissions, and letters] (Vol. 5). Tehran, Iran: Institute for Compilation and Publication of Imam Khomeini's Works.

Khomeini, S. R. (2010e). *Sahifeh Imam: Majmoe asar Imam Khomeini bayanat, payamha, mosahebeha, ahkam, ejazat sharei va nameha* [Sahifeh-Ye Imam: An anthology of Imam Khomeini's speeches, messages, interviews, decrees, religious permissions, and letters] (Vol. 11). Tehran: Institute for Compilation and Publication of Imam Khomeini's Works.

Khomeini, S. R. (2010f). *Sahifeh Imam: Majmoe asar Imam Khomeini bayanat, payamha, mosahebeha, ahkam, ejazat sharei va nameha* [Sahifeh-Ye Imam: An anthology of Imam Khomeini's speeches, messages, interviews, decrees, religious permissions, and letters] (Vol. 18). Tehran, Iran: The Institute for Compilation and Publication of Imam Khomeini's Works.

Khomeini, S. R. (2010g). *Sahifeh Imam: Majmoe asar Imam Khomeini bayanat, payamha, mosahebeha, ahkam, ejazat sharei va nameha* [Sahifeh-Ye Imam: An anthology of Imam Khomeini's speeches, messages, interviews, decrees, religious permissions, and letters] (Vol. 2). Tehran, Iran: The Institute for Compilation and Publication of Imam Khomeini's Works.

Khomeini, S. R. (2010h). *Sahifeh Imam: Majmoe asar Imam Khomeini bayanat, payamha, mosahebeha, ahkam, ejazat sharei va nameha* [Sahifeh-Ye Imam: An anthology of Imam Khomeini's speeches, messages, interviews, decrees, religious permissions, and letters] (Vol. 3). Tehran, Iran: The Institute for Compilation and Publication of Imam Khomeini's Works.

Khomeini, S. R. (2010i). *Sahifeh Imam: Majmoe asar Imam Khomeini bayanat, payamha, mosahebeha, ahkam, ejazat sharei va nameha* [Sahifeh-Ye Imam: An anthology of Imam Khomeini's speeches, messages, interviews, decrees, religious permissions, and letters] (Vol. 4). Tehran, Iran: The Institute for Compilation and Publication of Imam Khomeini's Works.

Khomeini, S. R. (2010j). *Sahifeh Imam: Majmoe asar Imam Khomeini bayanat, payamha, mosahebeha, ahkam, ejazat sharei va nameha* [Sahifeh-Ye Imam: An anthology of Imam Khomeini's speeches, messages, interviews, decrees, religious permissions, and letters] (Vol. 6). Tehran, Iran: The Institute for Compilation and Publication of Imam Khomeini's Works.

Khomeini, S. R. (2010k). *Sahifeh Imam: Majmoe asar Imam Khomeini bayanat, payamha, mosahebeha, ahkam, ejazat sharei va nameha* [Sahifeh-Ye Imam: An anthology of Imam Khomeini's speeches, messages, interviews, decrees, religious permissions, and letters] (Vol. 7). Tehran, Iran: Institute for Compilation and Publication of Imam Khomeini's Works.

Khomeini, S. R. (2010l). *Sahifeh Imam: Majmoe asar imam Khomeini bayanat, payamha, mosahebeha, ahkam, ejazat sharei va nameha* [Sahifeh-Ye Imam: An anthology of Imam Khomeini's speeches, messages, interviews, decrees, religious permissions, and letters] (Vol. 10). Tehran, Iran: The Institute for Compilation and Publication of Imam Khomeini's Works.

Khomeini, S. R. (2010m). *Sahifeh Imam: Majmoe asar Imam Khomeini bayanat, payamha, mosahebeha, ahkam, ejazat sharei va nameha* [Sahifeh-Ye Imam: An anthology of Imam Khomeini's speeches, messages, interviews, decrees, religious permissions, and letters] (Vol. 8). Tehran, Iran: The Institute for Compilation and Publication of Imam Khomeini's Works.

Khomeini, S. R. (2010n). *Sahifeh Imam: Majmoe asar Imam Khomeini bayanat, payamha, mosahebeha, ahkam, ejazat sharei va nameha* [Sahifeh-Ye Imam: An anthology of Imam Khomeini's speeches, messages, interviews, decrees, religious permissions, and letters] (Vol. 21). Tehran, Iran: The Institute for Compilation and Publication of Imam Khomeini's Works.

Khomeini, S. R. (2010o). *Sahifeh Imam: Majmoe asar imam Khomeini bayanat, payamha, mosahebeha, ahkam, ejazat sharei va nameha* [Sahifeh-Ye Imam: An anthology of Imam Khomeini's speeches, messages, interviews, decrees, religious permissions, and letters] (Vol. 9). Tehran, Iran: The Institute for Compilation and Publication of Imam Khomeini's Works.

Shariati, A. (2008). *Bazgasht* [Return] (Vol. 4). Tehran, Iran: Entesharat Elham.

Shariati, A. (2009a). *Miad ba Ebrahim* [The Vow with Abraham] (Vol. 29). Tehran, Iran: Enteshrat Agah.

Shariati, A. (2009b). *Tarikh va Shenakht Adiyan (1)* [History and Understand Religions (1)] (Vol. 14). Tehran, Iran: Sherkat Shami Enteshar.

Shariati, A. (2010). *Tarikh Tamadon (2)* [History of Civilization (2)] (Vol. 12). Tehran, Iran: Entesharat Ghalam.

Shariati, A. (2011a). *Ali* (Vol. 26). Tehran, Iran: Nashr Amon.

Shariati, A. (2011b). *Jahatgiri Tabghati Islam* [The Class Orientation of Islam] (Vol. 10). Tehran, Iran: Entesharat Ghalam.

Shariati, A. (2011c). *Vizhehgihai Ghoron Jadid* [New Features Century] (Vol. 31). Tehran, Iran: Chappakhsh.

Shariati, A. (2011d). *Zan* [Woman] (Vol. 21). Tehran, Iran: Enteshrat Chapakhsh.

CHAPTER 5

A Return to Innocence: The Resurgence of Shia Ideas

This chapter examines the viewpoints of Khomeini, Shariati and Bazargan through a critical comparison regarding the programme for returning to Shia Islamic culture. It concludes with a review of the concept of ideology to help illuminate the similarities and differences between the thought systems of Khomeini, Shariati and Bazargan.

KHOMEINI

Khomeini maintained that the Islamic world, and Iran, should return to the societal context and form predominance at the beginning of Islam. He believed that the most successful time of Islam was at its dawn. He added that Muslims, at the beginning of Islam, though limited in population, defeated the two great contemporary empires of Rome and Persia. From the outset, the Prophet Mohammad established principles that enabled people to maintain a humane society according to the Will of God (Khomeini 2010g, pp. 448–449).

While the population of the Muslim world is more than one billion, on the whole it appears to be dormant. For Khomeini all Third World countries needed to wake up to the reality of their situation based on the duty of all Muslim thinkers and people to maintain a proper Islamic human society. Thus, all Muslims required a movement that starts with reviewing their thoughts and what they have, then continues with the realisation of

© The Author(s) 2020
S. M. Lolaki, *Diverging Approaches of Political Islamic Thought in Iran since the 1960s*,
https://doi.org/10.1007/978-981-15-0478-5_5

those thoughts. He believed that this would be possible if they actively sought it (Khomeini 2010c, pp. 533–535).

To Khomeini Iranians should use their own terms and science in the context of the modern world. He observed, however, that some good points could be taken from the medical sciences and engineering in Western countries. He also asserted that countries like Japan and India pursued this path and used their own definitions of terms and indigenous philosophies to pursue the aspirations of their own societies (Khomeini 2010b, p. 228). Khomeini also regarded the best path for the emancipation of Iran and the Islamic world was to return to what he understood to be 'real' Islam. He asserted that, by returning to real Islam and the Qur'an, Iranian people would gain emancipation from colonisation (Khomeini 2010d, p. 423). He further maintained that the main subject of dispute between Iran and the West, including the Western-oriented Pahlavi dynasty, related to autonomy and freedom based on Islam (Khomeini 2010f, pp. 259–260). He asserted that Iran's motto must be 'Neither East nor West; but Islam and Iran'. Khomeini believed that Iran was a unique country in that it wants, and needs, to be independent of both the East and the West (Khomeini 2010a, p. 389).

Specific Duty of Jurists

Khomeini supported traditional and dynamic jurisprudence. Traditional jurisprudence is based on the resources of Shia jurisprudence, namely the Holy Qur'an, the Hadith, Reason and Consensus. However, in addition to the foundations of traditional jurisprudence, dynamic jurisprudence considers two important elements, namely time and place, when issuing new fatwas in the modern era. Khomeini denounced some jurists for not believing, and acting on, dynamic jurisprudence. Moreover, he maintained that jurists were responsible for all social, political, cultural, military and economic issues at any time or era (Khomeini 2010h, pp. 289–290). He said that during the struggles with the Shah Dynasty, some clerics rejected him for teaching Islamic philosophy. According to Khomeini, some illiterate clerics believed that learning a foreign language was heresy and the teaching and learning of Islamic philosophy and mysticism were sins. In fact, he thought that such clerics just believed in traditional jurisprudence and nothing else. Hence, he maintained that should this continue, seminaries would become like churches of the Middle Ages (Khomeini 2010h, pp. 278–279). Accordingly, it was necessary that knowledgeable jurists issue new fatwas about emerging and complicated subjects, including domestic and foreign trade, tax, banking, music, theatre, cinema, painting, photography, statutes, environment, the role of women in society and limitations to individual and social freedom. The 1979 Islamic revolution successfully brought to the fore different ideas, especially new fatwas by jurists, which came into the public sphere allowing people to recognise diverse ideas among jurists. These kinds of discussions were deemed highly appropriate for Iranian society (Khomeini 2010h, pp. 176–177).

Iranian Identity

Khomeini argued that it was vitally important for Iranian people to create an Iranian-Islamic society where they could be freed from cultural and intellectual dependency. He observed that Iranian people should understand that they could manage themselves based on their rich culture (Khomeini 2010g, p. 53). Also, he asserted that nationalism is detrimental to Muslims since it causes them to be confrontational with each other. He maintained that Islam ensures a unity among all races including Persian, Arab and Turk, based on piety. He regarded the Pahlavi dynasty as trying to return Iran to the pre-Islamic era and that this was a terrible blunder. Therefore, he thought that all Muslims should return to Islam for the sake of societal unity (Khomeini 2010c, pp. 87–88). Furthermore, he stated that Islam is a progressive religion and that it is ahead of liberalism and communism (Khomeini 2010e, p. 507). Certainly, Khomeini appreciated some aspects of the ancient Iranian heritage and Western modernity, as he employed some facets despite this distracting from his message of prioritising a return to a pristine form of Islam.

In sum, Khomeini had a focus on restoring to Islam as a framework and a comprehensive package of jurisprudential values, and greater clerical involvement in public life. Likewise, he wanted to create an Iranian-Islamic society forged into a new identity. He believed in Islamic-Iranian interests based on freedom and independence under the umbrella of Islam. He suggested an identity with the main focus on Islam but with some facets of ancient Iran and Western modernity.

SHARIATI

Shariati asserted that intellectuals in the Islamic world as well as all the intelligentsia of the Third World countries live in an era that poses two options: One is to maintain the traditions of past legacies and the other is to follow the ideologies of the West. He held that ordinary people believed in and followed tradition, which offered its own unique worldview and special philosophy of life, language and literature. In contrast, the other option is to live by imitating different ideologies of the West, which is the way taken by some intellectuals. He believed, however, that the intelligentsia should take a critical look at the imported ideologies from the West and contrast those with traditional Islamic religious ideas and, while recognising the positive and negative aspects of them, embark on creating a contemporary new Islamic self-identity (Shariati 2011c, pp. 305–308).

He believed that, as a first step, it was necessary to understand the West, a civilisation that takes a hegemonic stance and lifestyle. During the Middle Ages, Europe was a colony of the Islamic East since Christianity went from the East to the West and became prominent in Europe. According to Shariati, initially, Western intellectuals were interested with Muslim civilisation and gained much from Islam culturally. They then devised ways to stand against it. Shariati argued that Western intellectuals came to know their own philosophy, ancient science and even religion through studying the writings of some Muslim thinkers such as Avicenna, Averroes, Al-Farabi (Alpharabius), Ghazali and others. He believed that they then relearned their cultural and philosophical heritage, including that of Ancient Greece, kick-starting the Renaissance that led to a kind of rebirth of Europe after the Dark Ages. He observed that today, with a good understanding of the West, Iranian Muslims can return to their true selves and gain self-understanding and make a new era for themselves. To do so two actions were required: First, to understand the history of the West and the social transformation of European civilisation. Second, to study trends in the ideas of the West with an emphasis on the period from the Renaissance until the present day (Shariati 2007, p. 184).

According to Shariati, the aforementioned study must be comprehensive. First, it is necessary to understand the Renaissance and focus on its economic roots such as urban growth, class evolution and global trade. Second, there is a need to understand the Christian Protestant ideas and leaders such as Luther and Calvin, and their role in the development of industrial civilisation and science in Europe, and the explosion of reason that eclipsed medieval and Catholic ideas. Third, it is necessary to understand the ideas of major thinkers including Bacon, Kant, Descartes, Hegel, Fichte, Nietzsche, Spinoza, Pascal, Bergson, Voltaire, Sartre and Rousseau. Fourth, it is important to understand movements such as the great revolution of France, the industrial revolution of England and the

Russian revolution. Also, there is a need to be familiar with key political and social thinkers such as Durkheim, Fromm and J. S. Mill in the West, and Laozi, Confucius, Hinduism, Buddhism, Zoroaster, Manichaeism and Mazdak in the East (Shariati 2007, p. 185).

He asserted that, today, the main subject among African, Latin American and Asian intellectuals is a return to self or self-understanding directed by intellectuals such as Fanon and Ionesco who believe that every society should be enlightened in accordance with its own culture and history. Given this, it is the duty of Iranians to return to the Islamic culture and ideology of their heritage (Shariati 2008a, pp. 22–24). He also asserted that, after the eighteenth century, with the aid of its sociologists, historians, artists and even revolutionaries, the West tried to impose its civilisation on the rest of the world. According to Shariati, the West wanted the rest of the world to be a consumer of its produce in all aspects of life, even in terms of culture. According to Heidegger, every human being lives two existences: Existence per se which refers to a form of existence that all human beings have in common as members of a society; and what he refers to as 'genuine existence'. The latter forms civilisation and culture throughout history. In fact, it is a human being's true existence (Shariati 2008a, pp. 24–28).

Shariati is of the view that it is the duty of intellectuals to understand the type and form of their own people's culture. Examples of each type include Greek, Roman, Chinese, Indian and Iranian culture where ideas, respectively consist of philosophical, artistic and military-based, Sufic (historic culture), spiritual and Islamic. Cultural forms refer to the collection of information, emotions, traditions and ideals of a society. The intelligentsia of Iran should recognise their own culture as a religious and Islamic type and undertake the task of purifying the Islamic spirit (Shariati 2012a, pp. 284–290). A major mistake that an intellectual could make is to deem an idea eternal, absolute and universal. Since society and time are ever-changing and these types of concepts are essentially relative, then it follows that new ideas are needed to manage the society in every era (Shariati 2012a, p. 481). Following Gurvitch, Shariati asserted that Iran needs to conceptualise itself as an inclusive plurality of 'societies' and not simply as a singular, unitary 'society' (Shariati 2008a, p. 60).

For Shariati it is the duty of intellectuals to make Islam a vibrant ideology that stands against the static traditional ideas of the past as well as recognising the ideas imported from the West. This requires an informative and dynamic Islam to contrast with and be ahead of the two other ideas mentioned above (Shariati 2008a, p. 40). He argued that there have been two types of Shi'a during the history of Islam, namely Alawi and Safavid Shiism. During the history of Islam, Alawi Shiism has been based on the idea of infallible Imams and justice. Therefore, the Alawi Shi'a came to answer the suffering of people oppressed throughout the history of imperialism of the Sassanid dynasty, the Roman Empire and also the West today (Shariati 2009, p. 304). However, Safavid Shiism was a mixture of governmental regime, nationality and Sufism. It was devised by the Safavid dynasty in order for it to take and hold power (Shariati 2011a, p. 200). He believed that Shia culture has never been a static and conservative religion, but indeed a revolutionary ideology (Shariati 2009, p. 304). Furthermore, he claimed that it is necessary that Iran returns to the great and eminent spirits and characters of its own culture as they were the best patterns for people. By great and eminent spirits and characters he means the prophet Mohammad and his family. As he says, this is because these people showed us the true identity and valuable humanity (Shariati 2010, pp. 354–355).

Shariati believed that human beings were imprisoned in four areas of life: Nature, history, society and self. With regard to nature, they were captive to geographical parameters, that is, they are restricted by them, but they can set themselves free by understanding nature and using modern technologies. For example, we have overcome the force of gravity by technology. Regarding history, he said that we can release ourselves from the constraints of history to the extent we understand it and determinism. In terms of society, he observed that we were captured by society and we could rid ourselves of it by perceiving society in terms of traditions, types of government and different social classes. Finally, with regard to the self, he claims that we can release ourselves by managing our instincts, habits, individual hedonism and by strengthening religious faith. Following Toynbee, Shariati claimed that people such as Moses, Christ, Mohammad and Buddha were those who managed to free themselves from their own self-interest. Shariati believes that these kinds of people can release others from their temporal self (Shariati 2012b, pp. 327–330). He added that these people brought love for all human beings. He alleges that, in our culture, the best patterns to show this are Imam Ali and his successors. (Shariati 2011b, p. 162).

The Specific Duty of Intellectuals

Shariati believed that intellectuals are the successors to the prophets with the exception that they do not receive divine revelation. That is to say, the intellectuals' mission is, in essence, to give people awareness, freedom and humanity in contrast to ignorance and injustice (Shariati 2012a, p. 368). Thus, the two primary duties of intellectuals are to foster, firstly, self-awareness and, secondly, social awareness. With regard to the former, he held that intellectuals should know to which race, nation, history, culture, literature and time they belong. In connection with the second, he adds that intellectuals should understand the society to which they belong in order to guide and lead their society (Shariati 2012a, pp. 207–208).

For Shariati, a key duty of intellectuals is the production of thoughts and ideas. Intellectuals should not follow the 'form' of Western ideologies. Rather, they should follow their own methods and authentic behaviours. In this way they will produce authentic thoughts and useful ideas. So, he believed it is necessary that Iranian intellectuals be producers not just consumers (Shariati 2008b, p. 36). He added that civilisation is not like an imported good that can be purchased from abroad. It is created by thought and it can be achieved through a revolution in respect to views, ideas and thoughts (Shariati 2012a, p. 163).

Shariati supported Shia jurists because he believed that, throughout history, they had opened the door of Ijtihad (interpretation) to devise dynamic ideas that addressed emerging issues. He believed that this is a really positive point for jurists. However, he also encouraged intellectuals to engage in ijtihad (interpretation) with regard to the principles of Islam in order to keep Islam up to date as an ideology (Shariati 2012a, p. 399). He further maintained that it is the duty of Muslim intellectuals to create an Islamic 'Protestantism', rather like the Protestantism of Western Christianity which, in effect, terminated the Middle Ages and led to the creation of new dynamic ideas. According to Shariati, this would enable the immense cultural reserves of Shia Islam to be extracted and refined; the gap between intellectuals and masses would be bridged, in order to better understand each other; and the weapon of religion taken from those who are armed with it and who use it to exert their authority. In this way, the intelligentsia would gain sufficient power to mobilise people and relying on their shared authentic culture, they will revive the cultural character and social identity of Iran against any cultural invasion by the West (Shariati 2012a, pp. 294–296).

Iranian Identity

Shariati believed that Iranian identity comprised a mixture of two races, namely Semitic and Aryan. In his view, Semitic people are unidimensional and Aryans are multidimensional. Semitic people were impatient and Aryan people are patient. Semitics were extroverts while Aryans were introverts. Semitic people were realistic but Aryan people are fantasy-oriented (Shariati 2009, pp. 342–362). He denounced people who believed that Iranians should focus on the history of pre-Islamic Iran alone. He maintained that this mixture between Iran and Islam created a new civilisation that was really beautiful (Shariati 2009, pp. 362–363). Also, he was of the view that Iranian nationalism had always possessed an openness and outlook consistent with humanity. He believed that not only had Iran never tried to use its nationalism to humiliate other people, but in fact it had always respected other nations and religions (Shariati 2009, p. 153). In all, Shariati suggested that all religious people who, thanks to their knowledge and humanity, were responsible for the awakening and guidance of a people should gather together to protect them against the two pitfalls of static Islam and the ideologies imported from West. Furthermore, he believed that Iranian people should return to the beginning of Shia culture and extract and refine the immense spiritual and cultural Islamic reserves that were a legacy of the past. Finally, he proposed an Islamic renaissance that gave a new impetus to the original Islam: A revolutionary and dynamic impetus for the oppressed people.

Bazargan

Bazargan was of the opinion that after the constitutional revolution some imported ideologies, such as Liberalism, Socialism, Communism and some foreign terms and ideas, such as concepts of social justice and democracy, came into the public sphere of Iran. However, he believed that these kinds of Euro-centric terms were commonly put ahead of a vast wealth of indigenous ideas and concepts that had been present from the dawn of Islam; that they represented a drop of water compared to a vast ocean. The egalitarianism and freedom that came to Muslim people during the time of the Prophet Mohammad, and some of the first Caliphs were, and remain, unsurpassable. He posed the question as to whether it was it really necessary for Iranian people to follow imported ideologies. His answer was that Islam is wholly sufficient and really valuable because, since the dawn of Islam these kinds of ideas have existed and Muslims have followed and practised them (Bazargan 2009, pp. 129–131). Also, he maintained that prophets were the first people who recognised natural human rights.

All religions, and especially Islam, support the natural rights of all human beings (Bazargan 2009, p. 134).

Bazargan acknowledged that some Iranian intellectuals were of the view that Iran should be Westernised. He asked what they meant by that. Should Iranians become French, German, American or English? Such a development would be a terrible blunder. Western countries were different from each other in terms of attitude, culture and temperament. Western countries possessed good and bad aspects. The Iranian people should adopt the good aspects of the West but leave behind the bad and focus on the development of those positive aspects for themselves. He believed that some Iranian people were under the illusion that Western countries were heaven, which was a colossal mistake. According to Bazargan, social and economic problems were only increasing in Western countries and this was due to the loss of morality (Bazargan 2011, pp. 22–32).

For Bazargan, tradition is vitally important. He held that tradition was also really important to Europeans and, in particular, although not exclusively French people. He then asserted how some of the young Iranians imitate the mores, habits, morality, religion, script, language and wedding traditions of the West. He denounced the practice of imitating Western countries and suggested employing instead ideas and cultural forms based on Islamic-Iranian history. To achieve this, it was necessary for Iranians to have knowledge of their own history. Likewise, he asserted that Iranian people should distinguish between principles and derivative ideas, and their ideal life should be based on their own culture (Bazargan 2011, pp. 32–45). In one of his major books, namely '*Sazegari Iranian*' (Iranian Compatibility) (Bazargan 2011, pp. 415–480), Bazargan looked at Iranian history. He was aware that some people thought that Iran should be Westernised for this would be a really good solution to Iran's problems and could finally lead to much needed development. He observed, however, that there were others who believed that Iran's problems emanated from colonialism and foreign hegemony, from as long ago as the invasion of Alexander the Great from 331 to 334 BC, the Umayyad Caliphate between 633 and 651, which resisted the rise of Shi'ism; and, between 1219 and 1256, the invasion by Genghis Khan and his followers (Bazargan 2011, pp. 416–417). He also stated that studies of the changes which occurred in Iranian thought and behaviours over the past 2500 years was needed. He noted that Grousset, in his book *La Face de l' Asie* (Grousset and Deniker 1955), saw Iran at the 'crossroad of history', meaning that

Iran had always been in a situation that has had profound effects on Iranians' temperament and race (Bazargan 2011, pp. 422–423).

Moreover, Bazargan maintained that the ancestors of the Iranians were farmers, a fact that had directly and indirectly affected the Iranian spirit. He believed that the genesis of the Iranian spirit comes from the special geographical situation of Iran, a predicament that had brought insecurity, invasion and despotism for the Iranian people. He enumerated what he regarded as some drawbacks or deficiencies of the Iranian people: Indiscipline, irresponsibility, poor problem solving habits, demanding everything from the government, imitation and exaggeration in excessive ceremoniousness, negative individualism, poor work ethic and participation in the society, and finally Sufic ideas. He also believed that Iranians were weak in the concepts of nationality and nationhood (Bazargan 2011, pp. 435–466). At the same time, he enumerated some good points about the Iranian people including the priority of culture and spirituality. According to Bazargan, at times the people faced despotism and foreign invaders, but sometimes the dominant despot was broken and the people found opportunities to manage themselves through their strong culture and spirituality. He observed that the impact and effect of many foreign invaders gradually dissolved in Iranian culture due to the strength of this culture. The only exception to this is the acceptance of Islam by Iranians, which was due to the superiority of Islam over their former religion. Bazargan believed that the Shia version of Islam is indeed the 'brains' of real Islam. Furthermore, throughout history Iranian people have retained their culture and language. Being Shia has brought unity for them (Bazargan 2006, pp. 320–321).

Bazargan believed that the Iranian people were united behind the shield of Islam and Shiism always fought despotism. He maintained that Shia clerics had always been independent. Accordingly, in contrast to Sunni clerics who were reliant on governments, Shia clerics were independent and that is why they could stand against the Umayyad, Abbasid and Ottoman emperors during the course of history (Bazargan 2006, pp. 326–327). However, he believed that Shia clerics could have a negative role and this happened when, instead of dealing with Islamic commands and people's beliefs, they deem themselves to be the central pillar of Islam and thought that Islam without them means infidelity (Bazargan 2008, pp. 367–368).

Bazargan maintained that, in light of experience from the past, it was necessary to reach a general policy suitable for Iran today. First, the vast majority of Iranian people should support justice, freedom and independence for Iran. Second, the most important factor for Iranian people was been fighting against despotism and it was their duty to break with tyranny and find protection around robust freedom and democracy. Third, Iranians needed to reject foreign hegemony. Fourth, it was necessary that Iranians actually change their attitudes and behaviour. Fifth, with regards to this change in temperament and diplomacy, the Iranian people would be faced with some difficulties and thus they should be attentive and resistant. Moreover, Bazargan stated that the role of religion and clerics was the key point in Iran. Therefore, the Shia people, equipped with the two principles of Imamate and justice, had always had an important role in fighting tyrants during the history of Iran and in the course of the Constitutional Revolution. Finally, the Iranian people need a collective leadership based on goodwill, rationality and suitable tactics and strategies (Bazargan 2008, pp. 467–471).

Islamic Identity

Bazargan noted that since the beginning of the Islamic revolution of Iran in 1979 two different ideas have coexisted. On one side were the ideas of Khomeini and his followers who thought that the goal of the revolution was to serve Islam through Iran. On the other side were some nationalist individuals and Islamic groups who believed in serving Iran through Islam (Bazargan 2010, pp. 249–250). According to Bazargan, both he and the members of the provisional government of the 1979 Islamic revolution, as well as members of the freedom movement (party) of Iran, thought it was important to serve Iran through Islam. Therefore, this provided a general strategy for the creation of an Islamic state or Islamic culture and a system that superseded monarchy and determined the guiding ideology, constitution and lifestyle. The motif of serving Iran brought a new constitution, a transfer of power from the previous regime to the new system, emancipation from despotism and foreign hegemony, and a good relationship with other countries and neighbours based on law, autonomy and preserving territorial integrity of Iran (Bazargan 2010, pp. 251–253).

However, Bazargan also held views about an opposing idea, which was to serve Islam through Iran. First, since targeting Islam places religion ahead of Iranian identity, culture and nationhood, any concern about the nation, and also respecting the good customs that are legacy of the past, are deemed Nationalism and dismissed as a deviation and as representing polytheism. Second, there happen to be some similarities in form and method between Islam and modern philosophical schools coming from the West, such as Nationalism, Socialism and Marxism. One of the methods of contemporary philosophical, political and ideological schools is exclusivism and party-related discipline. Third, since the goal is to serve and advance Islam, the programmes of the Islamic revolution would become universal. For example, the motto of helping and supporting oppressed people all over the world had been added to the agenda. Thus, foreign policy has overridden internal policy. Finally, since the implementation of the programmes and managing the country's affairs and, in particular, government and policy need to be in accordance with Islam, naturally, these jobs must be done by Islamic experts and authorities (Bazargan 2010, pp. 252–257).

It is clear that Bazargan believed in Iran and Islam. However, he demands that his ideals in a framework for Iran consist of an Iranian-Islamic identity based on Iran's interests rather than global or regional concerns. Overall, Bazargan maintained the best role model for Iranian people were the Prophet Mohammad and his followers from the dawn of Islam. Also, Bazargan paid special attention to the holy book, the Qur'an. He believed that with regard to questions of ideology, Iranians should return to the Qur'an. From his standpoint, the Qur'an was a text which retains its relevance to the changing social conditions (Bazargan 2010, pp. 74–75). He rejected the Westernisation of Iran. He strongly criticised the tempers and attitudes of Iranian people during their 2500-year history. To recap, he maintained that two important critical points about Iranian people were a strong culture and Islam. He believed in an Iranian-Islamic identity with focus on the national interests of Iran.

Concluding Analysis

This chapter has outlined and discussed the ideas of the three political thinkers, in regards to the notion of a 'return to Shia Islamic culture'. Five concluding analytical points can be made.

First, in terms of an explanation of the situation they considered that the decline of Iran was related to two major factors: Thoughts and ideas on the one hand and some tangible issues such as despotism, exploitation, colonialism, poverty and corruption on the other hand. All three thinkers suggested Iran should return to its essential Shia principles and they also criticised any importation of Western ideologies into the Iranian society.

Second, referred to the system of knowledge, which they believed comprised a mixture of Islam, modernity and nationalism. For these three thinkers, terms and concepts should be based on Iranian-Islamic values. For Khomeini that meant a return to Shia principles, and was the main duty of jurists who needed to pay attention to traditional and dynamic jurisprudence with focus on the two elements of dynamic jurisprudential Islam, that is, time and place. If the jurists did not keep themselves up to date, then seminaries would become much like that of the Medieval Churches. However, Shariati believed that in order to return to Shia principles intellectuals had a duty to make new ideologies to inform an Islamic renaissance which he called an Islamic Protestantism similar to what happened between the two branches of Christian thought namely Protestant and Catholicism in Western countries. To achieve Islamic Protestantism, he relied on Iranian-Islamic values. Also, he believed that today it's more suitable that management of the Islamic society is done through ideological dynamic Islam supported by intellectuals rather than direct attendance of clergies. Bazargan's ideas were somewhat in line with those of Shariati with the difference being that Bazargan seemingly paid more attention to cooperation with clergies, in particular for a period before and after the 1979 Islamic revolution.

Third, concerned the system of norms. The decades between the 1960s and 1980s turned out to be very important in that some nativism and an independence movement ideas emerged within countries, in particular in Latin American, Asian and African states. These three thinkers pursued these ideas in Iran by establishing new concepts and norms. Terms such as a return to the Islamic-Iranian self, Iranian nativism, Iranian existence and Iranian original identity helped develop a genuine Iranian thought process to create a new identity for the Iranian people.

Fourth, with respect to the system of government, as was previously mentioned, within the decades 1960s to 1980s nativism ideas were popular among political thinkers including these three Iranian thinkers. However, the models differed. Shariati proposed his two theories namely 'The Theory of Ummah and Imamate' and 'Mysticism, Equality and Liberty'. Khomeini's model was Islamic Republic based on *Velayat-e Faqih* (the guardianship of jurisconsult). Bazargan suggested an Islamic Democratic Republic model.

Fifth, regarding domestic policy Khomeini, Shariati and Bazargan supported an Islamic-Iranian identity. Generally, the ideas of Khomeini swayed between Iranian and Islamic ideas; however, he preferred an

Islamic identity. However, Bazargan believed in serving Iran through Islam. With regards to foreign policy, Khomeini was more interested in transnational Islamic ideology between Muslim countries. However, Bazargan tended towards a national Islamic Ideology only in terms of Iran.

REFERENCES

Bazargan, M. (2006). *Modafeat* [Court Defenses] (Vol. 6). Tehran, Iran: Sherkat Shami Enteshar.
Bazargan, M. (2008). *Koba, Hendostan, Iran* [Cuba, India, Iran] (Vol. 15). Tehran, Iran: Sherkat Shami Enteshar.
Bazargan, M. (2009). *Mbahes Bonyadin* [Fundamental Topics] (Vol. 1). Tehran, Iran: Entesharat Ghlam.
Bazargan, M. (2010). *Bazyabi Arzesha (1)* [Recovery values (1)] (Vol. 25). Tehran, Iran: Sherkat Shami Enteshar.
Bazargan, M. (2011). *Maghalat Ejtemaei va Fani* [Social and Technical Articles] (Vol. 4). Tehran, Iran: Sherkat Shami Enteshar.
Grousset, R., & Deniker, G. (1955). *La face de l'Asie*. Paris: Payot.
Khomeini, S. R. (2010a). *Sahifeh Imam: Majmoe asar Imam Khomeini bayanat, payamha, mosahebeha, ahkam, ejazat sharei va nameha* [Sahifeh-Ye Imam: An anthology of Imam Khomeini's speeches, messages, interviews, decrees, religious permissions, and letters] (Vol. 16). Tehran, Iran: The Institute for Compilation and Publication of Imam Khomeini's Works.
Khomeini, S. R. (2010b). *Sahifeh Imam: Majmoe asar Imam Khomeini bayanat, payamha, mosahebeha, ahkam, ejazat sharei va nameha* [Sahifeh-Ye Imam: An anthology of Imam Khomeini's speeches, messages, interviews, decrees, religious permissions, and letters] (Vol. 11). Tehran: Institute for Compilation and Publication of Imam Khomeini's Works.
Khomeini, S. R. (2010c). *Sahifeh Imam: Majmoe asar imam Khomeini bayanat, payamha, mosahebeha, ahkam, ejazat sharei va nameha* [Sahifeh-Ye Imam: An anthology of Imam Khomeini's speeches, messages, interviews, decrees, religious permissions, and letters] (Vol. 13). Tehran, Iran: The Institute for Compilation and Publication of Imam Khomeini's Works.
Khomeini, S. R. (2010d). *Sahifeh Imam: Majmoe asar Imam Khomeini bayanat, payamha, mosahebeha, ahkam, ejazat sharei va nameha* [Sahifeh-Ye Imam: An anthology of Imam Khomeini's speeches, messages, interviews, decrees, religious permissions, and letters] (Vol. 3). Tehran, Iran: The Institute for Compilation and Publication of Imam Khomeini's Works.
Khomeini, S. R. (2010e). *Sahifeh Imam: Majmoe asar Imam Khomeini bayanat, payamha, mosahebeha, ahkam, ejazat sharei va nameha* [Sahifeh-Ye Imam: An anthology of Imam Khomeini's speeches, messages, interviews, decrees, reli-

gious permissions, and letters] (Vol. 4). Tehran, Iran: The Institute for Compilation and Publication of Imam Khomeini's Works.

Khomeini, S. R. (2010f). *Sahifeh Imam: Majmoe asar Imam Khomeini bayanat, payamha, mosahebeha, ahkam, ejazat sharei va nameha* [Sahifeh-Ye Imam: An anthology of Imam Khomeini's speeches, messages, interviews, decrees, religious permissions, and letters] (Vol. 7). Tehran, Iran: Institute for Compilation and Publication of Imam Khomeini's Works.

Khomeini, S. R. (2010g). *Sahifeh Imam: Majmoe asar imam Khomeini bayanat, payamha, mosahebeha, ahkam, ejazat sharei va nameha* [Sahifeh-Ye Imam: An anthology of Imam Khomeini's speeches, messages, interviews, decrees, religious permissions, and letters] (Vol. 10). Tehran, Iran: The Institute for Compilation and Publication of Imam Khomeini's Works.

Khomeini, S. R. (2010h). *Sahifeh Imam: Majmoe asar Imam Khomeini bayanat, payamha, mosahebeha, ahkam, ejazat sharei va nameha* [Sahifeh-Ye Imam: An anthology of Imam Khomeini's speeches, messages, interviews, decrees, religious permissions, and letters] (Vol. 21). Tehran, Iran: The Institute for Compilation and Publication of Imam Khomeini's Works.

Shariati, A. (2007). *Khodsazi Enghelabi* [Revolutionary Self monitoring] (Vol. 2). Tehran, Iran: Enteshrat Elham.

Shariati, A. (2008a). *Bazgasht* [Return] (Vol. 4). Tehran, Iran: Entesharat Elham.

Shariati, A. (2008b). *Islamshenasi (3)* [Islamology (3)] (Vol. 18). Tehran, Iran: Entesharat Elham.

Shariati, A. (2009). *Bazshenasi Hoviyat Irani Islami* [Recognition of Iranian and Islamic identity.] (Vol. 27). Tehran, Iran: Entesharat Elham.

Shariati, A. (2010). *Hosein Varese Adam* [Hosein Adam's heir] (Vol. 19). Tehran, Iran: Entesharat Ghalam.

Shariati, A. (2011a). *Islamshenasi (2)* [Islamology (2)] (Vol. 17). Tehran, Iran: Entesharat Ghalam.

Shariati, A. (2011b). *Niyayesh* [Invocation] (Vol. 8). Tehran, Iran: Entesharat Elham.

Shariati, A. (2011c). *Vizhehgihai Ghoron Jadid* [New Features Century] (Vol. 31). Tehran, Iran: Chappakhsh.

Shariati, A. (2012a). *Che Bayad Kard?* [What Must Do?] (Vol. 20). Tehran, Iran: Enteshrat Ghlam.

Shariati, A. (2012b). *Ensan* [Man] (Vol. 24). Tehran, Iran: Entesharat Elham.

CHAPTER 6

Rocking the Casbah: The Relationship Between Politics and Religion

In this chapter I examine the viewpoints of Khomeini, Shariati and Bazargan, and make critical comparisons between them, with regard to the relationship between politics and religion.

KHOMEINI

Definition of Religion

According to Khomeini, the Islamic religion is a comprehensive plan from God that provides for the temporal and spiritual happiness of all human beings in the social and private spheres. He asserted that, in contrast to non-monotheism socio-political paradigms, Islam is a complete belief system that has supervision and intervention in all aspects of individual, social, temporal, spiritual, cultural, political, military and economic affairs, and it does not neglect anything that can contribute to the nurturing of humans and their temporal and spiritual progress of society (Khomeini 2010k, pp. 402–403).

It is clear that Khomeini believed the school of Islam has a unique identity distinct from non-monotheism schools. Also, the Islamic school of thought is responsible for all aspects of life.

© The Author(s) 2020   101
S. M. Lolaki, *Diverging Approaches of Political Islamic Thought in Iran since the 1960s,*
https://doi.org/10.1007/978-981-15-0478-5_6

Definition of Politics

Khomeini divided politics into three different categories based on an Islamic worldview. Firstly, he refers to Satanic politics. This type of politics is based on lying, ruse and encroachment on people's properties and lives and is not related to Islamic politics but has a Satanic base (Khomeini 2010d, p. 431). During the conflict with the Pahlavi dynasty, Khomeini viewed politics as venal and did not want to be involved, stressing that he was not a follower of this type of politics and disagreed with the type of conduct (Khomeini 2010a, p. 269).

Secondly, incomplete or unilateral politics. Khomeini believed that this kind of politics was associated solely with temporal matters and social interests and lacked spiritualty making it one dimensional (Khomeini 2010d, pp. 431–432).

Thirdly, idealistic politics was the best type of politics, according to Khomeini. This type of politics considered both temporal and spiritual dimensions of life and was followed by Prophet Mohammad (in Medina city) and Imam Ali thereafter. Khomeini stated that, according to the Qur'an, idealistic politics was the so-called straight way (*Serat-e-Mostaghim*) and the way of the prophets (Khomeini 2010d, pp. 432–433). According to Khomeini, four characteristics denote idealistic politics: (1) Bringing happiness to a society; (2) establishing justice in all aspects of life and denying despotism and removing it from the society; (3) paying attention to both temporal and spiritual perspectives; (4) removing dishonesty and ruse from society.

Depoliticisation

Khomeini believed that the depoliticisation of society started at the beginning of Islam and was practised from the era of the Omayyad Caliphate and especially following the advent of the Abbasid Caliphate (Khomeini 2010b, p. 418). He believed that some Muslim countries experienced depoliticisation in contemporary times and cited the instance of Mustafa Kemal Ataturk in Turkey and the Pahlavi dynasty in Iran (Khomeini 2010a, p. 374) and the Pahlavi dynasty in Iran. The Pahlavi regime sought to remove clergy from the political and public scene in an effort to divert people's attention from their destiny. They disapproved of clerical participation or presence in the body politic of the nation, although Prophet Mohammad was a clergyman and a political figure (Khomeini 2010h, pp. 225–229). According to Khomeini Islamic monarchies were an obfuscation and needed to be abolished (Khomeini 2010g, p. 326).

Religion and Politics

Khomeini held several unique perspectives about the relationship between religion and politics. Sometimes, he referred to the dawn of Islam, sometimes the role of Islamic leadership such as Prophet Mohammad that had both spiritual and temporal qualities, and also the relationship between Islamic commandments and politics.

He asserted that the interference in politics was the highest priority for the prophets. The prophets had aimed to encourage people towards equity and justice and this was impossible for a society without interference in politics (Khomeini 2010e, pp. 216–217). Therefore, the task of prophets was simultaneously related to politics and religion and this is the correct way (Khomeini 2010d p. 433).

He posed the theoretical question of whether Prophet Mohammad interfered in wars from the dawn of Islam, and concluded it was the duty of God to put on his shoulders to encourage people towards justice, order and equity to create a good society (Khomeini 2010e, p. 218). From the beginning of Islam, politics was universal as seen in Prophet Mohammad's invitation to the emperors of his age to accept Islam. Prophet Mohammad then formed a government, and thus, since the beginning of Islam, it can be seen that politics and religion were intertwined (Khomeini 2010c, pp. 204–205). He then swore to God that Islam is totally political. He believed that Prophet Mohammad put the basis of politics into religion. Khomeini also said that his role in Islam is not like that of the Pope in Christianity which, as he claimed, is limited to holding ceremonies especially on Sundays (Khomeini 2010a, p. 270).

Khomeini then posed the question of whether politics and religion were separated in the era of Prophet Mohammad and Imam Ali. His response came in the idea of a separation of religion and policy presented by colonisers and their followers as they sought to remove clergies from the public sphere in order to dominate Muslims and plunder Islamic wealth (Khomeini 2000, p. 22).

Khomeini claimed that all Islamic commandments such as praying, Hajj (pilgrimage), Zakat (almsgiving) and Khums are mixed with politics. Thus, prayer and Hajj are mixed with politics and Zakat and Khums are for managing the society. In terms of collective praying and Hajj, Muslims talk with each other about political problems and other issues associated with Islam and Muslims. Khomeini believed that the devotional commandments of Islam are mixed with politics and are suitable for administrating society (Khomeini 2010i, pp. 16–18).

According to Khomeini, all the prophets from Adam to Mohammad have sacrificed themselves for the wider society around them and throughout history we have not seen people higher than the prophets and Imams who were dedicated to the establishment of equity and justice (Khomeini 2010e, pp. 212–213).

The Policy of Denying Both the East and the West

In light of his thoughts on Islam, Khomeini introduced the motto of "neither the West nor the East" into the political literature of Iran. He asserted that continuity and stability of the Islamic Republic of Iran should be predicated on a policy that denied both the East and the West, and this was the very slogan that guaranteed the independence of Iran (Khomeini 2010k, p. 155). He believed that the meaning of this phrase was that superpowers were not allowed to interfere in the affairs of Iran (Khomeini 2010j, p. 114). He added that this was a permanent motto for the Islamic Republic of Iran and all Muslim countries since it was an expression that articulated a moral course (*Serat-e-Mostaghim*) (Khomeini 2010f, p. 319).

In sum, Khomeini claimed that the political and religious players of the past were prophets and that today's jurists were successors to the prophets. As religion and politics were inseparable, it followed that politics came under the Sharia Law. Likewise, the best form of politics addressed both spiritual and temporal matters. This contrasted with the successful policy of separating politics and religion, that was supported by colonisers and followers of Western ideas.

SHARIATI

Definition of Religion

Shariati also believed that religion focused on either temporal or spiritual matters. If a society concentrated on temporal matters, then religion invited spiritual considerations. Similarly, if a society focused on spiritual matters, then religion invited temporal considerations. Islam is the only religion that invited, simultaneously both temporal and spiritual dimensions.

In this regard Islam formed a society that is evenly balanced (Shariati 2009, p. 296). In support of this thesis, Shariati expressed the idea that religion was a comprehensive programme of instruction.

Definition of Politics

Shariati believed in two different types of politics, namely Eastern and Western politics. He asserted that Western politics originating from ancient Greece had, as its main goal, the management of government or a society. Furthermore, the philosophy of government in Western politics pertained to the satisfaction of the people through serving and giving them goals towards a 'good' life. This contrasted, with Eastern politics where the philosophy of government aimed to help the population reach a high moral standard in thought and spirituality (Shariati 2011a, pp. 360–361).

Shariati believed that the terms Eastern and Western politics refer to two distinct styles of thought. The Western one referred to government and its administration whereby democracy, liberalism and the autonomy of individuals emanated from this ideology. The Eastern one referred to nurturing and guiding people. Shariati believed that Western intellectuals and supporters of liberal democracy were reviewing today their system and that some of them had tried to merge their ideas with Eastern ideas (Shariati 2011b, pp. 194–195).

Depoliticisation

He asserted the policies of the administration were sensitive about the public sphere and society, arguing that colonisers and despots fear the politicisation of society and the power of the masses. Therefore, they attempted to divert popular attention away from their destiny through a variety of social distractions as diverse as sports, sexual freedom, consumerism, economic and family problems, art, and entertainment (Shariati 2007, p. 174).

Moreover, he believed that this was not a feature of the modern era only. During the era of Prophet Mohammad and the four caliphs after him a political society existed. Both the Omayyad and Abbasid Caliphates tried to depoliticise Islamic society. Shariati argued that the reign of the Omayyad Caliphate was around one hundred years until the people became politically enlightened and finally overturned this empire. Similarly, the Abbasid Caliphate sought to depoliticise Islamic society with the development of culture, relying on science, temporal progress, wealth, political power and upholding religious values. Shariati stated that during the reign of Abbasid Caliphate, Muslim intellectuals were preoccupied with philosophy, theology, subjective and sectarian matters which distracted them from politics. For this reason the Abbasid Caliphate lasted around seven centuries (Shariati 2007, pp. 175–176).

Religion and Politics

Shariati maintained that in Islam no separation is made between religion and temporal matters, religious and non-religious sciences, worship and politics. The mosque of Prophet Mohammad was a place for devotional acts, a seminary for scientific discussion and a centre for government and the management of social, political and military affairs. It was a free place where people could participate in different aspects of Islamic society (Shariati 2012, pp. 393–394).

At the beginning of Islam, there was a social trend for resolving subjective and objective problems along with suffering and attending to needs in the public sphere. This was manifested by Imam Ali and his followers who supported the participation of people in the public sphere (Shariati 2008, pp. 87–88).

For Shariati, Islam does not support individualistic Sufic ideas rather Islam is the culture of Jihad and politics. Moreover, the social culture of Islam is based on collective responsibility, power, esteem, good government and leadership. Islam has an anti-aristocratic attitude. According to Shariati the main goal of Islam is to establish justice and equity in society (Shariati 2006, p. 107). Moreover, he believed that the social power of Islam is based on the two principles of *Nahi Anil Munkar* (forbidding evil) and *Amr Bil Mahroof* (ordering to do good things). He thought that it is the duty of all Muslims who believe in God, social actions and principles of *Nahi Anil Munkar* (forbidding evil) and *Amr Bil Mahroof* (ordering to do good things) to enter the public sphere and uphold Islamic society.

There are differences between Alawi and Safavid Shias. From Shariati's standpoint, in Safavid Shia, it is not the duty of people to interfere in politics or the public sphere because everything is up to the monarch. However, Alawi Shia people are encouraged to shape their destiny and participate in politics and the public sphere (Shariati 2011c, p. 234). Likewise, two different types of *Entezar* (waiting) in the absence of the last Imam of Shia Imam Mahdi: Negative and positive *Entezar* (waiting) are identified. According to Shariati, with negative waiting it was not the duty of people to participate in the public sphere while in positive waiting, it was the duty of people to come to the public sphere in order to shape their destiny (Shariati 2010a, p. 264). Similarly, Shariati identified two different types of *Taqiyeh* (reservation): Positive and negative. He asserted that in positive Taqiyeh, people covertly sought truth through justice and Imamate whereas in negative Taqiyeh, many people were marginalised because of their fear and irresponsibly towards other people and their society (Shariati 2010b, p. 319). Furthermore, Shariati believed that the duty of people in Islamic society was to be resolute concerning the gap between Western and the Eastern ideas. This was a universal mission upheld by the principles of jihad and martyrdom which was sensitive to the public sphere. The principle of martyrdom indicates that it was the duty of all Muslims to participate in the public sphere to support values for a good society with their lives and properties (Shariati 2010a, p. 206).

He asserted that intellectuals should follow two principles: Firstly, our society was an Islamic society and, secondly, Islam is social and dynamic. Furthermore, it was necessary to form movements and motivate people by creating awareness and social growth to encourage mass participation in the public sphere (Shariati 2006, p. 105).

He believed that in order for Islam to alter the social structure, it was necessary to change the human status with awareness about beliefs and consideration of revolutionary and ideological actions. Therefore, Islam puts the destiny of a nation on the shoulders of its people based on self-awareness while it was the duty of the intelligentsia to be responsible for changing the society by contributing to the public areas of life (Shariati 2006, pp. 168–169).

BAZARGAN

Definition of Religion

Bazargan gave two different meanings to the definition of religion—one dating back to the period between the 1940s and the 1980s and the other to his last years of life.

Bazargan maintained that two ideas be considered for the definition of religion: One that concerns individual-related commandments such as praying, fasting, pilgrimage and the other meaning involves thoughts, morality, beliefs, actions and guidance of nation (*Uma*) in order for them to manage their temporal and eternal life. Bazargan recognised the second meaning as the true definition of religion (Bazargan 1999, pp. 360–361). Furthermore, Bazargan believed that Islam was a comprehensive religion that addresses both spiritual and temporal matters (and also individual and social considerations), whereas Jewish culture and religion focus on temporal affairs with Christianity involving mainly spiritual issues (Bazargan 1999, p. 397).

Bazargan presented another definition of religion in his later years. He believed that the main reason for the presence of prophets was to teach people to believe in God and the eternal world. For him, most prophets had a spiritual mission. However being the exception Mohammad, Solomon, David and Joseph possessed both a pious and a temporal programmes (Bazargan 2009a, pp. 284–288). Further in Islam and the orders of Prophets there was no instruction about cooking, gardening, pastoralism, housekeeping, or economics, politics and the management of society. He believed that religions leave these subjects for people to contemplate and manage themselves (Bazargan 2009a, p. 330).

From the 1940s onwards, he set about articulating an ideology based on his comprehension of the orders of the prophets, by preparing a complete package for the management of both society and government. However, in an interview with *Keyhan Havaei* weekly in 1995—the year he passed away—he declared that religion is separate from ideology. So although it is true that ideology can take the principles and goals or framework from religion, Bazargan concluded that religion and ideology are two separate things (Bazargan 2009a, pp. 402–403).

Definition of Politics

Bazargan identified two different meanings for politics in the past and present: In the past, politics concentrated on subjects relating to individuals, families and classes where rights were exceptionally rare. The second definition for politics related to all dimensions of life and in both the East and West, inclusive of democratic or non-democratic governments. He believed that contemporary governments tried to manage the lives and destinies of the people from birth to death, although politics is affected by different ideologies, national goals and sometimes, personal views or classes' factors (Bazargan 1999, pp. 362–363). In this context, if the body politic is involved in trickiness and plundering, it has to be separated from religion. However, if politics enables public security and livelihood, and provides happiness to the nation (Umat), then it may be considered the true politics (Bazargan 2009b, p. 51).

Depoliticisation

Bazargan attributed the decline of Muslims in the world of Islam to not paying attention to participation in politics and the public sphere. At the dawn of Islam, people were political and attended to the public sphere and took care of the Islamic government and society in all aspects. However, in later epochs, Muslim attention shifted to poetry, theology, jurisprudence, philosophy and the myriad trivialities of daily life. Moreover, sophisticated people tended to avoid the public sphere and politics. Also, unfortunately, governments were led by bad politicians with most of the damage to Eastern states due to their focus on theoretical forms of utopia rather than addressing realpolitik. He then stated that in order for Muslim countries to be successful, they need both happiness and good management, and at the same time, the participation of people in the public sphere. Indeed, he believed that this is the real politics (Bazargan 1999, pp. 360–362).

Religion and Politics

Bazargan asserted that religion was related to all aspects of life and, in particular, politics. According to Bazargan's view, this is a one-way relationship meaning that religion may instruct morality and politics, giving aim and direction; however, if politics gives direction to religion it leads to evil and impurity. According to Bazargan religion holds a higher position than politics. Religion also determines the principles of politics and government but it does not clarify details such as the type of government (Bazargan 1999, pp. 379–380).

Bazargan claimed that a reaction to the efforts of the Church to dominate the State in the Middle Ages was the main cause of separation between religion, the state and politics in Western countries. However, he noted that this separation was not uniform across all Western countries.

He continued that governments formed in the dawn of Islam, by Prophet Mohammad and Imam Ali, offered good examples of the association between religion and politics. He observed, however, that after that era and at the time of the Omayyad, Abbasid and Ottoman Empires, politics overrode religion. Also, at that time Shias were in the minority and disagreed with the status quo of society. He asserted that at the time of the Safavid dynasty, when Shia became the official religion in Iran, and also at the era of Qajar Dynasty, there was a separation between politics and religion with the kings and clergies regularly interfering in the affairs of one another. However, since the Constitutional Revolution, clergies entered the public sphere and politics which continued until the Islamic Revolution in 1979 when the clergy finally assumed power and control of government (Bazargan 2010, pp. 112–114). Bazargan believed that some clerics thought that political power was their divine right, when indeed it was more broadly the right of jurists to take power. This resulted in a theocracy and the fusing of politics and religion (Bazargan 2012, p. 375). Bazargan then asserted that the main goal of religions was to encourage people to believe in God and the other world. For him individual rights became more important than establishing a religious society (Bazargan 2014, pp. 358–359).

It seems that that the ideas of Bazargan shifted from maximising Islam to minimising it. Thus, as mentioned above, he presented two definitions of religion. Also, in his view, true politics was the one that provides happiness and good management of society simultaneously. He disagreed with the absence of people in government and society because this lack of power leads to the depoliticisation of society. Moreover, he believed that religion and politics should not be separate from each other because religion stands higher than politics and religion should inform politics. In essence, if politics governs religion, impurity and corruption results in society.

Concluding Analysis

Individually and collectively, the largest source of misery for most nations is the pretence that reality if not really reality, is mutable but that the individuals involved are personally immutable. When governments fight against reality, whatever their original ideological origin or premise, they lose. The recognition of reality is axiomatic regardless of socio-political affiliation or preference. Five concluding analytical points can be drawn from the above text.

Firstly, with regards to an explanation of the situation: All three thinkers here believed that the true relationship between religion and politics emerged during the dawn of Islam, that is, at the time of Prophet

Mohammad and Imam Ali. Following that era, at the time of the Omayyad, Abbasid and Ottoman Caliphates, religion and politics were decoupled, a situation that they blame and deem wrong. In Iran, this situation existed during the eras of Safavid, Qajar and Pahlavi dynasties even though at that time the official religion of the vast majority of Iranians was Shia. All of the aforementioned intellectuals disagreed with the depoliticisation of the society and masses and its impact on the encouraging religious people to enter the public sphere and inform both government and society.

Secondly, concerning the system of knowledge and its focus on the role of religion in an Iranian context, Bazargan, in his later years, shifted his emphasis from Political Islam to Social Islam. As far as the differences between social Islam and Political Islam are concerned it is important to know that, in Political Islam, Islamist groups and thinkers first tried to take control of the government and political power and then administer social and cultural changes. This was the case in Iran at the time of the Islamic revolution in 1979. However, in Social Islam, Islamist groups and thinkers sought social change and reform by taking control of government in a democratic way (Feirahi 2015). All of these three thinkers, after returning to self (Shia principles), sought to make a robust relationship between politics and religion based on Islamic-Iranian values. Khomeini opted for jurisprudentialism; Bazargan selected the Qur'an and Shariati chose the history of Islam. As far as religion is concerned, their ideas were common although their methods and reference points differed.

Thirdly, in terms of the system of norms these three thinkers gave new meaning to key Shia concepts to forge new Islamic ideological ideas. Khomeini adopted new terms such as the oppressed Islam, Alawi justice and religious democracy. Shariati gave new meaning to some historic Shia concepts such as positive and negative *Entezar* (waiting), positive and negative *Taqiyeh* (reservation), martyrdom, Alawi and Safavid Shia. Bazargan utilised Islamic democracy and Islamic justice. By creating new meaning for some Shia concepts and ideas they sought to establish new norms in the context of Iran to encourage Iranian people to enter the public sphere.

Fourthly, with regard to the system of government, both Khomeini and Shariati placed emphasis on Political Islam but they pursued different forms of governance. Shariati proposed his two theories: 'The Theory of Ummah and Imamate' and 'Mysticism, Equality and Liberty'. Due to his untimely death, he could not fully articulate his ideas. Khomeini's model was an Islamic Republic based on *Velayat-e Faqih* (the guardianship of jurisconsult). Bazargan, on the other hand, supported the idea of an Islamic Democratic Republic. Initially, he showed interest in Political Islam; however, the experience he gained in post-revolution Iran and his marginalisation had a profound impact on his thinking causing him to support Social Islam in later life.

Fifthly, with regards to public policy, all of the above thinkers supported efforts towards a good society with both traditional values and modern ideas existed and where happiness is sought for the public, and at the same time, managing society in a proper manner. Khomeini supported the maximisation of Islamic lore oscillating between collectivism and individualism with more focus on collectivism. In contrast, Bazargan shifted from Political Islam to Social Islam and in later life supported the minimisation of Islam. He was also an advocate of individualism rather than collectivism. He opined that ideology take the principles and goals or framework of religion; however, religion and ideology remain two separate entities.

REFERENCES

Bazargan, M. (1999). *Mabahes elmi ejtemae Islami* [Scientific, social, Islamic controversy] (Vol. 8). Tehran, Iran: Sherkat Sahami Enteshar.

Bazargan, M. (2009a). *Besat (2)* [Prophetic mission (2)] (Vol. 17). Tehran, Iran: Sherkat Shami Enteshar.

Bazargan, M. (2009b). *Enghelab Eslami Iran (1)* [Islamic Revolution in Iran (1)] (Vol. 22). Tehran, Iran: Sherkat Shami Enteshar.

Bazargan, M. (2010). *Bazyabi Arzesha (1)* [Recovery values (1)] (Vol. 25). Tehran, Iran: Sherkat Shami Enteshar.

Bazargan, M. (2012). *Enghelab Eslami Iran (3)* [Islamic Revolution in Iran (3)] (Vol. 24). Tehran, Iran: Sherkat Shami Enteshar.

Bazargan, M. (2014). *Padideh Pyambari* [Phenomenon of Prophecy] (Vol. 27). Tehran, Iran: Sherkat Shami Enteshar.

Feirahi, D. (2015). *Islam siasi va Tahavolat Khavar Miyanh (Evolution of political Islam in the Middle East)* Retrieved from http://www.feirahi.ir/?article=252

Khomeini, S. R. (2000). *Velayt Faghih* [Islamic Government: Governance of the Jurist]. Tehran, Iran: Institute for Compilation and Publication of Imam Khomeini's Works.

Khomeini, S. R. (2010a). *Sahifeh Imam: Majmoe asar Imam Khomeini bayanat, payamha, mosahebeha, ahkam, ejazat sharei va nameha* [Sahifeh-Ye Imam: An anthology of Imam Khomeini's speeches, messages, interviews, decrees, religious permissions, and letters] (Vol. 1). Tehran, Iran: The Institute for Compilation and Publication of Imam Khomeini's Works.

Khomeini, S. R. (2010b). *Sahifeh Imam: Majmoe asar Imam Khomeini bayanat, payamha, mosahebeha, ahkam, ejazat sharei va nameha* [Sahifeh-Ye Imam: An anthology of Imam Khomeini's speeches, messages, interviews, decrees, religious permissions, and letters] (Vol. 16). Tehran, Iran: The Institute for Compilation and Publication of Imam Khomeini's Works.

Khomeini, S. R. (2010c). *Sahifeh Imam: Majmoe asar Imam Khomeini bayanat, payamha, mosahebeha, ahkam, ejazat sharei va nameha* [Sahifeh-Ye Imam: An anthology of Imam Khomeini's speeches, messages, interviews, decrees, religious permissions, and letters] (Vol. 17). Tehran, Iran: The Institute for Compilation and Publication of Imam Khomeini's Works.

Khomeini, S. R. (2010d). *Sahifeh Imam: Majmoe asar imam Khomeini bayanat, payamha, mosahebeha, ahkam, ejazat sharei va nameha* [Sahifeh-Ye Imam: An anthology of Imam Khomeini's speeches, messages, interviews, decrees, religious permissions, and letters] (Vol. 13). Tehran, Iran: The Institute for Compilation and Publication of Imam Khomeini's Works.

Khomeini, S. R. (2010e). *Sahifeh Imam: Majmoe asar Imam Khomeini bayanat, payamha, mosahebeha, ahkam, ejazat sharei va nameha* [Sahifeh-Ye Imam: An anthology of Imam Khomeini's speeches, messages, interviews, decrees, religious permissions, and letters] (Vol. 15). Tehran, Iran: The Institute for Compilation and Publication of Imam Khomeini's Works.

Khomeini, S. R. (2010f). *Sahifeh Imam: Majmoe asar Imam Khomeini bayanat, payamha, mosahebeha, ahkam, ejazat sharei va nameha* [Sahifeh-Ye Imam: An anthology of Imam Khomeini's speeches, messages, interviews, decrees, religious permissions, and letters] (Vol. 20). Tehran, Iran: The Institute for Compilation and Publication of Imam Khomeini's Works.

Khomeini, S. R. (2010g). *Sahifeh Imam: Majmoe asar Imam Khomeini bayanat, payamha, mosahebeha, ahkam, ejazat sharei va nameha* [Sahifeh-Ye Imam: An anthology of Imam Khomeini's speeches, messages, interviews, decrees, religious permissions, and letters] (Vol. 2). Tehran, Iran: The Institute for Compilation and Publication of Imam Khomeini's Works.

Khomeini, S. R. (2010h). *Sahifeh Imam: Majmoe asar Imam Khomeini bayanat, payamha, mosahebeha, ahkam, ejazat sharei va nameha* [Sahifeh-Ye Imam: An anthology of Imam Khomeini's speeches, messages, interviews, decrees, religious permissions, and letters] (Vol. 3). Tehran, Iran: The Institute for Compilation and Publication of Imam Khomeini's Works.

Khomeini, S. R. (2010i). *Sahifeh Imam: Majmoe asar imam Khomeini bayanat, payamha, mosahebeha, ahkam, ejazat sharei va nameha* [Sahifeh-Ye Imam: An anthology of Imam Khomeini's speeches, messages, interviews, decrees, religious permissions, and letters] (Vol. 10). Tehran, Iran: The Institute for Compilation and Publication of Imam Khomeini's Works.

Khomeini, S. R. (2010j). *Sahifeh Imam: Majmoe asar Imam Khomeini bayanat, payamha, mosahebeha, ahkam, ejazat sharei va nameha* [Sahifeh-Ye Imam: An anthology of Imam Khomeini's speeches, messages, interviews, decrees, religious permissions, and letters] (Vol. 8). Tehran, Iran: The Institute for Compilation and Publication of Imam Khomeini's Works.

Khomeini, S. R. (2010k). *Sahifeh Imam: Majmoe asar Imam Khomeini bayanat, payamha, mosahebeha, ahkam, ejazat sharei va nameha* [Sahifeh-Ye Imam: An anthology of Imam Khomeini's speeches, messages, interviews, decrees, religious permissions, and letters] (Vol. 21). Tehran, Iran: The Institute for Compilation and Publication of Imam Khomeini's Works.

Shariati, A. (2006). *Ma va Iqbal* [We and Iqbal] (Vol. 5). Tehran, Iran: Entesharat Elham.

Shariati, A. (2007). *Khodsazi Enghelabi* [Revolutionary Self monitoring] (Vol. 2). Tehran, Iran: Enteshrat Elham.

Shariati, A. (2008). *Islamshenasi (3)* [Islamology (3)] (Vol. 18). Tehran, Iran: Entesharat Elham.

Shariati, A. (2009). *Tarikh va Shenakht Adiyan (1)* [History and Understand Religions (1)] (Vol. 14). Tehran, Iran: Sherkat Shami Enteshar.

Shariati, A. (2010a). *Hosein Varese Adam* [Hosein Adam's heir] (Vol. 19). Tehran, Iran: Entesharat Ghalam.

Shariati, A. (2010b). *Mazhab Alihe Mazhab* [Religion versus religion] (Vol. 22). Tehran, Iran Entesharat Chappakhsh.

Shariati, A. (2011a). *Ali* (Vol. 26). Tehran, Iran: Nashr Amon.

Shariati, A. (2011b). *Asar Gonagon (1)* [Various Works (1)] (Vol. 35). Tehran, Iran: Nashr Didar.

Shariati, A. (2011c). *Tashyoe Alawi va Tashyoe Safavi* [Alawi Shiite and Safavid Shiite] (Vol. 9). Tehran, Iran: Entesharat Chappakhsh.

Shariati, A. (2012). *Che Bayad Kard?* [What Must Do?] (Vol. 20). Tehran, Iran: Enteshrat Ghlam.

CHAPTER 7

The Table Spread: The Ideals of Islamic Government

This chapter examines the viewpoints of Khomeini, Shariati and Bazargan, and makes critical comparisons between them with regard to the ideals of an Islamic Government.

KHOMEINI

Khomeini believed that Islam and Islamic government are divine phenomena that can bring happiness to people in this world and in the world to come (the afterlife). Islam offers ideas, advice and guidance about all aspects of life, including individual, social, temporal, spiritual, cultural, political, military-related and economic aspects. In summary, according to Khomeini, Islam and Islamic government are able to offer a complete package that has a detailed, and, at the same time, holistic outlook upon life here and now, and in the eternal life. For Khomeini this is distinctive from all non-theistic, indeed monotheistic, religions. These are the marks of a divine religion based on revelation (Khomeini 2010n, pp. 402–403).

© The Author(s) 2020   115
S. M. Lolaki, *Diverging Approaches of Political Islamic Thought in
Iran since the 1960s*,
https://doi.org/10.1007/978-981-15-0478-5_7

Evidence for Islamic Government in the Qur'an and Sunnah

Citing verses 44 to 50[1] of Surah Al-Ma'ida, Khomeini asserted that God has created this world embodied with discipline and wisdom. He then concluded that God has specified clearly defined duties and rights for people with the intention of leading them to form a just government based on these duties and rights (Khomeini 1942, p. 183).

Moreover, referring to verse 25[2] of Surah Al-Hadid, Khomeini argued that focusing on justice had been the primary duty of all prophets including Prophet Mohammad, as well as the Imams (of Shi'ism) and today's

---

[1] "It was we who revealed the law (to Moses): therein was guidance and light. By its standard have been judged the Jews, by the prophets who bowed (as in Islam) to Allah's will, by the rabbis and the doctors of law: for to them was entrusted the protection of Allah's book, and they were witnesses thereto: therefore fear not men, but fear me, and sell not my signs for a miserable price. If any do fail to judge by (the light of) what Allah hath revealed, they are (no better than) Unbelievers. (44) We ordained therein for them: 'Life for life, eye for eye, nose or nose, ear for ear, tooth for tooth, and wounds equal for equal.' But if any one remits the retaliation by way of charity, it is an act of atonement for himself. And if any fail to judge by (the light of) what Allah hath revealed, they are (No better than) wrong-doers. (45) And in their footsteps we sent Jesus the son of Mary, confirming the Law that had come before him: We sent him the Gospel: therein was guidance and light, and confirmation of the Law that had come before him: a guidance and an admonition to those who fear Allah. (46) Let the people of the Gospel judge by what Allah hath revealed therein. If any do fail to judge by (the light of) what Allah hath revealed, they are (no better than) those who rebel. (47) To thee we sent the Scripture in truth, confirming the scripture that came before it, and guarding it in safety: so judge between them by what Allah hath revealed, and follow not their vain desires, diverging from the Truth that hath come to thee. To each among you have we prescribed a law and an open way. If Allah had so willed, He would have made you a single people, but (His plan is) to test you in what He hath given you: so strive as in a race in all virtues. The goal of you all is to Allah; it is He that will show you the truth of the matters in which ye dispute; (48) And this (He commands): Judge thou between them by what Allah hath revealed, and follow not their vain desires, but beware of them lest they beguile thee from any of that (teaching) which Allah hath sent down to thee. And if they turn away, be assured that for some of their crime it is Allah's purpose to punish them. And truly most men are rebellious. (49) Do they then seek after a judgment of (the days of) ignorance? But who, for a people whose faith is assured, can give better judgment than Allah?" (50) (Yusuf Ali 2016, pp. 115–116).

[2] "We sent aforetime our messengers with Clear Signs and sent down with them the Book and the Balance (of Right and Wrong), that men may stand forth in justice"...(25) (Yusuf Ali 2016, p. 541).

jurists. He asserted that in verse 41[3] of Surah Al-Anfal, and also verse 103[4] of Surah At-Tawba, God ordered Prophet Mohammad to receive Khums[5] and Zakat from people and to spend it on promoting justice among people in the Islamic society. This was done only in the context of an Islamic government, as led by the prophets and Imams in the past, and today by jurists (Khomeini 2000, p. 70). According to verse 59[6] of Surah An-Nisa, obeying Prophet Mohammad and the Imams, and today the jurists, is indeed tantamount to obeying God. This is because God entitled Prophet Mohammad to appoint judges and governors (Khomeini 2000, p. 71).

In reference to the Sunnah, Khomeini remarked that in his day, Prophet Mohammad effectively ran or organised the government, appointed judges and ambassadors, and made treaties and covenants; furthermore, he was the commander of wars and received taxes, ransoms, Khums and Zakat while issuing decrees. In brief, he was a governor and, as a result, made orders and issued directives (Khomeini 2000, pp. 25–35). In addition, based on God's order, he appointed a governor to lead the government after his life ended. Hence, for Khomeini running the government is an essential religious obligation and all commandments, whether devotional or non-devotional, are effective in all places and all times for the Muslim community (Khomeini 2000, pp. 25–35).

Imam Ali, the first Shia Imam and governor had sworn to God that he had accepted the role of giving due consideration to people in society, and also understood that God required of the Imams that they always support oppressed people and fight cruelty. This was a duty of Muslims and Islamic scholars because the Islamic state was underpinned by the happiness of Muslims and the overthrow of tyrannical governments (Khomeini 2000, pp. 35–38). Furthermore, it was the duty of Imams and jurists to form a government based on the Islamic justice system. Thus, he believed that

---

[3] "And know that out of all the booty that ye may acquire (in war), a fifth share is assigned to Allah,- and to the Messenger, and to near relatives, orphans, the needy, and the wayfarer"...(41) (Yusuf Ali 2016, p. 182).

[4] "Of their goods, take alms, that so thou mightiest purify and sanctify them; and pray on their behalf"... (103) (Yusuf Ali 2016, p. 203).

[5] Khums is a 20% tax that must be paid on all items regarded as ghanima (The earned Profit). There are differing legal traditions within Islam about what constitutes ghanima, and thus how far-reaching Khums should be. In some jurisdictions, Khums included a 20% tax paid on business profit and minerals. Khums is different and separate from other Islamic taxes such as Zakat and Jizya.

[6] "O ye who believe! Obey Allah, and obey the Messenger, and those charged with authority among you"...(59) (Yusuf Ali 2016, p. 87).

the guardianship of a jurisconsult was a divine mission and duty (Khomeini 2000, pp. 54–56).

Guardianship of Jurisconsult *(Velayat-e Fagih)*

Citing a Hadith from Imam Jafar al-Sadiq, the sixth Shia Imam, Khomeini asserted that Islam is built on five pillars: prayer (Salat), almsgiving (Zakat), the fast during the month of Ramadan, Hajj (pilgrimage) and, lastly, guardianship. Indeed, this last one is the most important, given that, according to the hadith, guardianship means government and leadership, and forms a foundation for other divine commandments to be effective in an Islamic society (Khomeini 2010g, pp. 113–115).

Jurists have the same duty as Prophet Mohammad and the 12 Imams, except with respect to taking initiatives today for jihad. Moreover, he thought that guardianship meant government and administration within a territory based on Sharia laws which is, foremost, a duty of jurists (Khomeini 2000, p. 51). Khomeini enumerated three roles for a jurist: Firstly, political guardianship; secondly, adjudication; thirdly, the issuance of fatwa as divine commandments in the absence of Imam Mahdi, the 12th Shia Imam (Khomeini 1998, pp. 26–30). As mentioned in Chap. 2, Khomeini had different ideas about the guardianship of the jurisconsult (*Velayat-e Fagih*) in various contexts in Iran. His view changed at least four times between the 1940s and 1980s. However, clearly, Khomeini was a political jurist whose ideas moved from political realities to political ideals, and, indeed, he was a successful jurist politician who, in his life, finally achieved the ideals that he pursued for the Islamic Republic of Iran.

Characteristics of Islamic State According to Khomeini

Value-Orientedness

Khomeini believed that the Islamic Revolution of the Iranian people was an Islamic and human one. According to him, the Iranian nation sought to live their lives according to the Qur'an and Sunnah (Khomeini 2010m, p. 371). Moreover, he thought that the ordinary folk of Iran realised that Islam was for both temporal and spiritual matters and for their security and peace (Khomeini 2010b, p. 44). He asserted that the Islamic state did not allow people, youth in particular, to go to nightclubs or gamble. Likewise, the Islamic state opposed any type of cinema, or other venue, that advertised prostitution. Rather, according to Khomeini, the Islamic state supported a cinema that focused only on informative and moral subjects (Khomeini 2010i, p. 427).

Rule of Law
Khomeini believed that all Iranian people should show respect to the constitutional law of the Islamic Republic of Iran because they voted for it. The constitution defined all administrative positions and clarified duties and limitations associated with them. As a consequence, people violating constitutional law must be penalised (Khomeini 2010e, pp. 348–349).

Support of Oppressed People
Khomeini stated that the government should serve the entire population. The Islamic Revolution of Iran should support oppressed people against oppressors wherever they may be, all over the world (Khomeini 2010k, pp. 117–118). He declared that it was the duty of the government to focus on oppressed people, especially the poor (Khomeini 2010j, p. 488). In sum, Islam clearly focused on the needy and oppressed people (Khomeini 2010o, pp. 50–51).

Government of Justice
For Khomeini, the primary duty of a government was to establish justice. He stated that it was the duty of a government to establish welfare and equity (Khomeini 2010d, p. 328). Also, he observed that Islam objected to discrimination, tribalism and racism but supported the dignity of human beings (Khomeini 2010d, pp. 55–57).

Freedom and Independence
Khomeini asserted that Iran should be an independent country in terms of culture, economy and political affairs, and that there should be no other country that dominates Iranian people (Khomeini 2010l, pp. 246–247). The destiny of the common folk of Iran should be decided by themselves (Khomeini 2010i, p. 266). Moreover, they must have freedom within the framework of the constitutional law, a law which supports Islamic laws (Khomeini 2010k, pp. 535–536).

Culture and Civilisation
Culture forms the identity of a society and without an autonomous culture the independence of a country in all other aspects is not achieved. For

this reason, Khomeini claimed the first attack on colonised countries by colonising countries comes through culture. He stated that Iranian people need to have an Islamic, Iranian culture, not a 'Western' or 'Eastern' one (Khomeini 2010f, pp. 243–247). While Islam is the foundation of a new civilisation, it does not reject other civilisations; rather he believed that Islamic civilisation as such has its focus on both the spiritual and temporal dimensions of life (Khomeini 2010m, pp. 516–517).

Islamic Economy
In terms of the economy, Islam rejected with both Western capitalism, such as that of the US and Britain, and also the ideological systems of Marxism and Leninism. According to Khomeini, Islam respected and recognised private ownership; however, it offered a median solution as to private ownership and consumerism. Social justice was really important to an ideal Islamic government (Khomeini 2010n, pp. 444–445). He also paid attention to self-sufficiency in agriculture and other industries (Khomeini 2010c, pp. 294–296).

Foreign Policy
The foreign policy of Iran was based on protecting the freedom and independence of Iran and also preserving the national interest (Khomeini 2010i, p. 414). He argued that the Islamic Republic of Iran was interested in mutual respect with other countries (Khomeini 2010c, p. 257), but added that the most important principle in foreign policy was to repudiate both the West and the East, and to affirm the Islamic Republic of Iran, instead (Khomeini 2010n, p. 155).

Defending Islam and the Islamic System
Khomeini mentioned that since the dawn of Islam, there had been a conflict between Islam and non-Islamic ideas, and, in this regard, all Iranian people should defend Islam and the Islamic Republic of Iran as a duty (Khomeini 2010a, p. 414). Further, he stated that the Islamic Republic of Iran should export the Islamic Revolution to other countries in support of all oppressed populations all over the world (Khomeini 2010e, pp. 212–213).

The Characteristics of Administration of Islamic State
The administration of the Islamic state in Iran should be undertaken by and from the masses. Also, he stated that the staff, personnel and officials,

in charge of the administration should live simple lives like those of Prophet Mohammad and the Shia Imams (Khomeini 2010b, pp. 317–318). They should also deeply believe and practise Islam and be socially acceptable persons (Khomeini 2010c, p. 382).

Rights of People in Islamic State

Human Rights in Islam
The Islamic state centres on human rights and is based on freedom and democracy, which can be found within Islamic thought (Khomeini 2010c, p. 70). He added that the constitutional law of the Islamic Republic of Iran recognised universal suffrage for all (Khomeini 2010h, p. 503). He asserted that Islam respected the rights of minority religious groups such as Christians, Jews and Zoroastrians (Khomeini 2010j, p. 468). He recognised woman's rights (Khomeini 2010c, p. 70). Furthermore, he thought that all different ethnic groups have equal rights (Khomeini 2010o, p. 317).

The Right of Criticising the Government
Khomeini believed that all citizens participate in *Nahi Anil Munkar* (forbidding evil) and *Amr Bil Mahroof* (ordering for doing good actions) in terms of the Islamic government administration; indeed, it is the duty of Iranian people to uphold these principles. Further, all administrations were required to be responsible about their positions and accept criticism from the general public (Khomeini 2010o, pp. 469–470).

Political Parties and Media
Khomeini asserted that the constitutional law of the Islamic Republic of Iran guaranteed the freedom of political parties and the media to freely express ideas. They must, however, consider Islamic rules in all interactions (Khomeini 2010i, p. 266).

The Islamic Republic of Iran

In many respects, Khomeini was the founder of the Islamic Republic of Iran. He employed both modernity and traditional methods in this system. On the one hand, he adopted duty, guardianship and expediency; on the other hand, he paid attention to rights, freedom and law. These two sets of concepts form a political order in the Iranian context and are expressed through *fiqh*, that is, Islamic jurisprudence. As stated previously, Khomeini proved to be a successful political jurist who moved from political realities to ideals in his life within the context of Iran. He sought to combine traditional ideas, which are summarised as virtue, with modernity, which in turn is summarised as order, to devise a modern political order for this era. However, some paradoxes appear in this compromise. Sometimes Khomeini tended towards traditional ideas, and sometimes he tended towards modern ideas, and this is manifested in Iran's political order. Moreover, during his tenure as the supreme leader of the Islamic Republic of Iran, Khomeini issued some decrees, which demonstrated that his position was higher than the constitutional law of Iran. After his death in 1989, two different schools followed his ideas on political jurisprudential Islam. One supported divine legitimacy for Iran's supreme leadership, suggesting that, in the absence of Imam Mahdi, the supreme leader is a representative of him, and the popular vote is effectively a decoration. The other school, however, attributed this legitimacy to the votes of the general public (Feirahi 2012, pp. 275–280). The second is closer to modern ideas. This idea is a form of Social Islam in terms of political jurisprudence in the context of Iranian Islam.

SHARIATI

Shariati held two different views about the government. The first, the theory of Ummah and Imamate, was explained by him in speeches in Hussainieh-e-Ershad around 1970. His second theory was mysticism, equality and liberty, which he proposed in 1977.

Ummah and Imamate

Shariati believed that the Ummah refers to a people who have a common ideology and goals and who act to achieve those goals (Shariati 2011, p. 360). From an Islamic political perspective, the Imamate refers to political leadership based around guiding the society. He believed that this contrasted with Western political leadership, which merely sought to manage a society (Shariati 2011, pp. 361–362). Shariati posed the idea of 'gifted democracy' in contrast to liberal democracy. He claimed that this kind of democracy ended in corruption, whereas gifted democracy paid attention to morality and spirituality in society. The central argument of Shariati about gifted democracy emerged after the Bandung conference in

1954 (Shariati 2010, p. 599). He believed a leader could be elected but could not be dismissed by the people. According to Shariati, democracy had two contributions to make: (a) the public representative should be elected by the people and (b) the duration of the elected term must be extensive. Further, for Shariati, political leadership was synonymous with the Imamate (Shariati 1980, p. 232).

Shariati believed that the theory of Ummah and Imamate related especially to the revolutionary transition period, and that once the society developed and matured in its thinking, democracy then became a good model for it. However, underpinning the nature and model of his democracy was Shura and allegiance (Shariati 2009, pp. 275–276).

By referring to the Imamate, Shariati did not mean spiritual emulation or clerical rule. An Islamic government meant an administration legitimised by a particular (Islamic) ideology rather than a government that is simply ruled by Jurisconsults and Jurisprudentialists as such (Yosefi Ashkevari 1997, p. 277).

Mysticism, Equality and Liberty

Shariati saw mysticism, equality and liberty as the three major principles to guide humanity with other ideas branching out of this triad (Shariati 2007, p. 65). According to Shariati, mysticism is a spiritual trend and exists in both the East and the West. With regard to equality, he believed that equalitarianism was manifested in socialism, communism and other schools that deny discrimination in social relations (e.g. the relationship between farmer and master, or capitalism and labour). He thought liberty focused on freedom and the right of free choice, however, but that all these trends possessed some internal drawbacks: Mysticism could be reduced to Sufism, thereby causing people to think only of a supernatural power without making any effort in their lives to contribute. Socialism could sometimes connect to materialism and even the effective deification of government, as in the case of Stalinism. Liberty (existentialism) may sometimes end in extreme forms of individualism and nihilism, thus forgetting God (Shariati 2007, pp. 80–82). Despite these potential drawbacks, these three trends formed exciting dimensions for people and were necessary for a society. Clearly, mysticism contained the root and spirit of Islam (and other religions such as Christianity). Notably, Islam has a focus on social justice and freedom (Shariati 2007, pp. 90–91). Imam Ali provided a good role model—one who possessed these three dimensions at the same time (Shariati 2007, pp. 92–93).

After Shariati passed away in 1977, his first theory (with some changes) became the theory of Political Islam and was applied by jurists such as Ayatollah Hussein Ali Montazeri and Ayatollah Seyyed Mohammad Hossini Beheshti who were also followers of Khomeini. His second theory was adopted by the neo-Shariati school. Importantly, after the Islamic Revolution of 1979, liberal Islam divided into two schools: the Neo-Shariati or Left School that followed the ideas of Shariati and liberal Islam, which, more recently, has become Neo-Liberal Islam following Bazargan. In fact, Neo-Shariatism and Neo-Liberalism are both followers of Social Islam today.

BAZARGAN

Prior to the Islamic Revolution of 1979

Bazargan was agreeable to an Islamic government and cited verse 59[7] of Surah An-Nisa and verse 55[8] of Surah Al-Ma'ida to support his views. In this regard, and along with Khomeini, he also cited a Hadith from Imam Jafar al-Sadiq, the sixth Shia Imam, concerning the five cornerstones of Islam, prayer, Zakat, fasting, the Hajj, and guardianship, which is the primary feature in forming an Islamic government (Bazargan 2009, p. 304).

Theoretically, an Islamic government was focused on consultation and electing the government authorities by people, according to Islamic ideology. To support this, Bazargan referred to verses 38 and 39[9] of Surah Ash-Shura and also verse 159[10] of Surah Al-i-Imran and also a hadith from

---

[7] "O ye who believe! Obey Allah, and obey the Messenger, and those charged with authority among you"...(59) (Yusuf Ali 2016, p. 87).

[8] Your (real) friends are (no less than) Allah, His Messenger, and the (fellowship of) believers—"those who establish regular prayers and regular charity, and they bow down humbly (in worship)" (55) (Yusuf Ali 2016, p. 117).

[9] "Those who hearken to their Lord, and establish regular Prayer; who (conduct) their affairs by mutual Consultation; who spend out of what We bestow on them for Sustenance; (38) And those who, when an oppressive wrong is inflicted on them, (are not cowed but) help and defend themselves" (39) (Yusuf Ali 2016, p. 487).

[10] "It is part of the Mercy of Allah that thou dost deal gently with them Wert thou severe or harsh-hearted, they would have broken away from about thee: so pass over (Their faults), and ask for (Allah's) forgiveness for them; and consult them in affairs (of moment). Then,

Prophet Mohammad wherein he asked the people to engage him in consultation about the affairs of Islamic society (Bazargan 2009, pp. 324–325). According to Bazargan, Islam does not interfere in the precise details relating to the specific type of Islamic government, for such fine points are determined in the context of the time and space where Muslims live. It was the duty of all populations to choose a different type of government to the concept of an Islamic government, which reflected a specific Islamic ideology (Bazargan 2009, p. 334). Bazargan supported justice and freedom and believed that these were necessary for an Islamic government (Bazargan 2009, pp. 317–324). Importantly, he believed in *Maktab-e Vaseteh-e Islam* (Islam is a median school) between communism and capitalism characteristic of collectivism and individualism (Bazargan 2009, pp. 309–311).

Post-1979 Revolution

As was mentioned earlier, Bazargan believed in an Islamic state that expressed an Islamic ideology. However, after the 1979 Islamic Revolution, and with the domination of jurisprudential Islam in Iran, Bazargan gradually changed his views and moved from Political Islam to Social Islam. The following sections discuss the changes that occurred to some of Bazragan's ideas.

Bazargan identified two different types of governments: One that is formed by individuals or groups and consists of parties and classes, including the nobility. Monarchies, empires, fascist regimes, and communist governments fall into this category. In the second category, however, all people in a society have the chance for equal participation. Examples include some liberal democracies in the modern era and the governments of Prophet Mohammad and Imam Ali, the first Shia Imam (Bazargan 2010, pp. 25–26). Bazargan enumerated three characteristics that apply to the second one: freedom, equality and fraternity, which are central to the formation of a good government. Indeed, these slogans had been used in the context of the 1906 Constitutional Revolution of Iran (Bazargan 2010, p. 235).

Furthermore, Bazargan supported a free electoral system based on the participation of the general public when choosing a government. He believed that the national government is, indeed, God's government. This is because God wants populations to be free and honourable. Contrary to

when thou hast taken a decision put thy trust in Allah. For Allah loves those who put their trust (in Him)" (159) (Yusuf Ali 2016, p. 71).

this, Bazargan thought that individuals, parties, and class-based govern-ments are prone to ossified despotism that deny people freedom and dig-nity, and are, indeed, Satanic (Bazargan 2010, p. 235). Thus, he sought to describe his ideas through focusing on the ways that they differ from those of jurisprudential Islam.

An Explanation of Mutual Consultation
Bazargan cited verse 38 of Surah Ash-Shura and verse 159 of Surah Al-i-Imran (cf. footnotes 18 and 19, respectively) to explain the motif of mutual consultation. He believed that it was due to God's command that the Prophet Mohammad consulted with ordinary people on affairs relat-ing to all aspects of life. God advised Prophet Mohammad to forgive those who had negative attitudes towards him in respect of this mutual consulta-tion (Bazargan 2010, pp. 235–236). Bazargan demonstrated that Prophet Mohammad upheld consultation with people as integral to managing the Muslim communities.

The Explanation of Obeying the Authority
Bazargan cited verse 59 of Surah An-Nisa (cf. footnote 6) to explain the different interpretations of the various authorities. For example, with respect to Sunni interpretations, it was believed that the legitimate rulers of Islam were indeed the four first Caliphs followed by the Omayyad, Abbasid and Osman Caliphs. However, in Shia interpretations, the vast majority of jurists believed that the rightful authorities are, indeed, the 12 Shia Imams. Following 1979, a new interpretation was created by a few jurists who believed that the true authority over the Ummah was indeed the Guardianship of the Jurisconsult (*Velayat-e Faqih*). Accordingly, this inter-pretation became the predominant one in Iran. Bazargan argued that this authority had two conditions: firstly, it should be democratically selected, and, secondly, because it operated within the framework of the Qur'an and Sunnah, it must be followed and obeyed (Bazargan 2010, pp. 236–237).

The Definition of Guardianship
Citing verse 257[11] of Surah Al-Baqara, Bazargan put forward two distinct types of guardianship: That of God and that of Taghut (falsehood). Based

---

[11] "Allah is the Protector of those who have faith: from the depths of darkness He will lead them forth into light. Of those who reject faith the patrons are the evil ones: from light they will lead them forth into the depths of darkness. They will be companions of the fire, to dwell therein (Forever)" (257) (Yusuf Ali 2016, p. 43).

on this verse, managing a society should be undertaken through the application of Shura or collective consultation. He reinterpreted the hadith under Imam Jafar al-Sadiq, pertaining to the five pillars of Islam. According to Bazargan, guardianship meant government that was formed by way of Shura (or collective rationality) with the participation of all the people in a Muslim society (Bazargan 2010, p. 239).

Guidance by God
Bazargan cited verses 12 and 13[12] of Surah Al_Lail and also verse 120[13] of Surah Al-Baqarah to explain the differences between the two models of national sovereignty and democracy in a new century and linked it to the guardianship of human-divine relations offered by Shura or collective consultation. He believed that the former was created by some thinkers, based on their experience and studies, while the latter was taken from God and the Qur'an and the faith of the common people was the protector of this system (Bazargan 2010, p. 240).

Unity in Islamic Society
Bazargan cited verse 103[14] of Surah Al-i-Imran and verses 31 and 32[15] of Surah Ar-Rum to encourage unity within Muslim society. In this regard, he argued that God and Mohammad paid attention to two things: first, unity and solidarity among people; second, denial of division among people (Bazargan 2010, pp. 240–241).

Social Islam

People's Consent to the Form and Operation of Government
Bazargan saw prophethood and government as two separate roles, while regarding prophets such as Mohammad, Moses, David, Solomon and

---

[12] "Verily We take upon Ourselves to guide, (12) And verily unto Us (belong) the End and the Beginning" (13) (Yusuf Ali 2016, p. 595).

[13] ... "The Guidance of Allah,-that is the (only) Guidance" ... (120) (Yusuf Ali 2016, p. 19).

[14] "And hold fast, all together, by the rope which Allah (stretches out for you), and be not divided among yourselves"... (103) (Yusuf Ali 2016, p. 63).

[15] ... "And be not ye among those who join gods with Allah, (31) those who split up their Religion, and become (mere) Sects,—each party rejoicing in that which is with itself!" (32) (Yusuf Ali 2016, p. 407).

Joseph (who held both role simultaneously) as exceptions (Bazargan 2014, pp. 428–429). He commented that these prophets used to consult with their people on the affairs of government, but that God related to them with respect to their duty of prophecy only. He articulated that the role of inviting people to God and the eternal world is the main duty of prophets. He enunciated that God has not specified the form and type of government in the Qur'an and, in the present day, the consent of people about the form and also the operation of government is essential for managing a society (Bazargan 2014, p. 430).

The Separation Between the State and Religion
Bazargan cited verse 256[16] of Surah Al-Baqara, verse 65[17] of Surah Al-Isra and verse 22 of Surah Al-Ghashiya[18] to explain the separation between the state and religion. In his view, these verses imply that it was not the duty of the state to interfere in the popular comprehension of any given religion, especially with the use of force. He understood that this was the case, especially, in the period of Imam Ali's government. Moreover, he thought that it was not the duty of jurists to take power and control over a society, an action that he believed to be in substantial disagreement with both the Qur'an and the Sunnah (Bazargan 2014, pp. 429–430). Bazargan believed in a mixture of religion and politics wherein religion dominates politics. However, he favoured the separation of the state and religion.

Moving from Maktab-e Vaseteh-e Islam *(Islam Is a Median School)*
to Individualism
Before the Islamic Revolution of 1979, Bazargan attempted to strike a balance between the needs and roles of the individual and society (Bazargan 2009, pp. 309–311). After the Islamic Revolution of 1979, however, he was sympathetic towards individualism because, according to his interpretations, actions such as paying Zakat or performing *Nahi Anil Munkar* (forbidding evil) and *Amr Bil Mahroof* (ordering for doing good acts) were more individual duties rather than social duties (Bazargan 2014, pp. 441–447).

---

[16] Let there be no compulsion in religion…(256) (Yusuf Ali 2016, p. 42).
[17] "As for My servants, no authority shalt thou have over them: Enough is thy Lord for a Disposer of affairs" (65) (Yusuf Ali 2016, p. 288).
[18] "Thou art not one to manage (men's) affairs" (22) (Yusuf Ali 2016, p. 592).

The Islamic Democratic Republic of Iran

Bazargan identified two different types of governments: dictatorship and democracy. According to him, Islam supports the democratic model of government (Bazargan 2014, pp. 419–420). Around 1964, when he was in prison as a political activist, he came to the conclusion that the ideal Islamic polity had an innate ideology superior to other paradigms such as communism and socialism. He, thus, sought to propose an ideological model for an Islamic state; however, he critiqued his theory after the 1979 Islamic Revolution (Bazargan 2014, pp. 421–422) and adopted the Islamic Democratic Republic of Iran. In terms of content, he underwent a shift from Political Islam to Social Islam and came to express a belief in a government based on the consent of the people with respect to both form and management.

Concluding Analysis

This chapter has outlined and discussed the ideas of the three major political thinkers regarding the notion of 'the ideals of Islamic government'. Five concluding analytical points are made.

Firstly, with regard to an explanation of the situation, four significant ideas were espoused in the context of Iran during the 1960s and 1970s. First, there was a dichotomy between divine subjects and materialism; second, a dichotomy between the free market economy and a command economy; third, a dichotomy between democracy and despotism; and fourth, a dichotomy between independence and colonialism. These three thinkers sought to develop an Islamic state model that abandoned or resisted imported ideologies such as communism or liberalism, and also rejected the anachronistic—fundamentally nationalistic—notion of encouraging a cultural return to a conceptualisation of ancient Iran as it was promoted by the Shah Mohammed Reza. Accordingly, the content of this new Islamic state was an amalgamation of Islam, nationalism and modernity. After 1979, a new relationship between Islam and democracy emerged in the public sphere in Iran. Indeed, this new bifurcation reflects the differences that arose, from this date onwards, between groups and intellectuals who supported Political Islam on the one hand, and those who advocated Social Islam on the other.

Second, in connection with the system of knowledge, we have seen that, initially, all of these three thinkers believed in *Maktab-e Vaseteh-e*

Islam: that is, Islam as an intermediate model that falls between the two extremes of communism and capitalism (or between collectivism and individualism). However, Shariati's theories demonstrated a tendency towards communitarian ideas. Bazargan's theory, particularly in his later life, displayed a tendency towards social liberalism. On the other hand, Khomeini's ideas veered between collectivism and individualism. The beliefs of these three intellectuals were based on modern Islamic-Iranian thinking. In general, Khomeini and Shariati displayed a tendency towards equality, including emancipation of the masses. In later life, Bazargan had an underlying tendency towards supporting freedom and the freedom of people.

Third, with regard to the system of norms, these thinkers introduced new proposals into Iranian society by defining the characteristics of an Islamic state. Khomeini upheld characteristics such as support for the oppressed people, government-based justice, freedom and independence. On the other hand, Shariati referred to Shura-based democracy, equality, liberty and mysticism. Bazargan referred to Shura-based democracy, people's agreement on forming an Islamic government and separation between state and religion. In this regard, Khomeini and Shariati focused on the emancipation of society, while, Bazargan focused on the freedom of society.

Fourth, in terms of the system of government, Shariati developed two theories—first, 'The Theory of Ummah and Imamate', which was utilised, with some changes and as a theory of Political Islam, by some jurists who followed Khomeini; second, 'Mysticism, Equality and Liberty' which was applied by Neo-Shariatists or 'the left', especially those who believed in Social Islam. Bazargan, on the other hand, espoused the idea of an Islamic Democratic Republic of Iran. Prior to the Islamic Revolution of 1979, he supported the idea of an Islamic state, which was fully in accordance with Islamic ideology. Later on, however, he shifted from Political Islam towards Social Islam. This shift in his ideas arose from his observation of Islamic government and its policy initiatives in the context of Iran. Khomeini's model was an Islamic Republic based on the guardianship of jurisconsult (*Velayat-e Faqih*).

Fifth, with regard to public policy, all of these three intellectuals believed in synthesising Islamic traditional ideas with modern ideas to develop a hybrid political order suitable for the modern era. Today, Shariati's two theories are still valid in the context of Iran. In fact, his theory of 'Ummah and Imamate' was used as an Islamic theory by some followers of Khomeini. Likewise, his theory of 'Mysticism, Equality and Liberty' was applied by

Neo-Shariatists as a theory of Social Islam. Bazargan advocated social liberalism whilst minimising Islam. In Iran, his followers are now known as neo-liberalists. Khomeini's, jurisprudential Islam, proposed the theory of the Guardianship of the Jurisconsult (*Velayat-e Faqih*). After his death in 1989, political jurisprudential Islam groups and thinkers divided into two separate schools: One school supported divine legitimacy for Iran's supreme leadership, suggesting that, in the absence of Imam Mahdi, the supreme leader was a representative of him and the peoples' votes are irrelevant. The other school, however, supported the idea that legitimacy of the whole administration, including the supreme leadership, comes from the popular vote. The latter is a reflection of the capacity for the development of Social Islam in contemporary Iran.

REFERENCES

Bazargan, M. (2009). *Besat* [Prophetic mission] (Vol. 2). Tehran, Iran: Glam.

Bazargan, M. (2010). *Bazyabi Arzesha* [Recovery values] (Vol. 26). Tehran, Iran: Sherkat Shami Enteshar.

Bazargan, M. (2014). *Padideh Pyambari* [Phenomenon of Prophecy] (Vol. 27). Tehran, Iran: Sherkat Shami Enteshar.

Feirahi, D. (2012). *Nezam Sisasi va Dolat dar Islam* [Political System and State in Islam]. Tehran, Iran: Enteshrat Samt.

Khomeini, S. R. (1998). *Resaleh Ejtehad va Taghlid* [Ijtihad and imitation paper]. Tehran, Iran: The Institute for Compilation and Publication of Imam Khomeini's Works.

Khomeini, S. R. (2000). *Velayt Faghih* [Islamic Government: Governance of the Jurist]. Tehran, Iran: Institute for Compilation and Publication of Imam Khomeini's Works.

Khomeini, S. R. (2010a). *Sahifeh Imam: Majmoe asar Imam Khomeini bayanat, payamha, mosahebeha, ahkam, ejazat sharei va nameha* [Sahifeh-Ye Imam: An anthology of Imam Khomeini's speeches, messages, interviews, decrees, religious permissions, and letters] (Vol. 16). Tehran, Iran: The Institute for Compilation and Publication of Imam Khomeini's Works.

Khomeini, S. R. (2010b). *Sahifeh Imam: Majmoe asar Imam Khomeini bayanat, payamha, mosahebeha, ahkam, ejazat sharei va nameha* [Sahifeh-Ye Imam: An anthology of Imam Khomeini's speeches, messages, interviews, decrees, religious permissions, and letters] (Vol. 19). Tehran, Iran: The Institute for Compilation and Publication of Imam Khomeini's Works.

Khomeini, S. R. (2010c). *Sahifeh Imam: Majmoe asar Imam Khomeini bayanat, payamha, mosahebeha, ahkam, ejazat sharei va nameha* [Sahifeh-Ye Imam: An anthology of Imam Khomeini's speeches, messages, interviews, decrees, religious permissions, and letters] (Vol. 5). Tehran, Iran: Institute for Compilation and Publication of Imam Khomeini's Works.

Khomeini, S. R. (2010d). *Sahifeh Imam: Majmoe asar Imam Khomeini bayanat, payamha, mosahebeha, ahkam, ejazat sharei va nameha* [Sahifeh-Ye Imam: An anthology of Imam Khomeini's speeches, messages, interviews, decrees, religious permissions, and letters] (Vol. 11). Tehran: Institute for Compilation and Publication of Imam Khomeini's Works.

Khomeini, S. R. (2010e). *Sahifeh Imam: Majmoe asar Imam Khomeini bayanat, payamha, mosahebeha, ahkam, ejazat sharei va nameha* [Sahifeh-Ye Imam: An anthology of Imam Khomeini's speeches, messages, interviews, decrees, religious permissions, and letters] (Vol. 12). Tehran, Iran: The Institute for Compilation and Publication of Imam Khomeini's Works.

Khomeini, S. R. (2010f). *Sahifeh Imam: Majmoe asar Imam Khomeini bayanat, payamha, mosahebeha, ahkam, ejazat sharei va nameha* [Sahifeh-Ye Imam: An anthology of Imam Khomeini's speeches, messages, interviews, decrees, religious permissions, and letters] (Vol. 15). Tehran, Iran: The Institute for Compilation and Publication of Imam Khomeini's Works.

Khomeini, S. R. (2010g). *Sahifeh Imam: Majmoe asar Imam Khomeini bayanat, payamha, mosahebeha, ahkam, ejazat sharei va nameha* [Sahifeh-Ye Imam: An anthology of Imam Khomeini's speeches, messages, interviews, decrees, religious permissions, and letters] (Vol. 20). Tehran, Iran: The Institute for Compilation and Publication of Imam Khomeini's Works.

Khomeini, S. R. (2010h). *Sahifeh Imam: Majmoe asar Imam Khomeini bayanat, payamha, mosahebeha, ahkam, ejazat sharei va nameha* [Sahifeh-Ye Imam: An anthology of Imam Khomeini's speeches, messages, interviews, decrees, religious permissions, and letters] (Vol. 3). Tehran, Iran: The Institute for Compilation and Publication of Imam Khomeini's Works.

Khomeini, S. R. (2010i). *Sahifeh Imam: Majmoe asar Imam Khomeini bayanat, payamha, mosahebeha, ahkam, ejazat sharei va nameha* [Sahifeh-Ye Imam: An anthology of Imam Khomeini's speeches, messages, interviews, decrees, religious permissions, and letters] (Vol. 4). Tehran, Iran: The Institute for Compilation and Publication of Imam Khomeini's Works.

Khomeini, S. R. (2010j). *Sahifeh Imam: Majmoe asar Imam Khomeini bayanat, payamha, mosahebeha, ahkam, ejazat sharei va nameha* [Sahifeh-Ye Imam: An anthology of Imam Khomeini's speeches, messages, interviews, decrees, religious permissions, and letters] (Vol. 6). Tehran, Iran: The Institute for Compilation and Publication of Imam Khomeini's Works.

Khomeini, S. R. (2010k). *Sahifeh Imam: Majmoe asar Imam Khomeini bayanat, payamha, mosahebeha, ahkam, ejazat sharei va nameha* [Sahifeh-Ye Imam: An anthology of Imam Khomeini's speeches, messages, interviews, decrees, religious permissions, and letters] (Vol. 7). Tehran, Iran: Institute for Compilation and Publication of Imam Khomeini's Works.

Khomeini, S. R. (2010l). *Sahifeh Imam: Majmoe asar Imam Khomeini bayanat, payamha, mosahebeha, ahkam, ejazat sharei va nameha* [Sahifeh-Ye Imam: An anthology of Imam Khomeini's speeches, messages, interviews, decrees, religious permissions, and letters] (Vol. 14). Tehran, Iran: The Institute for Compilation and Publication of Imam Khomeini's Works.

Khomeini, S. R. (2010m). *Sahifeh Imam: Majmoe asar Imam Khomeini bayanat, payamha, mosahebeha, ahkam, ejazat sharei va nameha* [Sahifeh-Ye Imam: An anthology of Imam Khomeini's speeches, messages, interviews, decrees, religious permissions, and letters] (Vol. 8). Tehran, Iran: The Institute for Compilation and Publication of Imam Khomeini's Works.

Khomeini, S. R. (2010n). *Sahifeh Imam: Majmoe asar Imam Khomeini bayanat, payamha, mosahebeha, ahkam, ejazat sharei va nameha* [Sahifeh-Ye Imam: An anthology of Imam Khomeini's speeches, messages, interviews, decrees, religious permissions, and letters] (Vol. 21). Tehran, Iran: The Institute for Compilation and Publication of Imam Khomeini's Works.

Khomeini, S. R. (2010o). *Sahifeh Imam: Majmoe asar imam Khomeini bayanat, payamha, mosahebeha, ahkam, ejazat sharei va nameha* [Sahifeh-Ye Imam: An anthology of Imam Khomeini's speeches, messages, interviews, decrees, religious permissions, and letters] (Vol. 9). Tehran, Iran: The Institute for Compilation and Publication of Imam Khomeini's Works.

Khomeini, S. R. M. M. (1942). *Kashf al asrar* [Key to the secrets]. Qom, Iran: Bita.

Shariati, A. (1980). *Tarikh tamadon* [History of civilization] (Vol. 12). Tehran, Iran: Daftare Tanzim va Nashre Asar Shariati.

Shariati, A. (2007). *Khodsazi Enghelabi* [Revolutionary Self monitoring] (Vol. 2). Tehran, Iran: Enteshrat Elham.

Shariati, A. (2009). *Miad ba Ebrahim* [The Vow with Abraham] (Vol. 29). Tehran, Iran: Enteshrat Agah.

Shariati, A. (2010). *Islamshenasi Mashhad* [Mashhad Islamology] (Vol. 30). Tehran: Chappakhsh.

Shariati, A. (2011). *Ali* (Vol. 26). Tehran, Iran: Nashr Amon.

Yosefi Ashkevari, H. (1997). *Shariati va naghd sonnat* [Shariati and criticism of tradition]. Tehran, Iran: Yad Avaran.

Yusuf Ali, A. (2016). *Quran* [English translation]. Retrieved from http://tanzil.net/#trans/en.yusufali/1:1

PART III

Political Islamic Thought

CHAPTER 8

In the Beginning: Iran's Constitutional Law After the 1979 Islamic Revolution

This chapter critically examines the viewpoints of Khomeini, Shariati and Bazargan and their followers with regard to their influence on the development of the constitution and constitutional law of Iran following the 1979 Islamic Revolution. It elaborates the concept of ideology from five analytical perspectives.

The Philosophy of Codification of Constitution

In the modern sense, the codification of constitutional law began in eighteenth-century Europe. France codified its constitution after the 1791 revolution. Reigning in the power of the monarchy was one of the major reasons for the codification of constitutions. Other factors such as revolutions, coups d'état and gaining independence have contributed to the codifying of, or change to, constitutions in many countries in the era of late modernity. Iran was among the first Asian countries to codify a formal constitution. This happened after the Constitutional Revolution of 1906 (Ghazi Shariat Panahi 2005, pp. 20–40).

© The Author(s) 2020
S. M. Lolaki, *Diverging Approaches of Political Islamic Thought in Iran since the 1960s*,
https://doi.org/10.1007/978-981-15-0478-5_8

137

EVOLUTION OF THE DRAFT OF THE CONSTITUTION
OF THE ISLAMIC REVOLUTION

Khomeini believed that the constitutional law of Iran, which was a legacy of the Pahlavi Dynasty, was basically illicit. He enumerated several reasons for his claim. First, the Pahlavi dynasty had seized power from the Qajar Dynasty by a coup (reinforced by the Founders Assembly formed during the Pahlavi dynasty), in a rigged election. Second, since the adoption of Iran's constitution in 1906, neither the Qajar nor the Pahlavi Dynasty had implemented the second Article of the constitution that required the supervision by five jurists over the parliament in respect to its acts (Khomeini 2010a, pp. 286–289).

The first draft of the new constitution of the Islamic Republic of Iran was prepared upon an order from Khomeini in Paris given to Hassan Habibi and Ayatollah Seyed Mohammad Bagher Soltani Tabatabai Boroujerdi circa 1978. Hassan Habibi was an Iranian lawyer and Tabatabaei Soltani was a jurist (Tabatabaei 2009, pp. 131–132). In January 1979 Khomeini spoke publicly for the first time of the new constitution and its law (Hashemi 1995, p. 229). In February 1979, a committee comprising three lawyers—Mohammad Jafar Jafari Langrodi, Abdolkarim Lahiji and Naser Katoziyan—together with Fathollah Bani Sadr, Naser Minachi, and Hassan Habibi worked on the draft to elaborate it further (Katoziyan 2001, pp. 213–215). These six people, being close to Iran's Party of Freedom Movement (Nehzat-e-Azadi-e-Iran), were thus advocates of the interpretation of Islam advanced by Bazargan. They submitted a draft to the interim government of Iran which, in turn, sent it to the Council of Revolutionary Plans for further development. Next, the Council of Revolutionary Plans submitted it to the Council of the Islamic Revolution (Sahabi 2004, p. 222). It is noteworthy that the Council was established by an order from Khomeini. Its duties in order of importance included, but were not limited to, forming the interim government, conducting a referendum on the type of government and deciding on Iran's constitution. This council was composed of delegates who represented a broad spectrum of interpretations of political Islam (Saeli Koredh Deh 2005, p. 91). The Council brought the July draft up for discussion and finally decided to let the Iranian people select their representatives in the assembly of experts through an election. Subsequently, the draft was published in the newspaper *Kayhan* (Mosahebeh darbreh Pishnevis Ghanon Asasi ba Yadollah Sahabi [Yadollah Sahabi interview about the draft of constitutional law] 1979, p. 2).

DRAFT CONSTITUTION: DISCUSSIONS

Once the draft constitution of the Islamic Republic was published, it came under discussion from many quarters up to the election of the Assembly of Experts for the Constitution, held in August 1979. Notably these prominent grand Iranian ayatollahs, or Marjas (the source of emulations) namely Khomeini, Seyed Mohammad Reza Golpaygani, Seyed Shahbuddin Marashi Najafi and Seyed Mohammad Kazem Shariatmadari, had a profound influence on ordinary people.

Khomeini

Grand Ayatollah Khomeini invited members of the general public as well as scholars to put forward their ideas about this draft. Likewise, he asked all Iranian people to be attentive to the election of their representatives in the parliament claiming the nation needed a constitution based on the ideals of Islamic Republic of Iran. He stipulated that Iranians needed a constitution and law for their own land, not a copy of Western or Eastern constitutional law (Khomeini 2010c, pp. 218–221).

Seyed Mohammad Reza Golpaygani

Grand Ayatollah Golpayagani stated that the path of Iran was an Islamic one differing from those offered by both Western and Eastern ideas of governance and that Iran's government was based on monotheism, the Qur'an and human dignity. Moreover, the constitution ought to be codified in accordance with Sharia law and the government be based on the Imamate and the guardianship of jurisconsults *(Velayat-e Faqih)*. Any government that did not follow this rule must be dismissed as a government of falsehood (Byaniyeh Ayatollah Golpayagani dabreh Pishnevis Ghanon Asasi [The statement of Grand Ayatollah Golpayagani about the draft of constitutional law] 1979).

Seyed Shahbuddin Marashi Najafi

Grand Ayatollah Marashi Najafi commented on several of the articles of the draft constitution. He proposed adding five additional principles, namely the guardianship of the jurisconsults (*Velayat-e Faqih*); the right of *Marja-e-Taqlid* (the source of emulations) to reject a law enacted by parliament where it contradicted with Islamic laws; the agreement of Marja-e-Taqlids in respect to electing the president and prime minster; forming an organisation of the clergy that supervises all public institutions; the commitment of members of parliament to Islamic law; and finally that violation of those laws by them shall be deemed a crime (Naghdhai Ayatollah Marashi Najafi darbareh Pishnevis Ghanon Asasi [The comments of Ayatollah Marashi Najafi on the draft of constitutional law] 1979).

Sayyid Mohammad Kazem Shariatmadari

Grand Ayatollah Shariatmadari believed that it was better to retain the former framework of the constitution (that is from the Constitutional Revolution in 1906) while replacing the articles pertinent to the system of monarchy with new ones pertinent to the Islamic Republic (Mosahebeh ba Ayatollah Shariatmadari darbreh Pishnevish Ghanon Asasi [The interview about the draft of constitutional law with Grand Ayatollah Shariatmadari] 1979).

DRAFT CONSTITUTION: POLITICAL PARTIES AND CRITICAL IDEAS

The Mujahidin of Islamic Revolution Organisation (Sazman Mujahidin Enghelab Islami Iran)

This party published a statement declaring that, in the Islamic Republic, the right of legislation is with God who grants guardianship and leadership to the jurists. They also asserted that, in the absence of Imam Mahdi, the authenticity of the Islamic State is based on the guardianship of jurisconsults (Mujahidin of Islamic Revolution Organization 1979).

The Party of Diligent People of Iran's Nation (Hezb Zahmatkeshan Melat Iran)

For this party, the clergy—especially Khomeini himself and his disciples— had a great impact on the 1979 Islamic Revolution. They demanded the Imamate and the leadership position of Khomeini be incorporated into the constitution so that, as supreme leader, he could exercise supervision and guidance upon the president and judiciary (The Party of Diligent people of Iran's Nation 1979).

Movement of Militant Muslims (Jonbesh Mosalmanan Mobarez)

For this party, the constitution and its law should embody the essence of Islam and the main principles of the Muslim monotheistic system. Also, the constitution should embody an ideal of the public good, both at the level of the individual and the wider collective nation. Further, they argued that the constitution must have an anti-imperialist and anti-despotic orientation (Byaniyeh Jonbesh Mosalmanan Mobarez darbreh Pishnevis Ghanon Asasi [The statement of militant muslims movement about the draft constitutional law] 1979). These views were close to those of Shariati.

The People's Mujahidin of Iran (Mojahedin-e-Khalq Iran)

In general, this party believed that the spirit of the draft constitution supported Western capitalistic ideas. Moreover, they claimed that a true Islamic constitution features the following socialist oriented principles. It should be based on consultation which they saw as most suitable for managing society because it provided free education for all and advocates equality between men and women while supporting public health and insurance. A people-based and anti-imperialist army should underpin foreign policy based on a framework of non-alignment. It considered oppressed people as the main supporters of the Islamic State and recognised the right of nations to self-determination. Finally, it accepted the jurisdiction of the judiciary in all cases of crime and guarantees labour rights (Didgahhai Enteghadi darbreh Pishnevis Ghanon Asasi [The critical views to the draft of constitutional law] 1979).

The Tudeh Party of Iran (Hezb Tudeh Iran)

This party stressed an economic model based on public, private and cooperative systems with the foreign policy of Iran adopting non-alignment and good relationships with neighbours to attain peace and security. Parliament and local councils should support the constitution in terms of women's rights in the political, social, economic, cultural and civil contexts. The government should guarantee public insurance and workers' rights and ensure torture be eliminated. The seats of parliament and local councils should be distributed based on parties' votes (Tudeh Party of Iran 1979, pp. 136–137).

The National Front of Iran (Jebhei Meli Iran)

At first, this party sought to write a new draft; however, they rejected this task due to the revolutionary position of Iran. Their main source of criticism was related to changes in the authority of local councils and to the posts of president and prime minster (Naghdhai Jebhei Meli Iran darbreh Pishnevish Ghanon Asasi [The comments of The National Front of Iran on the draft of constitutional law] 1979). As was explained above, the grand ayatollahs influenced and their views impacted on ordinary people. Also, the vast majority of other clergy had the same role and they supported the idea of adding guardianship of the jurisconsult to the Constitution. While parties had different ideas, most tended towards leftist views such as anti-imperialism and affirming a further role for government in managing society. Only a few parties supported liberal ideas.

The election held in August 1979 saw the majority of the elected parliament following jurisprudential Islam. A minority followed the interpretations of Islam advanced by thinkers such as Bazargan and Shariati. The parliament also had four seats devoted to religious minorities, namely representatives of Zoroastrian, Christian and Jewish people; however, secular (non-religious) groups could not occupy any seat in this parliament (Edareh Kol Omor Farhangi Va Rvabet Omomi Majles Shorai Islami 1985c, pp. 332–413). Parliament started working immediately on the draft Constitution. Discussions were focused mainly on articles 5, 6, 56, 57, 107 and 110. I will examine the main arguments offered by advocates of jurisprudential and liberal Islam concerning these articles.

Article 5

This article states that during the absence of Imam Mahdi and in the context of Iran's theocratic religio-political self-understanding, the implementation of God's commands and the religious leadership of the community of believers is the responsibility of the jurisprudent who is just, pious, courageous, knowledgeable about his era. He must be a capable administrator, and should be accepted and recognised as the leader by the majority of the population. According to Article 107 of the Constitution, if a jurisprudent does not receive such a majority, the Leadership Council consisting of qualified jurisprudents will collectively assume the leader's responsibilities (Papan-Matin 2014, p. 167). Initially, this Article was not part of the draft but was put into discussion in the public session of the Assembly of Experts for the Constitution by Commission number one. Members of the Assembly of Experts for the Constitution were grouped into seven commissions whose task was to examine various articles and put them into discussion in the public session of the Assembly (Edareh Kol Omor Farhangi Va Rvabet Omomi Majles Shorai Islami 1985c, pp. 325–327). The basis of this Article was formed when some members of the Assembly discussed the values of the system (concerning the State existing as an Islamic Republic). They believed that within the Islamic Republic its values must be under the supervision of the guardianship of the jurisconsult (*Velayat-e Faqih*) (Edareh Kol Omor Farhangi Va Rvabet Omomi Majles Shorai Islami 1985b, pp. 61–91). Ayatollah Hussein Ali Montazeri, the head of this Assembly and a follower of jurisprudential Islam, asserted that a constitution that does not include the principle of guardianship of the jurisconsult was totally unacceptable. He held that it was necessary that all Islamic rules be based on the Qur'an and Sunnah and that without these principles, including the principle of guardianship of the jurisconsult, the constitution would be invalid (Edareh Kol Omor Farhangi Va Rvabet Omomi Majles Shorai Islami 1985b, p. 107).

Ayatollah Haeri, a follower of jurisprudential Islam, asserted that the guardianship of the jurisconsult is an indelible principle in Islam. From his perspective, a jurist plays three roles in a Muslim society: First, political guardianship; second, judgeship; third, issuing fatwa in the absence of Imam Mahdi, the twelfth Shia Imam (Edareh Kol Omor Farhangi Va Rvabet Omomi Majles Shorai Islami 1985b, pp. 610–611). Ayatollah Seyyed Mohammad Hosseini Beheshti, the deputy of the Assembly of Experts for the Constitution and an advocate of jurisprudential Islam, defended Article 5. He argued that there were two social systems. First, the liberal or democratic system which was based on the votes of the people. According to him, even though in such a system government must accept the ideas of the majority, in effect a few feudal or capitalist people orient the others' as they like. Second, that a social system is one wherein the people follow a particular or single school or ideology. In fact, he believed that in such a society, people accept freely a school and limit themselves to its framework of rules. He asserted that the Iranian people were (for the most part) Muslim and that they had voluntarily limited themselves to the framework of Islamic rules or law. He added that it was important to underscore that the Iranian system was not a Democratic Republic but an Islamic Republic. He argued that, according to Islamic rules, the central pillar of the Islam Republic was a knowledgeable jurist who is selected by the people. According to Ayatollah Beheshti, in Marxist societies such as those of Soviet Union, China, Bulgaria, their Constitutions and constitutional law limit their governments to the framework of Marxism, Leninism and Maoism. He also believed that in such societies someone who is more knowledgeable about the principle of *Maktab* (school) and ideology was the pivot of society. Thus, in Iranian society a jurist was, ideally, the pivot of the society (Edareh Kol Omor Farhangi Va Rvabet Omomi Majles Shorai Islami 1985b, p. 380).

Discussions Between Advocates and Opponents of Article 5

The Difference Between Articles 5 and 3
Hamidoallah Mir Morad Zehi, a Sunni representative of Parliament, stated that Article 5 contradicted Article 3 which stipulates that the basis for managing government was the general suffrage of the Iranian people (Edareh Kol Omor Farhangi Va Rvabet Omomi Majles Shorai Islami 1985b, p. 404). By contrast, Seyed Hassan Ayat, a follower of jurispru-dential Islam, responded by arguing that the Supreme Leader was elected by the popular vote and thus by the majority of people. Furthermore, some requirements must be met by a person who was to hold the position of Supreme Leader. Moreover, supreme leadership is not an inherited position, and consequently, it cannot deny people suffrage (Edareh Kol Omor Farhangi Va Rvabet Omomi Majles Shorai Islami 1985b, p. 405).

This Article Ends in the Hegemony of Jurists over All the People
Rahmatoallah Moghdam Maraghei, a follower of liberal Islam, asserted that Article 5 recognised the right of rulership exclusively for jurists, giv-ing them a special privilege, while also providing a right for all people. He stated that despotism did not belong in the framework of religion (Edareh Kol Omor Farhangi Va Rvabet Omomi Majles Shorai Islami 1985b, pp. 374–375). Seyed Ahmad Norbaskhsh, a fellow traveller, asserted that it was necessary for all the people of any class to participate in determining their destiny. He thought that concentrating power in the hands of jurists would not be suitable for society, arguing that there would be no guaran-tee that, say 20 years later, some jurists would not have remained as benign as they are today. Thus, he concluded that no special privilege should be given to jurists by the Constitution (Edareh Kol Omor Farhangi Va Rvabet Omomi Majles Shorai Islami 1985b, p. 557). In response, Ayatollah

Mohammad Yazdi, a follower of jurisprudential Islam, stated that anyone can study and become a jurist. He supported his view with an example: When someone was appointed as a physician this did not grant him a monopoly on the position (Edareh Kol Omor Farhangi Va Rvabet Omomi Majles Shorai Islami 1985b, p. 560).

The Main Duty of Jurists Is Just Giving Fatwa for Divine Commandments
Ezzatollah Sahabi, who had been influenced by Shariati, asserted that the jurist's role is suitable only for issuing fatwa on the divine commandments, not for political guardianship as such (Edareh Kol Omor Farhangi Va Rvabet Omomi Majles Shorai Islami 1985b, pp. 89–90). Likewise, Abolhassan Banisadr asserted that political guardianship is exclusive to Khomeini because Iran could not find another comprehensively learned jurist like him (Edareh Kol Omor Farhangi Va Rvabet Omomi Majles Shorai Islami 1985b, p. 93). However, Ayatollah Beheshti responded in the same manner as Ayatollah Haeri (as noted above), namely that a jurist plays three roles in a Muslim society: First, political guardianship; second, judgeship; third, giving fatwa as divine commandments in the absence of Imam Mahdi, the twelfth Shia Imam. In fact, Beheshti believed that there were different points of view about political guardianship though it was nevertheless required by jurisprudence (Edareh Kol Omor Farhangi Va Rvabet Omomi Majles Shorai Islami 1985b, p. 93). Article 5 was finally passed in the parliament with 53 votes for and 8 votes against it and 4 abstentions (Edareh Kol Omor Farhangi Va Rvabet Omomi Majles Shorai Islami 1985b, p. 384).

Article 6

This article asserted that in the Islamic Republic of Iran, the affairs of the country must be handled through public elections, namely presidential elections, parliamentary election, election of the members of the councils and other such institutions, or via referendums (Papan-Matin 2014, p. 168).

Discussions Between Advocates and Opponents of Article 6

Hamidoallah Mir Morad Zehi, the Sunni representative in Parliament, asserted the main problem with this Article is again a paradox between basing government on the popular vote and the principle of the guardianship of the jurisconsult (*Velayat-e Faqih*). According to him, Imam Ali accepted the initial caliphate (*of the Rashidun*) owing to the consensus that had then formed among the people around him. Thus, Zehi holds that God did not grant the right of rulership to a certain individual, but rather to all the people collectively (Edareh Kol Omor Farhangi Va Rvabet Omomi Majles Shorai Islami 1985b, pp. 403–404).

However, Ayatollah Mousavi Esfahani, a follower of jurisprudential Islam, stated in response that the principle of guardianship of the jurisconsult was not inconsistent with the rights of general suffrage. According to Ayatollah Mousavi Esfahani, once the people in Medina came into *Bay'ah* (allegiance) with Prophet Mohammad, the Prophet sought to leave management of the tribes to themselves; the prophet Mohammad used to receive consultation from these tribes. Thus, Ayatollah Mousavi asserted that, in the modern world, no government could attain autonomy without the will of the people. He stated that without the participation of people, a government would face developing corrupt practices because in Islam all people were responsible for their society (Edareh Kol Omor Farhangi Va Rvabet Omomi Majles Shorai Islami 1985b, pp. 361–362). Article 6 was finally passed with 54 votes for and 3 votes against it and 3 abstentions (Edareh Kol Omor Farhangi Va Rvabet Omomi Majles Shorai Islami 1985b, p. 407).

Article 56

This article asserts that absolute sovereignty over the world and humans belongs to God. And it is He who has granted the people freedom to determine their own social destiny. No one can take this divine right away from human beings or apply it to the interests of a special person or group. The nation exercises this God-given right in ways that are specified in the following articles. (Papan-Matin 2014, p. 175)

Article 56, with some changes from the initial draft, was brought into the public session of the Assembly of Experts for the Constitution by commission number three. Ayatollah Naser Makarem Shirazi, a follower of jurisprudential Islam, referring to Surah Ar-Rad verse 11[1] claiming the destiny of all people lay in their own hands and every change in their life,

---

[1] Allah does not change people's situation unless they change themselves... (11) (Yusuf Ali 2016, p. 250).

whether negative or positive, was made by them. According to him, people determine their social destiny by electing a president, the prime minister, a head of the judiciary and jurists (Edareh Kol Omor Farhangi Va Rvabet Omomi Majles Shorai Islami 1985b, p. 527).

Discussions Between Advocates and Opponents of Article 56

The Meaninglessness of This Article as a Result of the Principle
of Guardianship of the Jurisconsult (Velayat-e Faqih)
Hujjat al-Islam Seyed Abdolkarim Hasheminezhad, a follower of jurisprudential Islam, alleged that with the inclusion of articles number 5 and 6 there was no need for this Article (Edareh Kol Omor Farhangi Va Rvabet Omomi Majles Shorai Islami 1985b, p. 513). Seyed Mohammad Kiyavash, a follower of jurisprudential Islam, posed the question of how the right of rulership can be transferred from God to jurists and people simultaneously (Edareh Kol Omor Farhangi Va Rvabet Omomi Majles Shorai Islami 1985b, pp. 518–519). Ayatollah Jafar Sobhani, also a follower of jurisprudential Islam, responded that, according to Surah Yusuf verse 40,[2] the command is meant for Allah (God) to exercise, but God entitles some of His righteous servants to have and discharge this right. He thus believed that Article 56 fell within the series dealing with the guardianship of the jurisconsult, and a leader may transfer this guardianship (*Velayat*) to the people. According to him, this had led to referring to the popular right of rulership with orders from the jurists. He held the view that the people's power was exercised in two ways: First, directly through *Nahi Anil Munkar* (forbidding evil) and *Amr Bil Mahroof* (enjoining good) or uprising; second, indirectly via participating in parliamentary and presidential elections (Edareh Kol Omor Farhangi Va Rvabet Omomi Majles Shorai Islami 1985b, pp. 514–515).

Likewise, Ayatollah Mohammad Yazdi, another advocate of jurisprudential Islam, in support of this Article asserted in support of this Article that it explained the right of the nation and divine rulership and the relationship between them. According to Ayatollah Yazdi, God created human beings free yet necessarily restricted them under the framework of Sharia or Divine law. He believed that everybody, using their common sense, would find this limitation quite reasonable. Thus, in reality, people had

---

[2] ... The command is for no one but Allah... (40) (Yusuf Ali 2016, p. 240).

sovereignty over all aspects of their lives and this was achieved through parliamentary and presidential elections under the auspices Islamic law (Edareh Kol Omor Farhangi Va Rvabet Omomi Majles Shorai Islami 1985b, pp. 517–518). Ayatollah Beheshti argued that there was no contradiction here since the whole administration, including the Supreme Leader, was elected by the popular vote. Indeed, the system loses its legality if there is no participation by the people (Edareh Kol Omor Farhangi Va Rvabet Omomi Majles Shorai Islami 1985b, p. 523).

This Principle Emanates from the Third Principle of the Statement of Human Rights
Abdolrahman Heidari, also a follower of jurisprudential Islam, in citing Sura An-Nisa verse 58[3] asserted that this was similar to a principle in the French constitution wherein God recommends the nation's rulership (Edareh Kol Omor Farhangi Va Rvabet Omomi Majles Shorai Islami 1985b, p. 519). Ayatollah Beheshti declared that the Article demonstrated the mindfulness of mankind's culture and this was important in the world today. Thus, he stated that existence of such a principle in the constitution was fine and must not be deemed a problem (Edareh Kol Omor Farhangi Va Rvabet Omomi Majles Shorai Islami 1985b, p. 523). The Article was approved by parliament with 51 votes for and 6 against it, with 9 abstentions (Edareh Kol Omor Farhangi Va Rvabet Omomi Majles Shorai Islami 1985b, p. 536).

Article 57

This article states that the governing powers in the Islamic Republic of Iran consist of the legislative, executive and judiciary bodies. They operate according to the relevant articles of the Constitution under the supervision of the authority of the religious leadership (Imamate) of the community of believers. These powers are independent of each other and the President of the Islamic Republic of Iran establishes the association among them. (Papan-Matin 2014, p. 175)

In the draft of constitution, only these three powers had been proposed. However, two additional powers, that is the power of the nation

---

[3] …"Allah doth command you to render back your Trusts to those to whom they are due"…(58) (Yusuf Ali 2016, p. 87).

and the power of the leader were recommended to be added by commission number two of the Assembly of Experts for the Constitution and these were discussed in a later public session of Assembly.

Discussions Between Advocates and Opponents of Article 57

Some representatives in the Parliament stated there are three separate powers which function with respect to the exercise of people's right of rulership. Likewise, Ayatollah Hussein Ali Rahmani, a follower of jurisprudential Islam, observed that the efficacy of the three separate powers came in fact from the power of the nation and there was no need to refer to it as a separate power (Edareh Kol Omor Farhangi Va Rvabet Omomi Majles Shorai Islami 1985b, p. 557). Ayatollah Naser Makarem Shirazi, a follower of jurisprudential Islam, replied by arguing that every society has different values and for Iran it was not limited to three separate powers (Edareh Kol Omor Farhangi Va Rvabet Omomi Majles Shorai Islami 1985b, p. 541). The final Article was approved with the inclusion of four separate powers, namely the legislative, judiciary, executive and leadership powers. These are independent yet mutually connected to each other through the President (Edareh Kol Omor Farhangi Va Rvabet Omomi Majles Shorai Islami 1985a, p. 1697).

Article 107

Whenever any jurist, qualified under the fifth principle of this law, is recognised and accepted as Marja and leader by the majority of the people, as was the case for Imam Khomeini, this leader will have the responsibility of commanding. Otherwise, the Experts elected by the people will decide which people are qualified for being leader and Marja. In the event they find a Marja with distinguished qualifications, they will introduce him to people as the Leader. If none is found, they will appoint a Leadership Council consisting of three or five Marjas and present them to the people (Papan-Matin 2014, p. 184).

Chapter eight of the Constitution in which Article 107 is located included six articles that did not exist in the initial draft of the constitution. Ayatollah Mohammad Yazdi, a follower of jurisprudential Islam, in support of Article 107 asserted that the Islamic government of Iran was a conjoint God–People government. He believed that determining who was qualified as a real jurist was a matter of popular decision through the election of their representatives in the Assembly of Experts. In case the necessary leadership characteristics were not met by any one jurist, three or five jurists should manage this system. He also asserted that a jurist leader could reconcile common laws with Sharia laws. Although in the past some governments operated in this manner, or were formed by various jurists, he added that today we have an Islamic state governed by a jurist or a jurists' council, and therefore Iranian society was united (Edareh Kol Omor Farhangi Va Rvabet Omomi Majles Shorai Islami 1985a, pp. 1069–1070).

In this regard, Ayatollah Taheri Khoramabadi, a follower of jurisprudential Islam, stated that in Iran the people were responsible and chose the leadership to avoid an internal dictatorship on the one hand, and colonialism from abroad, on the other (Edareh Kol Omor Farhangi Va Rvabet Omomi Majles Shorai Islami 1985a, p. 1088). Seyed Hassan Ayat, also a follower of jurisprudential Islam, supported the article and argued that without it the Islamic state could not have been established. He added that there were many rational and notated reasons supporting this approach in jurisprudential books, in particular Khomeini's authored 'Guardianship of the Jurisconsult' (Edareh Kol Omor Farhangi Va Rvabet Omomi Majles Shorai Islami 1985a, pp. 1092–1093).

Discussions Between Advocates and Opponents of Article 107

Concerns About Taking of This Position by Jurists

Hojatoleslam wal-muslemin Ali Golzadeh Ghafuri, an advocate of liberal Islam, expressed two serious concerns with this article. First, for jurists these positions were new and they lacked any precedent. Second, there was uncertainty associated with the future of this position (Edareh Kol Omor Farhangi Va Rvabet Omomi Majles Shorai Islami 1985a, p. 1087). In response, Ayatollah Mohammad Yazdi, a follower of jurisprudential Islam, argued it would be improper to ignore the duties of forming an Islamic State and Republic because of worries about the future (Edareh Kol Omor Farhangi Va Rvabet Omomi Majles Shorai Islami 1985a, pp. 1089–1090).

What Is the Legal Position of Leadership?

Hojatoleslam wal-muslemin Mohammad Javad Hojati Kermani, a follower of jurisprudential Islam, posed the question of the role of leadership given the fact that, in international law, the highest person within the state was the president. How would he interact with international organisations? (Edareh Kol Omor Farhangi Va Rvabet Omomi Majles Shorai Islami 1985a, pp. 1094–1095). Seyed Hassan Ayat, a follower of jurisprudential Islam, responded by arguing that the leadership of the Supreme Leader was at the heart of the Iranian government and it carried the role of Imamate. He continued that some countries, such as China, had different power structures and appeared to have no problem with this role. The President communicates with international organisations and it was not a matter of concern (Edareh Kol Omor Farhangi Va Rvabet Omomi Majles Shorai Islami 1985a, p. 1094). Ayatollah Beheshti asserted that the Iranian system was a system of Ummah and Imamate with which the world would become acquainted. (Edareh Kol Omor Farhangi Va Rvabet Omomi Majles Shorai Islami 1985a, p. 1095).

Is the Leader Accountable for His Actions?
Because leaders are not infallible Seyed Ahmad Norbaskhsh, a follower of liberal Islam, posed the question of whether a leader was accountable for his actions, and if so, to whom he was responsible and accountable, and who will consider his violations of law, should he commit them? (Edareh Kol Omor Farhangi Va Rvabet Omomi Majles Shorai Islami 1985a, p. 1085). Ayatollah Beheshti replied that a leader was responsible to the nation in the same way as Members of Parliament. Furthermore, he declared that should a leader offend against the law, he would be held responsible as would be the case with other people (Edareh Kol Omor Farhangi Va Rvabet Omomi Majles Shorai Islami 1985a, p. 1090).

The Leadership Council Is Better
Abolhassan Banisadr, an advocate of liberal Islam, commented that a leadership council would preclude feudal tendencies and alleviate concerns about appointing just one individual as leader (Edareh Kol Omor Farhangi Va Rvabet Omomi Majles Shorai Islami 1985a, p. 1096). Ayatollah Montazeri, the head of this Assembly and a follower of jurisprudential Islam, observed that if a unique jurist can be found, it would be better, though a leadership council is fine as well. Therefore, we should not limit ourselves by basing our argument on either a person or council (Edareh Kol Omor Farhangi Va Rvabet Omomi Majles Shorai Islami 1985a, pp. 1096–1097).

Does the Term Ummah Include Religious Minorities As Well?
This question was posed by Aziz Danesh Rad, a representative in the
Parliament of the Jewish people (Edareh Kol Omor Farhangi Va Rvabet
Omomi Majles Shorai Islami 1985a, p. 1094). Ayatollah Beheshti replied
by stating that the term Ummah denotes all Iranian people (Edareh Kol
Omor Farhangi Va Rvabet Omomi Majles Shorai Islami 1985a, p. 1094).
Finally this Article was passed with 59 votes for and 3 votes against with 6
abstentions (Edareh Kol Omor Farhangi Va Rvabet Omomi Majles Shorai
Islami 1985a, p. 1098).

Article 110

This article enumerated the authorities and responsibilities of the supreme
leader as:

1. Appointing the jurist members of the Guardian Council;
2. Appointing the country's supreme judicial authority;
3. Commanding the armed forces as follows:

   A. appointment and dismissal of the chief of the general staff,
   B. appointment and dismissal of the commander-in-chief of the
   Islamic Revolutionary Guards Corps,
   C. establishing a Supreme National Defence Council, consisting of
   the following seven members:

   - The President,
   - The prime minister,
   - The defence minister,
   - The chief of the general staff,
   - The commander-in-chief of the Islamic Revolutionary
     Guards Corps,
   - Two advisors appointed by the leader,
   - Appointing the supreme commanders-in-chief of the three
     national forces, upon the recommendation of the Supreme
     National Defence Council.

   D. Declaring war, peace and mobilising national forces upon the
   recommendation of the Supreme National Defence Council;

4. Signing the appointment of the President of the Republic, after his
   election by the public. The qualifications of the candidates for presi-

dency, with respect to the criteria set forth by the Constitution, must be confirmed by the Guardian Council prior to the general elections and approved by the leader for the first term;

5. Dismissing the President of the Republic, with regard to the best interests of the country, after either the Supreme Court has issued a ruling convicting him of deviating from his legal duties, or the National Consultative Assembly has cast a vote against his political competence;

6. Pardoning or reducing the sentences of convicts, within the framework of Islamic criteria, upon the recommendation of the Supreme Court. (Papan-Matin 2014, p. 186).

The draft Constitution assigned most of these duties to the President and Prime Minister. The parliament, however, assigned them to the Supreme Leader. The main discussion among members of the parliament over the 1979 constitution concerned two important items: The precise rights of the leadership based on the principle of guardianship of the jurisconsult, and the legitimacy of the entirety of the Islamic Republic of Iran. It is necessary to mention that after the election of the Assembly of Experts, followers of jurisprudential Islam gained the majority. They sought to incorporate the principle of guardianship of the jurisconsult into several articles of the Constitution. However, a minority followed the interpretations of Islam advanced by thinkers such as Bazargan and Shariati, and also some secular politicians from outside the Assembly, objected. This objection caused Khomeini to interfere and strongly espouse the aforementioned principle in several cases, although before the election he merely had some general ideas and invited people to participate in the election by voting for their representatives. Khomeini asserted that the principle of guardianship of the jurisconsult was an anti-dictatorship principle and the minority groups, who did not obtain sufficient votes in the election, had sought to set this principle aside acting dictatorially (Khomeini 2010e, pp. 528–529). He also argued that this principle granted legitimacy insofar as without it the system lost its legitimacy and became a falsehood (Khomeini 2010b, p. 221). The members of the parliament finished their task of finalising the draft in August 1979, coming up with 175 Articles. Subsequently, the new Islamic constitution was approved by 99.5% of voters, with a 75.56% turnout (Abrahamian 2008, pp. 168–169).

REVISION OF IRAN'S CONSTITUTION BY ORDER OF KHOMEINI IN APRIL 1989

Khomeini believed the changing atmosphere post-revolution and the lack of sufficient knowledge about administrative issues prevailing at that time, meant the founding constitution had some major drawbacks. Thus, in April 1988, after 10 years of experience using the constitution, a committee comprising 20 followers of jurisprudential Islam were appointed by Khomeini together with five people selected by the Parliament to undertake the task of modifying the constitution. (Khomeini 2010d, pp. 363–364). It is noteworthy that the constitution had not included any mechanisms for its own later modifications.

Khomeini asked the committee to work on eight items, namely the precise role of the Supreme Leader; the centralisation of management of executive power; the centralisation of the management of judiciary power; the centralisation of the management of the broadcasting system of Iran; the number of parliamentary members; the formation of the Expediency Discernment Council (*Majmae Tashkhis Maslahat Nezam*); determining the method of revising the constitution in the future and the renaming of the National Consultative Assembly into the Islamic Consultative Assembly (Khomeini 2010d, p. 364). The most important part of the revision seemed to be the one related to the duties of the Supreme Leader of Iran. This subject will be discussed next.

Revision of Article 5

During the absence of the Lord of the Age—the hidden Imam—a jurist who was just, pious, knowledgeable about his era, courageous, and a qualified and efficient administrator, as indicated in Article 107 was responsible for the execution of the commands of God as well as religious leadership of the community [of believers] in the Islamic Republic of Iran (Papan-Matin 2014, pp. 167–168). The revision council of the constitution made two changes to this article: First, it eliminated reference to a leadership council; second, the process of electing the Supreme leadership was changed from direct election by the people into an election by the Assembly of Experts (Edareh Kol Omor Farhangi Va Rvabet Omomi Majles Shorai Islami 1990, p. 1451). The members of this council must be jurists (*Mujtahid*) and elected by the Iranian people and can appoint or dismiss an individual as Supreme Leader.

Revision of Article 6

In the Islamic Republic of Iran, the country's affairs must be administered by reliance on the public vote, and through elections. These will include the election of the president, the deputies of the Islamic Consultative Assembly (*Majles*), the members of the councils, and other such institutions, or through a referendum in such instances as are determined in other articles of this document. (Papan-Matin 2014, p. 168)

In order to modify this Article of the Constitution, the term National Consultative Assembly was supplanted by the term Islamic Consultative Assembly.

Revision of Article 57

This article states the governing powers in the Islamic Republic of Iran consist of the legislative, the executive, and the judiciary powers. They operate under the supervision of the absolute authority of the command (*Velayat-i amr*) and religious leadership (Imamate) of the community of believers and according to the forthcoming articles of this law. These powers are independent of one another. (Papan-Matin 2014, p. 175)

The revisionary council for the constitution made two changes: First, it added the term 'absolute' to the phrase 'authority of the command (*Velayat-i amr*) and religious leadership (Imamate) of the community of believers'; second, it removed the statement declaring the President of the Republic establishes the association among powers (leadership, executive, legislature and judiciary powers).

Discussions Between Advocates and Opponents of Revision of Article 57

Ayatollah Mohammad Mousavi Khoeiniha stated that should this revision be made, Iranians and others would think that Iran has concentrated all power in the hands of just one person (the supreme leadership). According to Ayatollah Khoeiniha, the revised version of the article permitted the Supreme Leader to make whatsoever changes to the Constitution, and dissolve the Parliament, therefore it was not necessary to change this Article (Edareh Kol Omor Farhangi Va Rvabet Omomi Majles Shorai Islami 1990, pp. 1633–1644). Ayatollah Ahmad Azari Qomi responded by arguing that this system took its legitimacy from the principle of guardianship of the jurisconsult *(Velayat-e Faqih)*. He added that according to Article 110, signing the appointment of the President of the Republic, after his election by people, was undertaken by the Supreme Leader. Thus, it was necessary to revise this article (Edareh Kol Omor Farhangi Va Rvabet Omomi Majles Shorai Islami 1990, p. 1636).

Revision of Article 107

This article was revised to assert that Article 107: after the honourable source of emulation, the great leader of the global Islamic Revolution, and the founder of the Islamic Republic of Iran, the venerated Grand Ayatollah, Imam Khomeini, may his noble character be sanctified, who was acknowledged and accepted by the undisputed majority of the people as the *marja* and the leader, the responsibility for designating the leader shall be with the Experts who are appointed by the people. The Experts consider all the qualified jurisprudents as discussed in Articles 5 and 109,[4] and consult with one another about them. If they find one of them, the most knowledgeable about the rules and subjects of jurisprudence, or political and social issues, or acceptability by the public, or significance in any one of the qualifications indicated in Article 109, that person shall be selected as the leader; otherwise, one of the Experts is chosen and declared as the leader. The leader who is appointed by the Experts is in charge of the sovereignty of the command and all the responsibilities that derive from it. Before the law, the leader is equal to other people in the country. (Papan-Matin 2014, p. 184)

The revisionary council for the Constitution made several changes into this article; first, completion of the section devoted to the role played by Khomeini in the 1979 Islamic Revolution; second, that Khomeini was directly elected by the Iranian people as the Supreme Leader whereas his successors for the leadership were to be indirectly

---

[4] "The qualifications and attributes of the leader are as follows:

1—scholarly qualification for issuing religious ruling (fatwa) concerning various discussions in jurisprudence; 2—required justice and piety in leading the Islamic community; 3—sound political and social perspective, prudence, courage, sufficient administrative capability, and power for leadership. In case there are a number of candidates who meet these qualifications, the person with a more efficacious political and jurisprudential insight has priority." (Papan-Matin 2014, pp. 184–185)

elected by the jurisprudents council; third, removing the requirement that the Leader shall be a *Marja* as well; fourth, the elimination of the alternative of the leadership council; finally, that the Leader is the same as other people before the law.

Discussions Between Advocates and Opponents of Revision of Article 107

The Concern About Separation Between Leadership and Marja'iat
For Ayatollah Mohammad Yazdi politics and religion that not mutually exclusive. According to him, some people were concerned that if someone becomes the Leader and someone else the *Marja*, then in the long term this separation will lead to the separation of religion and politics given that the leadership role of the Supreme Leader was indeed the manager of society and the *Marja* acted as a religious leader for those who emulate him (Edareh Kol Omor Farhangi Va Rvabet Omomi Majles Shorai Islami 1990, p. 184). Ayatollah Sayyed Ali Hosseini Khamenei argued that this is not problematic as the Leader was a just jurist elected by the Assembly of Experts for the Leadership, and he was the person who signed the appointment of the President of the Islamic Republic upon being elected by the Iranian people. Moreover, the Leader was elected based on Sharia law and all the country's affairs are indeed related to the leadership role of the Supreme Leader because he had the highest position and rank in the country (Edareh Kol Omor Farhangi Va Rvabet Omomi Majles Shorai Islami 1990, p. 194). Hojatoleslam wal-muslemin Akbar Hashemi Rafsanjani asserted that Khomeini believed that a command given by a just jurist was indeed a command from the religion. He added that the council of jurisprudents supported the leadership. He thus concluded that no source of emulation (*Marja-e-Taqlid*) could challenge the Supreme Leader or the position of the supreme leadership (Edareh Kol Omor Farhangi Va Rvabet Omomi Majles Shorai Islami 1990, p. 255).

The Discussion on Temporariness or Permanence of the Leader's Tenure
Ayatollah Ibrahim Amini asserted that if every jurist were to be entitled to rule, then chaos would result. He stated that was why people elected the Jurisprudents Council and then this council elected the Leader. According to Ayatollah Amini, Khomeini believed that the reason that a just jurist could influence Iranian society was his election by the Assembly of Experts

to the leadership. Furthermore, he asserted that the jurisprudents' council could set a limit of 10 years to the leader's tenure (Edareh Kol Omor Farhangi Va Rvabet Omomi Majles Shorai Islami 1990, p. 1210). Ayatollah Mohammad Momen responded by expressing the position that leadership in Islamic government was a divine matter and the jurisprudents' council must identify the right person for the task and introduce him to the people. Therefore, he thought, it was not proper to set a limit to the tenure of the Leader's tenure (Edareh Kol Omor Farhangi Va Rvabet Omomi Majles Shorai Islami 1990, p. 1215).

Also, Ayatollah Taheri Khoramabadi asserted that in the absence of Imam Mahdi, the Supreme Leader is indeed his deputy and if a limit is set on his tenure, people would question how he could be the deputy of Imam Mahdi for a limited period—say 10 years—and after this time period has elapsed, he was no longer. Therefore, he believed that the tenure of the leader must be lifelong (Edareh Kol Omor Farhangi Va Rvabet Omomi Majles Shorai Islami 1990, pp. 1210–1211). Moreover, Ayatollah Ali Meshkini asserted that the role of supreme leadership is a holy position and it was not suitable in the public sphere to dismiss a person from this position or set a limit to his tenure except in the cases specified in Article 109 and 111[5] (Edareh Kol Omor Farhangi Va Rvabet Omomi Majles Shorai Islami 1990, p. 1214).

---

[5] "The leader will be dismissed from his position in case he is incapable of performing his legal responsibilities, becomes deficient in one of the qualifications mentioned in Article 5 and 109; or it becomes evident that from the offset he has been lacking in some of the qualifications. This issue shall be determined by the Council of Experts, as mentioned in Article 108. In the aforementioned case, or in case of the death, resignation, or dismissal of the leader, the Experts are responsible for designating a new leader as soon as possible. Until the leader is introduced, a council consisting of the President of the Republic, the head of the judiciary power, and one of the jurisprudents of the Guardian Council, selected by the Expediency Council, will temporarily assume all the responsibilities of the leadership. If during this time any of them, for any reason, cannot fulfil his duties, another individual will be assigned in his place according to the vote of the assembly and with respect to maintaining the majority of the jurisprudents in the council. The council must obtain three-fourths approval of the members of Expediency Council, in order to fulfil the responsibilities that are outlined in Article 110, sections 1, 3, 5, 10, and segments 'd,' 'e,' 'f' of section 6. Whenever the leader, due to illness or other incidents, is temporarily unable to fulfil the duties of leadership, the council mentioned above in this Article assumes his responsibilities" (Papan-Matin 2014, pp. 186–187).

Revision of Article 110

The revision of this article asserts that the authorities and responsibilities of the Leader are in respect to:

1. Determining the overall politics of the Islamic Republic system of Iran after consultation with the Expediency Council;
2. Supervising the proper implementation of the general policies of the system;
3. Issuing referendums;
4. Commanding the armed forces;
5. Declaring war, peace and mobilising forces;
6. Issuing appointments, dismissals and accepting the resignation of:

   A. the jurisprudents of the Guardian Council,
   B. the highest position of the judiciary power,
   C. the president of the mass media of the Islamic Republic of Iran,
   D. the chief of the general staff,
   E. the commander-in-chief of the Islamic Pasdaran Revolutionary Corps,
   F. the supreme commanders-in-chief of the security and armed forces;

7. Coordinating the relationship among the three branches of the government and resolving any conflict among them;
8. Resolving issues in the system that cannot be settled by ordinary means through the Expediency Council;
9. Signing the appointment of the President of the Republic, after his election by the public. The qualifications of the candidates for presidency, with respect to the conditions set forth by the constitution, must be confirmed by the Guardian Council prior to the general elections and approved by the leader for the first term;
10. Dismissing the President of the Republic, with regard to the best interests of the country, after either the Supreme Court has issued a ruling convicting him of deviating from his legal duties, or the Islamic Consultative Assembly, based on Article 89, has cast a vote against his competence;
11. Pardoning or reducing the sentences of convicts, within the framework of Islamic criteria, after the head of the judiciary power has recommended such a motion. The leader can transfer some of his duties and authorities to another person. (Papan-Matin 2014, p. 185).

In conclusion, the main discussion about the revision of the constitution in 1989 was related to the centralisation of power, especially with regards to the Supreme Leader of Iran. The new Islamic constitution was approved by 97.57% of voters, with a 54.51% turnout (Abrahamian 2008, p. 183).

CONCLUDING ANALYSIS

This chapter outlined and discussed the influence of the ideas of three Iranian thinkers and their followers on Iran's Constitution after the 1979 Islamic Revolution. Five analytical points can be made. Firstly, the historical coup against Prime Minister Mohammad Mosaddegh on 19 August 1953 by Mohammad Reza Shah (assisted by the governments of the United States and the United Kingdom) gave rise to profound political implications for Iran. When History repeats, the first time is a tragedy, the second time a farce. Notably the Shah suspended his relations with political opposition activists and focused on the intelligence agency (SAVAK) to cement political power. This led opposition groups, especially political Islamic groups, towards the idea of changing the political regime from the dynasty of the Shah to something different. This idea gained traction among political Islamist groups as jurisprudential Islam based on the ideas of Khomeini and his followers, and also Shia ideological ideas proposed by Shariati and Bazargan and their disciples, found support. In the 1960s and 1970s these kinds of ideas became more popular among the Iranian and were reflected in the constitutions of Iran in 1979 and 1989. It is critically important to comprehend the significance of this transformation, from a monarchy to an Islamic Republic given the new system offered a new model of government based on the ideas of political Islamic groups.

Secondly, in terms of the system of knowledge, Bazargan as Prime Minister of the interim government brought a draft of the constitution into the inauguration of the 1979 Assembly of Experts for the Constitution stating all the articles, and particularly those related to national sovereignty, freedom and the right of majority's vote, were not foreign ideas, but grounded in the principles of the Qur'an (Edareh Kol Omor Farhangi Va Rvabet Omomi Majles Shorai Islami 1985b, p. 7). He wanted to distinguish this with other secular social, and nationalist ideologies. For, Ezzatollah Sahabi, who had been influenced by Shariati, the draft was based on the ideas of Ayatollah Mohammad Hossein Naini's ideas about government (Edareh Kol Omor Farhangi Va Rvabet Omomi Majles Shorai

Islami 1985b, p. 90). The latter was an outstanding thinker interested in the 1906 Constitutional Revolution who believed that, in the absence of Imam Mahdi, a jurist plays two roles in a Muslim society: Judgeship and issuing fatwa. A jurist had a third duty—that of political guardianship as found in the second article of the Constitutional Revolution Law. Here, supervision by five jurists over the actions of parliament, was sufficient in the absence of the Imam Mahdi (Hosainizadeh 2007, p. 88). In contrast, followers of jurisprudential Islam believed that a jurist played three roles in a Muslim society: First, political guardianship; second, judgeship; third, issuing fatwa in the absence of the Imam Mahdi, the 12th Shia Imam (Edareh Kol Omor Farhangi Va Rvabet Omomi Majles Shorai Islami 1985b, p. 93). Obviously, Bazargan and the followers of liberal Islam had focused on the Qur'an as the basis and main principle of the constitution, whereas the advocates of jurisprudential Islam had focused on *fiqh*.

Thirdly, with regard to the system of norms, by 1979, all opposition groups whether religious or non-religious wanted to eliminate the dynasty of the Shah from public life in Iran. However, the political Islamist groups differed from secular groups—such as communist or nationalist groups—in terms of the formation of an Islamic government. After the revolution, the gap between the religious and secular communities was evident when the secular groups lost out in the election of the Assembly of Experts for the Constitution to the followers of jurisprudential Islam (which achieved the majority), and a minority followed the interpretations of Islam advanced by thinkers such as Bazargan and Shariati. According to the interpretation of jurisprudential Islam, the draft of the constitution was secular in that it lacked the principle of guardianship of jurisconsult (*Velayat-e Faqih*). In jurisprudential Islam, it was believed that the principle of guardianship of jurisconsults ensures the Islamic nature of the Islamic Republic system. Also, followers of jurisprudential Islam believed that the Iranian government was a God-centred people's government.

Fourthly, the system of government, adopted was Khomeini's model of an Islamic Republic based on *Velayat-e Faqih* (the guardianship of jurisconsult). Shariati, put forward his two theories, namely 'The theory of Ummah and Imamate' and 'Mysticism, Equality and Liberty' and Bazargan, espoused the idea of an Islamic Democratic Republic of Iran. With regards to these ideas, Davood Feirahi, an Iranian scholar, believed that Ayatollah Seyyed Mohammad Hosseini Beheshti, the deputy of the Assembly of Experts for the Constitution in 1979, made a major contribution to the development of the Iranian constitution. Beheshti took the idea of 'Ummah and Imamate' from Shariati but made two modification: First, while Shariati applied it merely in referring to the era of infallible Imams, Ayatollah Beheshti used it for the establishment of a political system (the Islamic Republic) during the absence of Imam Mahdi. Second, he extended its use to the role of leadership in the revolution and made it integral to the state apparatus of the Islamic Republic of Iran. Also, Ayatollah Beheshti as one of the major players in the Assembly applied it to the Constitution, especially to Articles 5, 56, and 107 (Feirahi 2014, pp. 358,359). According to Davood Feirahi, Ayatollah Beheshti is among the major intellectuals who sought to extend the *fiqh*-based theory of the Guardianship of Jurisconsult into the dialectical concept of Ummah and Imamate. Therefore, he thought that the Islamic Republic of Iran is clearly a system of Ummah and Imamate with a triple structure of jurisconsult, leadership and election (Feirahi 2014, p. 343).

Fifthly, with regard to public policy, the term 'Islamic Republic' consists of two parts: The former refers to the democratic side and the latter to *Ijtihad* (interpretation). As mentioned previously, the theory of Guardianship of Jurisconsult proposed as a *fiqh*-related idea by Khomeini was extended into the dialectic theory of Ummah and Imamate proposed by Shariati. This was revealed in Iran's constitution, in particular in Articles 5, 56 and 107. Also, political jurisprudential Islamic groups and thinkers have divided into two separate schools. One school supported the divine legitimacy of Iran's supreme leadership and suggested that, in the absence of Imam Mahdi, the Supreme Leader stands as his representative and therefore the peoples' votes are irrelevant here. The other school, however, supported the idea that legitimacy of the whole administration including the supreme leadership stemmed from the popular vote. The latter contained capacity for building on Social Islam in contemporary Iran. There have been robust discussions and competition between these two groups in the public sphere. Those disciples of Shariati who followed his second theory, 'Mysticism, Equality and Liberty', and also followers of Bazargan who adhered to the idea of an Islamic Democratic Republic, have been identified as marginalised groups in the context of Iran.

References

Abrahamian, E. (2008). *A history of modern Iran*. New York, NY: Cambridge University Press.

Byaniyeh Ayatollah Golpayagani dabreh Pishnevis Ghanon Asasi [The statement of Grand Ayatollah Golpayagani about the draft of constitutional law]. (1979, July 22). *Jomhori Islami*, p. 4.

Byaniyeh Jonbesh Mosalmanan Mobarez darbreh Pishnevis Ghanon Asasi [The statement of militant Muslims movement about the draft constitutional law]. (1979, August 8). *Omat*, p. 7.

Didgahhai Enteghadi darbreh Pishnevis Ghanon Asasi [The critical views to the draft of constitutional law]. (1979, August 6). *Nashriyeh Mojahed*, p. 6.

Edareh Kol Omor Farhangi Va Rvabet Omomi Majles Shorai Islami. (1985a). *Sorat Mashroh Mozakerat Majles Baresi Nhaei Ghanon Asasi Jomhori Islami* [The Final Review of Constitutional Law of Islamic Republic] (Vol. 2). Tehran, Iran: Edareh Kol Omor Farhangi Va Rvabet Omomi Majles Shorai Islami.

Edareh Kol Omor Farhangi Va Rvabet Omomi Majles Shorai Islami. (1985b). *Sorat Mashroh Mozakerat Majles Baresi Nhaei Ghanon Asasi Jomhori Islami* [The Final Review of Constitutional Law of Islamic Republic] (Vol. 1). Tehran, Iran: Edareh Kol Omor Farhangi Va Rvabet Omomi Majles Shorai Islami.

Edareh Kol Omor Farhangi Va Rvabet Omomi Majles Shorai Islami. (1985c). *Sorat Mashroh Mozakerat Majles Baresi Nhaei Ghanon Asasi Jomhori Islami* [The Final Review of Constitutional Law of Islamic Republic] (Vol. 4). Tehran, Iran: Edareh Kol Omor Farhangi Va Rvabet Omomi Majles Shorai Islami.

Edareh Kol Omor Farhangi Va Rvabet Omomi Majles Shorai Islami. (1990). *Sorat Mashroh Mozakerat Shuorai Baznegari Ghanon Asasi* [The Revision of the Constitutional Law]. Tehran, Iran: Edareh Kol Omor Farhangi Va Rvabet Omomi Majles Shorai Islami.

Feirahi, D. (2014). *Fiqh va Siyasat dar Iran Moaser* [Jurisprudence and politics in contemporary of Iran] (Vol. 2). Tehran, Iran: Nashr Nei.

Ghazi Shariat Panahi, S. A. (2005). *Bayestehai Ghanon Asasi* [Necessary for the Constitutional Law]. Tehran, Iran: Mizan.

Hashemi, S. M. (1995). *Hoghogh Asasi Jomhori Islami Iran* [The fundamental rights of the Islamic Republic of Iran] (Vol. 1). Tehran, Iran: Daneshgah Shahid Beheshti.

Hosainizadeh, S. M. A. (2007). *Islam siasi dar Iran* [Political Islam in Iran]. Qom, Iran: Mofid University.

Katoziyan, N. (2001). *Gami besoye Edalat* [A step toward Justice] (Vol. 1). Tehran, Iran: Entesharat Daneshgah Tehran.

Khomeini, S. R. (2010a). *Sahifeh Imam: Majmoe asar Imam Khomeini bayanat, payamha, mosahebeha, ahkam, ejazat sharei va nameha* [Sahifeh-Ye Imam: An anthology of Imam Khomeini's speeches, messages, interviews, decrees, religious permissions, and letters] (Vol. 4). Tehran, Iran: The Institute for Compilation and Publication of Imam Khomeini's Works.

Khomeini, S. R. (2010b). *Sahifeh Imam: Majmoe asar imam Khomeini bayanat, payamha, mosahebeha, ahkam, ejazat sharei va nameha* [Sahifeh-Ye Imam: An anthology of Imam Khomeini's speeches, messages, interviews, decrees, religious permissions, and letters] (Vol. 10). Tehran, Iran: The Institute for Compilation and Publication of Imam Khomeini's Works.

Khomeini, S. R. (2010c). *Sahifeh Imam: Majmoe asar Imam Khomeini bayanat, payamha, mosahebeha, ahkam, ejazat sharei va nameha* [Sahifeh-Ye Imam: An anthology of Imam Khomeini's speeches, messages, interviews, decrees, religious permissions, and letters] (Vol. 8). Tehran, Iran: The Institute for Compilation and Publication of Imam Khomeini's Works.

Khomeini, S. R. (2010d). *Sahifeh Imam: Majmoe asar Imam Khomeini bayanat, payamha, mosahebeha, ahkam, ejazat sharei va nameha* [Sahifeh-Ye Imam: An anthology of Imam Khomeini's speeches, messages, interviews, decrees, religious permissions, and letters] (Vol. 21). Tehran, Iran: The Institute for Compilation and Publication of Imam Khomeini's Works.

Khomeini, S. R. (2010e). *Sahifeh Imam: Majmoe asar imam Khomeini bayanat, payamha, mosahebeha, ahkam, ejazat sharei va nameha* [Sahifeh-Ye Imam: An anthology of Imam Khomeini's speeches, messages, interviews, decrees, religious permissions, and letters] (Vol. 9). Tehran, Iran: The Institute for Compilation and Publication of Imam Khomeini's Works.

Mosahebeh ba Ayatollah Shariatmadari darbreh Pishnevish Ghanon Asasi [The interview about the draft of constitutional law with Grand Ayatollah Shariatmadari]. (1979, July 31). *Bamdad*, p. 9.

Mosahebeh darbreh Pishnevis Ghanon Asasi ba Yadollah Sahabi [Yadollah Sahabi interview about the draft of constitutional law]. (1979, June 16). *Kayhan*, p. 9.

Mujahidin of Islamic Revolution Organization. (1979). *Byaniyeh Shomareh 14 [The Political Party Statement 14].* Tehran, Iran: Mujahidin of Islamic Revolution Organization.

Naghdhai Ayatollah Marashi Najafi darbareh Pishnevis Ghanon Asasi [The comments of Ayatollah Marashi Najafi on the draft of constitutional law]. (1979, July 22). *Jomhori Islami*, pp. 1–2.

Naghdhai Jebhei Meli Iran darbreh Pishnevish Ghanon Asasi [The comments of The National Front of Iran on the draft of constitutional law]. (1979, July 18). *Bamdad*, pp. 1–3.

Papan-Matin, F. (2014). The Constitution of the Islamic Republic of Iran (1989 edition). *Iranian Studies, 47*(1), 159–200.

Saeli Koredh Deh, M. (2005). *Shuorai Enghelab Islami Iran* [The Council of the Islamic Revolution of Iran]. Tehran, Iran: Markaz Asnad Enghelab Islami.

Sahabi, E. (2004). *Nagoftehai Enghelab va Mabahes Bonyadi Meli* [Untold Revolution and National foundamental Topics]. Tehran, Iran: Game Noe.

Tabatabaei, S. (2009). *Khaterat sisasi ejtemaei doctor Sadeq Tabatabaei* [Social and Political memoirs doctor Sadeq Tabatabaei] (Vol. 3). Tehran, Iran: Nashr Oroj.

The Party of Diligent people of Iran's Nation. (1979). *Noghteh Nazrat darbreh Pishnevis Ghanon Asasi [The views on the draft of Constitutional Law].* Tehran, Iran: The Party of Diligent people of Iran's Nation.

Tudeh Party of Iran. (1979). *Majmoeh Byanieha va Etelaeihai Hezb Tudeh Iran* [The collection of Statements and Notifications of Tudeh Party of Iran]. Tehran, Iran: Hezb Tudeh Iran.

Yusuf Ali, A. (2016). *Quran* [English translation]. Retrieved from http://tanzil. net/#trans/en.yusufali/1:1

The Final Cut: Authority and Democracy in Contemporary Iran: From National Borders to the Idea of Islamic Empire

This chapter examines two different schools of jurisprudential Islam, given there have been various interpretations derived from the ideas of Khomeini with respect to the constitutional law of Iran, which became more prominent after his death. Since 1989, these two schools have been the main players in the political scene of Iran. One is based on the ideas of Ayatollah Seyyed Mohammad Hosseini Beheshti, Ayatollah Hussein Ali Montazeri, Ayatollah Nematollah Salehi Najafabadi and Hojatoleslam wal-muslemin Davood Feirahi, who consider people to be the source of political legitimacy. The other school is based on the ideas of Ayatollah Abdollah Javadi Amoli, Ayatollah Mohammad Momen and Ayatollah Mohammad Taqi Mesbah Yazdi, who believe political legitimacy derives from a divine source. Both schools have presented themselves in the framework of jurisprudential Islam.

LEGITIMACY OF THE POPULAR SCHOOL

Ayatollah Seyyed Mohammad Hosseini Beheshti

Ayatollah Beheshti (1929–1981) was a prominent jurist and political activist. He was the deputy of the Assembly of Experts for the Constitution in 1979. According to Seyed Habib (Abdul Karim)

© The Author(s) 2020
S. M. Lolaki, *Diverging Approaches of Political Islamic Thought in Iran since the 1960s*,
https://doi.org/10.1007/978-981-15-0478-5_9

167

Hashemi Nezhad, a member of assembly of experts, Article 5[1] of the constitution was prepared in 1979 and added to the draft constitution by Ayatollah Beheshti in commission number one and discussed in the public session of the Assembly (Edareh Kol Omor Farhangi Va Rvabet Omomi Majles Shorai Islami 1985b, p. 376). Also, in public sessions, Ayatollah Beheshti strongly defended this article. He explained the rationale behind his support of the Article by stating that independence and freedom were ideal additions, following the establishment of the Islamic Republic of Iran. He argued that the pillars of this system should be jurists, who were knowledgeable about Islam, capable of practising Islam in all individual, political, familial and social aspects and were good role models for other Muslims. Comparing Islamic society with other ideological systems led him to argue that there were two social systems. On the one hand was the liberal or democratic system based on the popular vote where the government accepted the wish of the majority; however, in effect, a minority (feudal or capitalistic) held power and oriented the others as they want. On the other hand, there was the social system wherein people follow a particular, or single, school or ideology. According to Beheshti, in such a society, people freely accepted and limited themselves to its framework of rules. He asserted that the Iranian people were (for the most part) Muslim, and that they had voluntarily disciplined themselves to the framework of Islamic rules or laws. He added that it was important to underscore that the Iranian system was not a Democratic Republic but an Islamic Republic.

Beheshti argued that, according to Islamic rules, the central pillar of the Islamic Republic was a knowledgeable jurist who was elected by the people. In such societies, someone who was more knowledgeable about the principle of *Maktab* (school) and Ideology is a jurist who embodied a

---

[1] "Article 5 (1979 Edition): In the Islamic Republic of Iran, during the absence (ghayba) of his holiness, the Lord of the Age, May God all mighty hasten his appearance, the sovereignty of the command [of God] and religious leadership of the community [of believers] is the responsibility of the jurisprudent who is just, pious, courageous, knowledgeable about his era, and a capable administrator, and is recognised and accepted by the majority of people as leader. In case no jurisprudent receives such a majority, the leader or the Leadership Council, consisting of qualified jurisprudents, as mentioned above and in accordance with Article 107, assumes these responsibilities" (Papan-Matin 2014, p. 167).

pivotal role in society (Edareh Kol Omor Farhangi Va Rvabet Omomi Majles Shorai Islami 1985b, pp. 376–381). Ayatollah Beheshti believed that the supreme leader should thus be a jurist and also a *Marja* (the source of emulation) simultaneously (Hosseini Beheshti 2012, pp. 190–192).

The Ummah and Imamate System
From an Islamic political perspective, the Ummah and Imamate system differs from other systems referred to in political or constitutional law books around the world (Hosseini Beheshti 2012, p. 39).

Similar to Shariati, Ayatollah Beheshti believed that the Ummah refers to a community sharing an ideology and goal, and which moves forward to achieve that objective. He asserted that from an Islamic political perspective, the Imamate refers to a political leadership that seeks to move people forward and to guide the society (Hosseini Beheshti 2012, pp. 39–40). Furthermore, Beheshti posed the question of how the leader should be elected. He then identified two systems in Islamic society—one which derives its legitimacy from the people and another whose legitimacy is from a divine source. He advocated the system that derived its legitimacy from the divine source whereby the leader is directly chosen by God, as was the case for Prophet Mohammad and the infallible Imams. On the other hand, in a system which regarded the people as the direct, or even indirect, source of legitimacy, the leader was elected by people (Hosseini Beheshti 2012, pp. 185–186). For the present era and in the absence of Imam Mahdi, Ayatollah Beheshti preferred a system whose legitimacy emanated from the people. Therefore, he compared the method of choosing the leader with that of choosing the *Marja-e-Taqlid* (the source of emulation) in the historical tradition of Shi'ism and which was performed in two ways. Firstly, by imitators using their personal recognition. Secondly, by some trusted experts (Hosseini Beheshti 2012, pp. 107–108). This method was based on research about an individual's performance. The second occurred when two *Mujtahids* (jurists) approved by the people for this purpose suggested someone as a *Marja-e-Taqlid* (the source of emulation). Also, it is clear that this model of selection by the people offered somewhat different options for selecting a *Marja-e-Taqlid* (the source of emulation) in a Shia framework. It seems that Ayatollah Beheshti sought to extend this idea to the means by which the supreme leader was elected in Iran. This is reflected in Articles 5, 107[2] and 108[3] in the 1979 constitutional law.

The Guardianship of Jurisconsult (Velayat-e Faqih) *and Sovereignty of the People*
In connection to the relationship between the guardianship of a jurisconsult and the sovereignty of the people, Ayatollah Beheshti supported Articles 5, 6[4] and 56[5] of the Constitution. In the course of public sessions of the Assembly of Experts, and in support of Article 56 and its consistency with Article 5, Ayatollah Beheshti argued that Article 5 stated that a fully qualified jurist (or board of jurists) be elected by a majority vote of the people, while Article 56 recognised people's right of self-determination. Thus, the Iranian people are the key point in both articles (Edareh Kol Omor Farhangi Va Rvabet Omomi Majles Shorai Islami 1985b, p. 523).

---

[2] "Article 107 (1979 Edition): Whenever one of the jurisprudents who fulfils the qualifications discussed in Article 5 of this constitution is acknowledged and accepted by the undisputed majority of the people as the leader and the exalted source of religious conduct (marja'-i taql-id)—as has been the case with the exalted source of religious conduct and the leader of the Revolution, Imam Khomeini, may his noble character be sanctified—this leader is in charge of the sovereignty of the command and all the responsibilities that derive from that. Otherwise, the Experts, who are elected by the people, consider and consult with each other about all the persons who have the qualifications to be the marja and the leader. If they find one Marja possessing of special significance for leadership, they introduce him to the people as the leader; otherwise, they designate three or five marja's, who are qualified for the leadership, and introduce them to the people as members of the Leadership Council" (Papan-Matin 2014, p. 184).

[3] "Article 108 (1979 Edition): The law on the number and qualifications of the Experts, the manner of their selection, and the internal guideline for their meetings of the first term, must be prepared by the jurisprudents of the first Guardian Council, it must be ratified by their majority vote, and submitted to the leader for the final approval. Whence, any change or review of this law falls within the authority of the Assembly of Experts" (Papan-Matin 2014, p. 184).

[4] "In the Islamic Republic of Iran, the country's affairs must be administered by reliance on the public vote, and through elections. These will include the election of the president, the deputies of the Islamic Consultative Assembly (Majles), the members of the councils, and other such institutions, or through a referendum in such instances as are determined in other articles of this document" (Papan-Matin 2014, p. 168).

[5] Absolute sovereignty over the world and human being belongs to God. And it is He who has made people sovereign over their social destiny. No one can take this divine right away or apply it to the interests of a special person or group. The nation exercises this God-given right in ways that are specified in the following articles (Papan-Matin 2014, p. 175).

The Authority of the Leader

Beheshti objected to the idea that the guardianship of the jurisconsult (*Velayat-e Faqih*) falls outside the framework of the constitution. In fact, Beheshti believed that the constitution differs from all other laws, in that it is an all-inclusive law that provides for everything with the supreme leader and his authorities not being exceptions. In other words, he argued that the constitution limited the latitude of government of which the guardianship of the jurisconsult formed an integral part. Thus, he supported the view that the supreme leader was to be held responsible for his performance within the framework of the constitution, and that the supreme leader is not higher than the constitution itself (Edareh Kol Omor Farhangi Va Rvabet Omomi Majles Shorai Islami 1985a, p. 870). In terms of Article 80, he asserted that the role of the supreme leader, or the leadership council, is general and that the members of the Assembly should note that the supreme leader or leadership council should not interfere in all matters of the state (Edareh Kol Omor Farhangi Va Rvabet Omomi Majles Shorai Islami 1985a, p. 873). Also, in a public session of the Assembly of Experts, considering the authority of the supreme leader (Article 110), Beheshti complained that some members behaved by ignoring any mistake made in the country as that of the people, and that the supreme leader or leadership council were regarded as infallible. He added that some members of the Assembly saw leadership as an organ separate from other organs of the government, and that the two form parallel governments separate from each other (Edareh Kol Omor Farhangi Va Rvabet Omomi Majles Shorai Islami 1985a, pp. 1175–1176).

Ayatollah Beheshti[6] was a pragmatic jurist and, together with some other important revolutionists, was one of the founders of the Islamic Republican Party in 1979. He was the first general secretary of this party between 1979 and 1981. On 28 June 1981, when attending a meeting of the Islamic Republican party, he and 72 other members were assassinated in a bomb attack by groups opposing the Islamic Republic of Iran. This act was widely thought to have been the responsibility of the People's Mujahidin of Iran (*Mojahedin-e-Khalq Iran*) (Moin 2000, pp. 234–243). The main goal of Beheshti was to support the idea of the Ummah and

---

[6] It is worth mentioning that from 1965 to 1970, he led the Islamic Centre in Hamburg where he was responsible for the spiritual leadership of religious Iranian students in Germany and Western Europe. He knew English and German very well and did his PhD in Islamic philosophy at Tehran University.

Imamate system (Hosseini Beheshti 2013, p. 226). He was critical of both Western and Eastern ideas and an advocate of the idea of *Maktab-e Vaseteh-e Islam* (Islam is a median school), which took an intermediate path between the two extremes of communism and capitalism. He proposed the Ummah and Imamate system, and correspondingly in the Assembly of Experts, he supported the idea of an Islamic Republic against secular republicanism and the spectre of those who supported the idea of an Islamic in the framework of what is known today as the divine legitimacy school. Ayatollah Beheshti espoused the view that the people were the source of legitimacy in contemporary-day Iran, and he believed that the role of the supreme leader fell within the framework of the constitution.

Ayatollah Hussein Ali Montazeri

Ayatollah Montazeri (1922–2009) was a major Iranian jurist and political activist, with considerable theoretical expertise in Islamic government and the guardianship of the jurisconsult. He was the first head of the Assembly of Experts for the 1979 Constitution and also the deputy supreme leader of Iran between 1986 and 1989. Furthermore, Ayatollah Montazeri was a *Marja-e-Taqlid* (the source of emulation) at the seminary of Qom from 1984 until his demise in 2009. With regard to the theory of the guardianship of the jurisconsult and the role of the supreme leader in contemporary Iran, he shifted his mindset over time from upholding divine legitimacy to that of the legitimacy of the people as its source.

In the early years from 1945 to 1985, Montazeri espoused divine legitimacy and followed the ideas of Grand Ayatollah Seyyed Hossein Borujerdi (Shia's leading *Marja* in Iran from approximately 1947 to his death in 1961) about the right of divine legitimacy for jurists. Khomeini influenced him and was effective in supporting sweeping powers, given to the supreme leader in the constitution of Iran (Montazeri 2009a, p. 25).

Ayatollah Montazeri offered two messages concerning the draft constitution before the election for the Assembly of Experts. In both, he asserted jurists must have a strong presence in the Islamic Republic of Iran, especially with respect to the constitution. In his first message, he declared that the president and prime minister must be Shia and preferably jurists, while judges must be chosen by jurists. Moreover, members of Guardian Council should have the right to veto parliament's bills (Montazeri 2001a, pp. 888–902). In his second message, he provided more detail. His main proposals included that the Islamic Republic of Iran should have three distinct powers, and that a just jurist, who is familiar with the issues of the day connected them to each other. It was better that the president be a just jurist or appointed by a just jurist. Members of parliament must be just jurists, and the laws and bills they pass approved by just jurists. The judges should be just jurists or appointed by just jurists and be familiar with Islamic laws (Montazeri 2001a, pp. 896–902).

While preaching at the Friday prayer in Tehran in September 1979, he referred to the lessons taken from the 1906 Constitutional Revolution, stipulating that it was not enough that some jurists supervise the bills from parliament, since this did not provide sufficient guarantee for an Islamic system. He recommended a just jurist who attained this government position came from God. According to Ayatollah Montazeri, this provided the Islamic system with a better option, for the just jurist could then transfer part of his power to other jurists and to the people; however the final decision was to be made by him (Kadivar 2012, pp. 2–3).

In a discussion about Article 110, Montazeri stated that, even if all the people vote for a particular president, but the supreme leader had not signed off this presidency, then this presidency was not valid in terms of Sharia law. The Iranian government was an Islamic Republic, meaning that rules must conform to Islam and be executed by one who is knowledgeable about Islamic ideology with respect to the discharge of the Divine Will (Edareh Kol Omor Farhangi Va Rvabet Omomi Majles Shorai Islami 1985b, p. 107).

Again, at another Friday prayer held in Tehran in September 1979, Montazeri, stated that there were two social systems: The liberal or democratic system which is based on popular votes without interference from any school, ideology or religion; a social system in which people follow a particular or single school or ideology (Kadivar 2012, p. 1). In fact, his views on the social structure of society had currency to those of Beheshti.

Ayatollah Montazeri initially supported the idea of divine legitimacy, and this was reflected especially in his comments on the draft constitution. This point was reinforced when he became the head of the Assembly of Experts for the Constitution, where he played an important role in adding several articles to the constitution to strengthen the role of jurists. The draft of the constitution had a primary focus on national sovereignty. However, Montazeri believed that *Marjas* (the source of emulations) and just jurists should hold the pivotal roles in Islamic government although in the draft there was no role assigned to them in this regard. Similar to Ayatollah Beheshti, Ayatollah Montazeri believed that there must be coherence between leadership and *marja'iat*. He also thought that the supreme leader must be a just jurist. Ayatollah Montazeri further asserted that he and Ayatollah Beheshti had a key role by way of adding the principle of guardianship of the jurisconsult to the draft of the constitution, to which other members of the Assembly of Experts then join. The rationale behind his action was to support the Islamic dimension of the Islamic Republic of Iran by way of affirming the importance and role of the supreme leader (Montazeri 2001a, p. 455). According to Ayatollah Montazeri, in the draft of the constitution, the president had great powers and the members of the Assembly of Experts were concerned about this as experience from the past had proved that the rule by one individual could lead to despotism. Hence, a majority of members of the Assembly of Experts sought to hand over this power from the president to Khomeini as a function of supreme leader (Montazeri 2009a, pp. 25–27). Furthermore, in response to the question on the role of Khomeini in terms of the addition of the principle of guardianship of the jurisconsult, Ayatollah Montazeri asserted that, as the head of The Assembly of Experts for the Constitution in 1979, he did not seek to interfere in this matter; however, Khomeini gave a positive vote to the revised constitutional law after its passage by the Assembly of Experts (Montazeri 2001a, p. 459).

By 1985, Montazeri had revised his position. He changed from supporting the principle of divine legitimacy to supporting the principle of legitimacy being derived from the people. He stated publicly that should a plural number of jurists be equally qualified, then five possibilities existed to determine their divine legitimacy. First, if several jurists had simultaneous potential qualifications for guardianship, then they also had the right to apply for this guardianship and sovereignty. Second, in cases where all had guardianship qualifications in general, only one possessed divine legitimacy to apply the right of guardianship. Third, where just one had divine legitimacy for applying this right. Fourth, all have divine legitimacy, but the utilisation of this guardianship is to be restricted by way of coordination and consensus between them. Finally, all have divine legitimacy, so they should act as a singular unified Imamate. (This position would also necessitate application with coordination and consensus amongst themselves.)

According to Ayatollah Montazeri, the outcome of the fourth and fifth possibilities were the same (Montazeri 2001b, pp. 195–196). He criticised all of the five aforementioned possibilities and rejected them, claiming these kinds of possibilities caused chaos within Muslim society, especially under critical situations such as war and where social tensions exist. He argued that a government was formed on the basis of either divine legitimacy, by the use of brute force or by way of legitimacy derived from the people. Rejecting the five possibilities noted earlier, he believed that it was impossible today to form a government with divine legitimacy. Likewise, he viewed as unreasonable the formation of a government based on force. Therefore, the best government was one which derived legitimacy from the people (Montazeri 2001b, pp. 195–202). He concluded it was necessary that during the absence of Imam Mahdi, jurists were capable of managing Muslim society. Likewise, he thought that it was necessary that people come to the public sphere and elect only one of the jurists to manage society. In sum, he believed that the people must know that making this choice is obligatory for them and avoiding it is a great sin. Furthermore, he thought that the people must know that not having a strong government resulted in the hegemony of unbelievers within Muslim societies (Montazeri 2001b, pp. 202–203).

The author believes that Montazeri still valued authority and the centralisation of power for the supreme leader despite thinking that this person must be selected by virtue of the popular vote. This conclusion about Montazeri is due to the fact that Montazeri endorsed both the election of supreme leader by the people and at the same time an absolute guardianship of jurisconsult. By 2008, Montazeri had extended his ideas, claiming that within the framework of the popular legitimacy school, individuals could choose government, based on perceived benefits, a separation of powers for political guardianship, judgeship and the issuance of fatwa. This guardianship could be granted to one jurist or to different jurists, although in the current context of Iran the centralisation of power in the hands of one jurist would, he believed, end in despotism and corruption. Ultimately, everything ought to be based on the consent of the people, who give power to the supreme leader to supervise the execution of Islamic directives within the Islamic society. Furthermore, he claimed that if people did not choose a religious government, the jurists' duty would then be a case of only giving advice to the Muslim society (Montazeri 2009b, pp. 22–25). It is clear that during his later life, Ayatollah Montazeri espoused the notion of a supervisory role for the supreme leader in political guardianship. However, he believed that the supervisory role of the supreme leader in the Islamic society fell within the category of school of popular legitimacy (Montazeri 2009b, p. 25).

In sum, Ayatollah Montazeri believed in divine legitimacy between 1945 and 1985, where the supreme leader acted as an ideologue, which displayed a structural similarity to socialist societies. He thought that the supreme leader should be a jurist and also a *Marja* (the source of emulation) simultaneously. After 1985, he shifted from divine legitimacy towards legitimacy derived from the people and gave more weight to the role of the common people in Islamic society. In his later life, he believed more in the supervision of the supreme leader with respect to Islamic religious directives and the necessity of popular consent about the form or type of government. It seems that he shifted from Political Islam to Social Islam and from an ideological society to a society wherein people played a more important role and had national sovereignty.

Ayatollah Nematollah Salehi Najafabadi

Ayatollah Salehi Najafabadi (1923–2006) was a well-known Iranian jurist and historian. He believed that the popular legitimacy and the divine legitimacy schools were essentially different and are, indeed, opposed to each other (Salehi Najafabadi 1985, p. 45). For him, it was impossible that all jurists, at the same time, could hold guardianship from God with respect to forming a government. Instead, he believed that by virtue of having a focus on rational and natural reasons, people should choose, by way of voting, a jurist for an Islamic government (Salehi Najafabadi 1985, pp. 178–179). The value of the people's votes was critical as was their choice of the supreme leader based on Article 5 of the constitution (Salehi Najafabadi 1985, pp. 46–47).

Ayatollah Salehi Najafabadi expressed some of Khomeini's ideas in support of the popular legitimacy school and the formation of government through the votes of the people (Salehi Najafabadi 1985, p. 47). Salehi Najababadi cited one of Khomeini's speeches before the formation of the Assembly of Experts for the Constitution that the main pillar of the Islamic Republic of Iran is the vote of the people (Khomeini 2010c, pp. 173–174). According to Salehi Najafabadi, a government irrefutably based on the popular vote gave every Iranian a sense that their vote contributed to their destiny and country (Salehi Najafabadi 1985, pp. 47–48). Salehi Najafabadi observed that at the final stages of the 1979 Islamic Revolution, when Khomeini arrived in Iran, his first speech in Behest-e-Zahra cemetery declared that he was able to form a government since he had been accepted by the Iranian people as the supreme leader. Thus, according to

Salehi Najafabadi, as far as formation of government was concerned, Khomeini believed in the votes of majority (Salehi Najafabadi 1985, p. 49). Furthermore, Salehi Najafabadi believed that the validity of the opinions of the members of the Assembly of Experts was derived from people's natural reason and, in the final analysis, it was the people who were the determining factor (Salehi Najafabadi 1985, p. 108). Therefore, referring to the message that Khomeini sent to the members of the second Assembly of Experts of the Leadership (Khomeini 2010a, pp. 3–7), Salehi Najafabadi asserted that the main point of the message was that the supreme leader who was to manage the Islamic government is elected by the people's votes and an Assembly of Experts. Therefore, the supreme leader who was not representative of the people would indeed be a counterfeit one (Salehi Najafabadi 1985, p. 73). Salehei Najafabadi believed that according to the ideas of Khomeini, a jurisprudent leader had authentic political guardianship. A supreme leader was elected by the votes of the people and that was why and how the leader had legitimacy. Thus, Khomeini emphasised the votes of the people and, accordingly, he formed the Assembly of Experts, since without it every jurist could form an Islamic government, and this would result in chaos in Muslim society (Salehi Najafabadi 1985, pp. 73–74).

Hojatoleslam wal-muslemin Davood Feirahi

Hojatoleslam wal-muslimin Davood Feirahi believes in the school of popular legitimacy and the leader's political guardianship through the will of the people as electors of the leader. Followers of this school noted Articles 6, 56, 107, 111[7] and 142[8] as particularly important (Feirahi 2012, p. 286). In Article 6, it stated that the whole administration of the Islamic Republic, and the supreme leader in particular, were to be elected by the votes of the people. Article 56 was devoted to right of national sovereignty. Article

---

[7] "The leader will be dismissed from his position in the case he is incapable of performing his legal responsibilities, becomes deficient in one of the qualifications mentioned in Articles 5 and 109; or it becomes evident that from the outset he has been lacking in some of the qualifications" (Papan-Matin 2014, p. 186).

[8] "The wealth of the leader, the President of the Republic, his deputies, the ministers, and their spouses and children, will be examined by the head of the judiciary before and after their term of office, in order to determine if it increased illegitimately" (Papan-Matin 2014, p. 194).

107 stated that members of the Assembly of Experts were elected by the people and were responsible for appointing or deposing the supreme leader. Article 111 demonstrated the means of the deposal of the supreme leader by the Assembly of Experts. Finally, Article 142 illustrated the supervisory properties of Iran's supreme leader (Feirahi 2012, pp. 286–287).

Feirahi provides evidence that Khomeini supported the school of popular legitimacy, especially in his later life (Feirahi 2012, p. 285). Ayatollah Ali Meshkini, the head of revision council of Iran's Constitution, in April 1989, asked Khomeini whether it was possible for the supreme leader to be a jurist only, and not a Grand Ayatollah and *Marja* (the source of emulation). Khomeini replied that from the time of the first constitution, he (Khomeini) had disagreed with the idea that the supreme leader should have the conditions of a *Marja* (the source of emulation) since, in the long term, this may cause trouble for Iranian people not wanting their society to live without a supreme leader. According to Khomeini, it was necessary for a supreme leader to be someone (jurist) who was able to defend the Islamic international of Iran in today's complicated world. For Khomeini, the Iranian people elected the members of the Assembly of Experts, and then this assembly in turn chose the supreme leader. Hence, the supreme leader was accepted by the people as well (Khomeini 2010d, p. 371). For, Khomeini when the selection of a supreme leader was necessary, it must be undertaken by the Assembly of Experts; this was the case, for example, after the death of the previous one. Also, it seems that he thought some of the current *Marjas* lacked political knowledge and the managerial skills necessary. Several preachers at the Friday prayers across the country asked the rhetorical question of Khomeini: When does a fully qualified jurist have guardianship of the Islamic society? Khomeini responded that a fully qualified jurist has guardianship in all aspects, namely politics, judgeship and issuing fatwa in the absence of Imam Mahdi (the 12th Shia Imam). However, he thought that forming an Islamic government must be based on majority votes—a fact recognised in Iran's constitutional law and, which in the dawn of Islam, was reflected in a statement of allegiance to Islamic rulers (Khomeini 2010b, p. 459). According to Feirahi, the above evidence indicated that Khomeini and some articles of the constitution supported the popular legitimacy school. It should be noted that in the later ideas of Ayatollah Montazeri and Hojatoleslam wal-muslimin Feirahi, they both became interested in the corpus of Ayatollah Naini.

THE DIVINE LEGITIMACY SCHOOL

Ayatollah Abdollah Javadi Amoli's Ideas

Ayatollah Javadi Amoli is an influential jurist and Qur'an interpreter, and advocate for the ideas of the divine legitimacy school ideas. He was also a member of the Assembly of Experts for the 1979 Constitution. He is a *Marja-e-Taqlid* (the source of emulation) at the seminary of Qom today.

Two Types of Guardianship
Ayatollah Javadi Amoli identified two different types of guardianships, namely cosmic (*Takvini*) and legislative (*Tashriei*). Cosmic guardianship involves the creation by God of the universe and all creatures therein. He divided legislative guardianship into two parts: In the first, there was the right of legislation given to Prophet Mohammad through revelation. This was the right of God, which was a universal command concerning human life over time. The second involved the explanation and implementation of this legislation by Prophet Mohammad and the Imams and jurists today (Javadi Amoli 2012, pp. 123–125). According to Ayatollah Javadi Amoli, the guardianship of the jurisconsult was associated with the latter (explanation and implementation of this legislation by Prophet Mohammad and the Imams and jurist today). He then argued that some interpreters believed that in the Qur'an and the Sunnah, the second guardianship involved only guardianship with respect to insane, weak or immature individuals. However, some other interpreters claimed that this guardianship in reality involved the management of Islamic society. For Ayatollah Javadi Amoli, the second interpretation was correct and the guardianship of jurisconsult was indeed the wise management of society (Javadi Amoli 2012, pp. 25–29).

Delegation and Guardianship
Ayatollah Javdi Amoli believed that, in Islam, affairs and rules addressing them divided into three different categories: individual, social and those pertinent to the particular school of Islam. As far as individual and social affairs were concerned, he argued that it was possible for the people to give their delegation to others, as was the case when one gave delegation to someone else in respect of their personal matters, or when citizens delegate to some representatives affairs related to their city. With regard to ideologically related issues, however, he stated that all decisions must be

made by those in the Imamate and guardianship positions (Javadi Amoli 2012, pp. 217–218). Citing verse 38 of Surah Ash-Shura,[9] verse 159 of Surah Al-i-Imran[10] and verse 59 of Surah An-Nisa[11] he noted that some societal concerns should be addressed by a leader consulting with the people; however, some affairs must be dealt with directly by the one in position of guardianship. He continued that it was sometimes difficult to distinguish between the people's duties on the one hand, and the leader's duties on the other. According to Ayatollah Javadi Amoli, the Islamic Republic of Iran completely conforms with the above-mentioned verses (Javadi Amoli 2012, p. 136). His answer to the question of whether the selection of the leader must be made by people was negative. He continued that in the light of the aforementioned verses and many other verses of the Qur'an, it was the duty of the Islamic Ummah to understand the Islamic rules and help the leader with that which God ordered (Javadi Amoli 2012, p. 420). He then argued that the Assembly of Experts was not representative of the people, but the Iranian people elect some jurist experts who, in turn, identify the right jurist to be the supreme leader (Javadi Amoli 2012, p. 425).

Ayatollah Javadi Amoli, also distinguished between a government based on delegation and one based on guardianship, stating that in the former everything was reliant on the votes of the people, and every law was founded on reason. If, however, a leader in an Islamic government had received his position from God, such as Prophet Mohammad and the Imams, such a government was indeed one with divine guardianship. He stated that—with the exception of the Islamic Republic of Iran, which is based on divine guardianship—all other democratic or pseudo-democratic countries were in fact only delegation-based (Javadi Amoli 2012, pp. 210–212). Essentially, a qualified jurist had been delegated by Imam Mahdi and played four roles including protecting the Qur'an and Sunnah, political guardianship, judgeship and the issuance of fatwa. He then concluded that

---

[9] "Those who hearken to their Lord, and establish regular Prayer; who (conduct) their affairs by mutual Consultation; who spend out of what We bestow on them for Sustenance" (38) (Yusuf Ali 2016, p. 487).

[10] "It is part of the Mercy of Allah that thou dost deal gently with them Wert thou severe or harsh-hearted, they would have broken away from about thee: so pass over (Their faults), and ask for (Allah's) forgiveness for them; and consult them in affairs (of moment). Then, when thou hast taken a decision put thy trust in Allah. For Allah loves those who put their trust (in Him)" (159) (Yusuf Ali 2016, p. 71).

[11] "O ye who believe! Obey Allah, and obey the Messenger" (59) (Yusuf Ali 2016, p. 87).

a qualified jurist did not receive these positions from the popular vote and did not need the votes of the people in this regard (Javadi Amoli 2012, pp. 225–226). It seemed he acknowledged a double sovereignty in the constitutional law, and he believed that the legitimacy of this system stemmed from the supreme leader (Javadi Amoli 2012, p. 452) who has three characteristics: absolute Ijtihad, absolute justice and political headship (Javadi Amoli 2012, pp. 137–140). Clearly, Ayatollah Javadi Amoli differentiated between delegation and guardianship, which were related matters. Also, he believed that the jurist guardian (*Vali-e Faqih*), after consultation with the people in some social affairs, made the final decision at his sole discretion. Furthermore, according to him, the position of the guardianship of jurisconsult did not require the people's vote. Rather, Ayatollah Javadi Amoli supported the centralisation of power bestowed on a qualified jurist.

Ayatollah Mohammad Momen's Views

Ayatollah Momen (1938–2019) was one of the important theoretical jurists of the divine legitimacy school in Iran. From 1982 to 2019, he had been an influential member of the Guardian Council and an important member of the Assembly of Experts covering four periods. Also, he was a member of the 1989 constitutional law revision council.

The Authority of the Muslims Stewardship (Vali-e Amr Moslemin)
Ayatollah Momen has used the term 'Muslims stewardship' (*Vali-e Amr Moslemin*) as a basis for his ideas when referring to Prophet Mohammad, the Imams and the supreme leader of Iran. For Momen, a jurist plays three roles in a Muslim society: first, that of political guardianship; second, the responsibility of judgeship; and third, issuing fatwa in the absence of Imam Mahdi. According to Momen, the first role, namely political guardianship, is the most important one linked to the Imam of the (Shi'a) Islamic Ummah (Momen 1995, p. 14). From his perspective, this results in today's jurists, especially the supreme leader, having the same position of rank and status within the Ummah as that of Prophet Mohammad and the Imams.

The Muslims Stewardship (Vali-e Amr Moslemin) and Allegiance/Vote
Ayatollah Momen believed that the guardianship of the jurisconsult was a subject related to divine legitimacy in that God gave this position to jurists;

it was, therefore, not pertinent to the rights of the people as such (Momen 2000, p. 19).

He believed that *bay'ah* (allegiance) was not a necessary condition for political guardianship (Edareh Kol Omor Farhangi Va Rvabet Omomi Majles Shorai Islami 1990, pp. 1313–1314). Furthermore, he asserted that, today, compliance with the Imams and stewardship was necessary for the whole Ummah, and that the Ummah must swear allegiance to Muslims stewardship (*Vali-e Amr Moslemin*) without any preconditions (Momen 1999, p. 36). In response to the question of whether political legitimacy of the present Iranian system was derived the votes of the people or the guardianship of jurisconsult, he stated based on his interpretation of Qur'an and Sunnah, that the legitimacy of this system was associated with Muslim stewardship. He also believed that Muslim stewardship (*Vali-e Amr Moslemin*) must be endowed by the Assembly of Experts (Momen 2000, pp. 12–13). In sum, the votes of the people were utterly superficial, and the Iranian people should just swear allegiance to the guardianship of the jurisconsult.

*The Muslims Stewardship (*Vali-e Amr Moslemin*) and Shura*

For Momen, Islamic law is permanent and universal. This makes it the duty of any administration to govern and guard these Islamic laws. Momen argued that should modifications be required to these laws, they became the duty of Muslim stewardship (*Vali-e Amr Moslemin*) as the main guardians and ones responsible for those laws (Momen 2009b, pp. 73–75). Similarly, the Shura or parliament falls under the dominance of Muslim stewardship today and the validity, legitimacy and restrictions on the authority of parliament's bills resides in the will and decision making of Muslims stewardship (Momen 2009b, pp. 76–79).

Referring to the verse 38 of Surah Ash-Shura and the verse 159 of Surah Al-i-Imran, Momen argues that the former relates to current affairs amongst Muslims and is not a matter for the political guardianship of Muslim stewardship, while the latter pertains to the battle of Uhud and so is not relevant to the consultation of the Prophet Mohammad with Muslims about all governance-related affairs (Momen 2009a, pp. 82–84).

Responsibilities and Duties of the Supreme Leader in the Absence of Imam Mahdi

First, Ayatollah Momen believed that the realm of the rulership of the supreme leader was similar to the mandate of Prophet Mohammad and the Imams, namely, the whole world (Momen 2000, p. 12). Obviously, Momen believed in the traditional idea of a religious empire, which is far different from the modern idea of nation-state.

Second, he believed that the sovereignty of the supreme leader remained general and absolute and could not be subject to popular opinion nor their votes. He maintained that limiting the guardianship of jurisconsult was as inappropriate as is limiting that of the Prophet Mohammad and the Imams. Thus, during a session of the 1989 constitutional law revision council, he objected to adding the term 'absolute' to the term 'Guardianship' in the constitution arguing that it would not change any-thing since the jurisconsult was not to receive his guardianship from law and addition of the term 'absolute' would imply otherwise (Edareh Kol Omor Farhangi Va Rvabet Omomi Majles Shorai Islami 1990, p. 700). In fact, he believed that the power of the supreme leader was absolute and general already; that the supreme leader was of a higher rank than the constitutional law and, indeed, not bound by the framework of the consti-tution itself. It was noteworthy that, eventually the term 'absolute' was added to the 'guardianship of jurisconsult' in the body of the constitu-tional law. Thus, Ayatollah Momen defines 'absoluteness' of the guardian-ship of the jurisconsult as not being restricted by profane law or national territories.

Third, with regard to financial resources, he believed that all revenue from Anfal,[12] Khums (one fifth), Zakat (Alms Tax), Zakat al-Fitr,[13] Waqf[14](donation) and tax must be under the control of the supreme leader for he knew best how these monies should be spent for the benefit of the people (Momen 2007, pp. 3–26).

For Ayatollah Momen, the dichotomy of duties and rights in Shia cul-ture demonstrated a strong bias towards duties and espoused the centrali-sation of power by the Muslim stewardship. This centralisation of power comes with a religious authority, and the legitimacy of this system derives from stewardship, not people's votes. Indeed, the validity of the electoral system is also tied to Muslim stewardship.

---

[12] It's of Arabic origin, it was mentioned on the Qur'an. The meaning of Anfal is the spoils or treasures of war.

[13] Zakat al-Fitr is charity given to the poor at the end of the fasting in the Islamic holy month of Ramadan.

[14] An endowment made by a Muslim to a religious, educational, or charitable cause.

Ayatollah Mohammad Taqi Mesbah Yazdi

Ayatollah Mesbah Yazdi is an influential jurist and Islamic philosopher and also an adherent of the divine legitimacy school. He was also an important member of the Assembly of Experts for four terms.

Like Ayatollah Javadi Amoli, Ayatollah Mesbah Yazdi divided guardianship into two different types: Cosmic (*Takvini*) and legislative (*Tashriei*). He believed the former was associated with all creatures of this world and their creation by God. In this regard, he believed that miracles performed by the Prophet Mohammad, the Imams and probably some jurists were associated with cosmic guardianship as conferred by God. However, legislative guardianship (*Velayat Tashriei*) related to the management of the Islamic society by Prophet Mohammad, the Imams and jurists for today (Mesbah Yazdi 2011, pp. 79–80).

The Role of People in an Islamic State

Ayatollah Mesbah Yazdi stated that an important question in political philosophy was that of who should manage the government; in other words, who should rule the society and whose government orders should be obeyed by the people. This was something related to what he called 'possessing legitimation'. He argued that it was the right of God to grant such position to whoever He wills. Thus, he thought that it was a right granted to Prophet Mohammad, the Imams and today, to qualified jurists. Following this explanation, Ayatollah Mesbah Yazdi made a distinction between legitimation and acceptability (Mesbah Yazdi 2011, p. 51). In his view, legitimation was opposite to usurpation so that any government not having this legitimacy from God was an illegitimate government (Mesbah Yazdi 2011, p. 53). In connection to acceptability, he stated that acceptability meant the acceptance of a government by the people such that the people were content with it. He then identified two types of governors and governments: first, governors and government that were accepted by the people and supported them and, second, governors and government that force the people to obey them (Mesbah Yazdi 2011, p. 53). He argued that from a Shia perspective, the Prophet Mohammad received his legitimacy from God and thereafter the people accepted him by *Biyah* (the swearing of allegiance). He argued that the Imams had their legitimacy from God and that the formation of a government by them was with the acceptance of the people. He argued that, today, the legitimacy of a qualified jurist is derived from God and also the Imam Mahdi. Likewise, according to him, a qualified jurist was somehow appointed by the Imam Mahdi. But he thought that the establishment of the government was also with the acceptance of the people (Mesbah Yazdi 2011, pp. 59–65). In addition, he believed that the Assembly of Experts was elected by the people in order to discover the right jurist for the supreme leadership role; that is to say, the duty of the Assembly of Experts was indeed to discover the supreme leader (Mesbah Yazdi 2010a, pp. 51–53). He thus concluded that the Iranian people could not of themselves grant legitimacy to the supreme leader of Iran (Mesbah Yazdi 2010b, p. 25).

The Guardianship of the Jurisconsult and Constitutional Law
Referring to Articles 5, 57 and 107 of the constitution (especially in its revised 1989 form), he stated that the role of the supreme leader and the Assembly of Experts was to support the idea of divine legitimacy (Mesbah Yazdi 2010a, pp. 59–61).

Ayatollah Mesbah Yazdi posed the question as to whether the supreme leader was higher than the constitutional law, or vice versa. His view was that the supreme leader was definitely in a higher position than the constitutional law since the supreme leader was indeed appointed by God and Imam Mahdi. The constitutional law then derived its legitimacy from the supreme leader. He also noted that the supreme leader ratified the constitutional law, and it was this that gave legitimacy to it, not the popular vote. Nevertheless, he stipulated that it was important that the supreme leader was not higher than the orders of God, and, indeed, the supreme leader was limited in function to the framework of Sharia law (Mesbah Yazdi 2011, pp. 116–117). In 1989 he argued the term 'absolute' should be added to the 'guardianship of jurisconsult' in the revised version of the constitutional law in order to indicate that the supreme leader was indeed ranked higher than the constitution (Mesbah Yazdi 2011, p. 118). He supported his reasoning by mentioning that when Khomeini appointed Bazargan as the Prime Minster of the Islamic Republic of Iran, Khomeini said to Bazargan "in light of the guardianship that I received from God, I appointed you (Bazargan) as Prime Minster". He argued that according to Khomeini, the government of Bazargan was thus a lawful administration. Around two years before the revision of constitution in 1989, upon the order of Khomeini, the Expediency Discernment Council of the System was formed. It was originally set up to resolve disagreements between the parliament and the Guardian Council. According to Ayatollah Mesbah Yazdi, Khomeini formed this council even though it was not part of constitutional law and this action indicates that Khomeini was higher than the constitution. Moreover, according to Ayatollah Mesbah Yazdi, when Khomeini signed the presidency decree of some of the presidents of the Islamic Republic of Iran (for example, Ablohassan Banisadr, Mohammad Ali Rajai and Ayatollah Sayyed Ali Khamenei), he wrote to them that: "I *appointed* you for the presidency of the Islamic Republic of Iran". Ayatollah Mesbah Yazdi argued that this means the authority of Khomeini was higher than what was specified in the constitution, namely merely issuing a validating decree for a president after the election by people. He thought that this was due to the absoluteness of guardianship of the jurisconsult (Mesbah Yazdi 2010a, pp. 42–44). As further evidence for his view, also referred to some institutions such as the Supreme Council of the Cultural Revolution[15] and the Special Clerical Court,[16] which were not part of the constitution but were formed on the direct orders of Khomeini's further sanction (Mesbah Yazdi 2011, p. 119).

It is clear that Ayatollah Mesbah Yazdi believed that the legitimacy of the supreme leader of Iran derived from God and the Imam Mahdi, and the Assembly of Experts did no more that discover the one who was a qualified jurist for the supreme leadership of Iran. The popular votes were thus superficial in this regard. Mesbah Yazdi's ideas as a political activist have had a profound effect on his followers for whom he is a 'spiritual father'.

Concluding Analysis

This chapter has outlined and discussed the influence of Political Islam and the ideologies of some important thinkers who were adherents of two different schools, namely the divine legitimacy and the people legitimacy schools, which increased in significance following the 1979, in particular, after Khomeini's passing. Five concluding analytical points can be made.

Firstly, with regard to the explanation of the situation, after the 1979 Islamic Revolution, the advocates of jurisprudential Islam dominated

---

[15] The Supreme Cultural Revolution Council that was formed in December 1984 was in fact continuation of the Cultural Revolution Headquarters. The declared goal of the Supreme Council of the Cultural Revolution is to ensure that the education and culture of Iran remains '100% Islamic' as Ayatollah Khomeini directed. This includes working against outside 'cultural influences' and ideologies.

[16] The Special Clerical Court is an Iranian court system for examining transgressions within the clerical establishment. It was formed by Khomeini in 1979.

Iranian government and society. They effectively removed or marginalised all other political groups and parties in Iran from the organs of power (e.g. the liberal Islamic or secular factions). This was done with reference to the constitutional law of Iran, as it quickly established the supreme religious leader as the highest rank and position. This new regime managed the war between Iraq and Iran in spite of the fact that this conflict caused huge loss of life and property for the Iranian people. Moreover, they managed to defeat key secessionist groups in the outer regions and provinces of Iran. As mentioned previously, the three decades from the 1960s to the 1980s were ideologically driven decades in Iran. However, in subsequent decades there has been a slow shift from the dominance of ideology to an era where people play a participatory role based on their electoral votes. Despite an ideological stance still manifested in some Iranian administrations and thinkers, it is not as strong as it was from the 1960s to the 1980s. Also, after Khomeini's death, the two important schools of divine legitimacy and popular legitimacy have become part of the ongoing public discussion in Iran. The main argument between them concerns the role of people in terms of the legitimacy of the system and the management of society. Moreover, it is important to mention that in contemporary Iran, the followers of liberal Islamic schools, including followers of Bazargan and Shariati, have been generally known as marginalised groups; this is the case, for instance, *Shourai Falan Meli-Mazhabi Iran* (the Council of Nationalist-Religious Activists of Iran) (Arjomand 2009, p. 99). In general, they have supported popular legitimacy school in these kinds of arguments.

Secondly, with regards to the system of knowledge, thinkers of both schools of divine legitimacy and people legitimacy recognised the important role of jurisprudential Islam. Major thinkers of the two schools believed that jurisprudential Islam could manage an Islamic society in both spiritual and temporal matters. Also, both of these schools believed that forming an Islamic government was necessary, since, firstly, without a government the Islamic society may be plunged into chaos and, secondly, without a government, most of the Islamic laws were not implemented. Also, both schools believed that a fully qualified jurist who was to manage an Islamic society should be *mujtahid* (jurist), just, knowledgeable and with managerial capabilities in political matters.

Thirdly, with regard to the system of norms, thinkers of the divine legitimacy school believed that the role of the people is superficial, and that the people should just accept a supreme leader to form an Islamic government. Adherents of the divine legitimacy school focus only on the duty of the people and think that it is their obligation to accept an Islamic government. In this regard, they emphasise terms such as obedience, followership, raison d'état and public well-being in an Islamic society. However, those in the popular legitimacy school believe that, within the framework of Islam, it is up to the people to elect the supreme leader. Further, these thinkers believe in both duties and rights for Iranian people. In this regard, they stress terms such as freedom, democracy and the right to self-determination, the right to hold elections and the role of national interest in Islamic society.

Fourthly, regarding the system of government, thinkers in the divine legitimacy school believed that a fully qualified jurist's legitimacy derived from God and Imam Mahdi. Thus, the Islamic government is formed from the top-down. However, thinkers in the popular legitimacy school believe that a fully qualified jurist's legitimacy is granted by the Iranian people such that an Islamic government is formed from the bottom-up, in the framework of Islamic law.

Thinkers of the divine legitimacy school also believed in the principle of the legitimacy of government and sovereignty of the jurist on behalf of God and the Imam Mahdi. According to them, the Assembly of Experts is tasked to simply discover the supreme leader and the acceptance of this by the people results in the establishment of an Islamic government. However, the popular legitimacy school has two ideas. First, Ayatollah Beheshti articulated a notion that the origin of the legitimacy of the government and the sovereignty of the jurist is from God and the Imam Mahdi via general appointment—meaning that a fully qualified jurist who has the characteristics of being *mujtahid* (jurist), *Marja-e-Taqlid* (the source of emulation), fair, knowledgeable and with managerial capabilities in political matters, received this position as a general appointment from God and Imam Mahdi. However, the election of a person as supreme leader and the establishment of legitimacy of an Islamic government should be left up to the people through the Assembly of Experts. Second, Ayatollah Montazeri, especially in his later life, believed that in the absence of the Imam Mahdi even the basis of the legitimacy of the jurist and his governance is contingent upon the people's acceptance and approval. Ayatollah Montazeri believed that his idea is in line with the popular legitimacy school.

Furthermore, thinkers in the divine legitimacy school have posed the question of who should rule an Islamic society. This is a question generally raised by classical political philosophers who believe that the answer is a fully qualified jurist. The divine legitimacy school has a greater focus on duties in the answer to this question. However, in the popular legitimacy school, the main question is how to rule an Islamic society. This seems to be the main question proposed by modern political philosophers. To answer this question, thinkers in this group seek to form a model that lies between the duties and rights for the Iranian people.

Fifthly, with regard to public policy, and in connection with domestic decision making, thinkers from the divine legitimacy school generally believed in controlling policy whereas those from the popular legitimacy school believed in representative policies. In this regard, thinkers in the divine legitimacy school believed that the power of the supreme leader was higher than the constitutional law and that the constitutional law derived its legitimacy from the supreme leader. On the other hand, thinkers from the popular legitimacy school claimed that the power for the supreme leader was founded within the framework of constitutional law, the legitimacy of which was derived from the people. Also, thinkers in the divine legitimacy school suggest a lifelong tenure for the supreme leader. However, intellectuals from the popular legitimacy school posit that it is better to limit the length of tenure of any given supreme leader to ten years.

So far as foreign policy is concerned, thinkers from the divine legitimacy school, based on traditional idea of Islamic empire, opine that the territories of governance of the supreme leader include all areas occupied by Muslims. Generally, they sought to emphasise the role of the enemy and, in particular, the confrontation of Western civilisation with Muslim civilisation. However, thinkers from the popular legitimacy school, based on the modern idea of nation-statehood, consider that the territory is restricted to Iran only and generally advocate the idea of leadership is limited to Iran only. Furthermore, they generally advocate the idea of dialogue between different civilisations.

REFERENCES

Arjomand, S. A. (2009). *After Khomeini: Iran Under His Successors*. New York, NY: Oxford University Press.

Edareh Kol Omor Farhangi Va Rvabet Omomi Majles Shorai Islami. (1985a). *Sorat Mashroh Mozakerat Majles Baresi Nhaei Ghanon Asasi Jomhori Islami* [The Final Review of Constitutional Law of Islamic Republic] (Vol. 2). Tehran, Iran: Edareh Kol Omor Farhangi Va Rvabet Omomi Majles Shorai Islami.

Edareh Kol Omor Farhangi Va Rvabet Omomi Majles Shorai Islami. (1985b). *Sorat Mashroh Mozakerat Majles Baresi Nhaei Ghanon Asasi Jomhori Islami*

[The Final Review of Constitutional Law of Islamic Republic] (Vol. 1). Tehran, Iran: Edareh Kol Omor Farhangi Va Rvabet Omomi Majles Shorai Islami.

Edareh Kol Omor Farhangi Va Rvabet Omomi Majles Shorai Islami. (1990). *Sorat Mashroh Mozakerat Shuorai Baznegari Ghanon Asasi* [The Revision of the Constitutional Law]. Tehran, Iran: Edareh Kol Omor Farhangi Va Rvabet Omomi Majles Shorai Islami.

Feirahi, D. (2012). *Nezam Sisasi va Dolat dar Islam* [Political System and State in Islam]. Tehran, Iran: Enteshrat Samt.

Hosseini Beheshti, S. M. (2012). *Mabani Nazari Ghanon Asasi* [The Theoretical Foundations of Constitutional Law] (Vol. 3). Tehran, Iran: Entesharat Bogheh.

Hosseini Beheshti, S. M. (2013). *Hezb Jomhori Eslami (Goftarha, Goftegoha va Neveshtarha)* [Islamic Republican Party (Speeches, Talks and Texts)]. Tehran, Iran: Entesharat Rozaneh.

Javadi Amoli, A. (2012). *Velayat-e Faghih Velayat-e Feghhahat va Edalat* [The Guardianship of Jurisconsult the Guardianship of Jurisprudence and Justice]. Qom, Iran: Nashre Asrae.

Kadivar, M. (2012, 2016). *Seir Tahavol Andisheh Ayatollah Montazeri ghesmat chaharom [The Evolution of Thought Ayatollah Montazeri Part 4]* Retrieved from http://mkadivar.wpengine.com/?p=4013

Khomeini, S. R. (2010a). *Sahifeh Imam: Majmoe asar Imam Khomeini bayanat, payamha, mosahebeha, ahkam, ejazat sharei va nameha* [Sahifeh-Ye Imam: An anthology of Imam Khomeini's speeches, messages, interviews, decrees, religious permissions, and letters] (Vol. 18). Tehran, Iran: The Institute for Compilation and Publication of Imam Khomeini's Works.

Khomeini, S. R. (2010b). *Sahifeh Imam: Majmoe asar Imam Khomeini bayanat, payamha, mosahebeha, ahkam, ejazat sharei va nameha* [Sahifeh-Ye Imam: An anthology of Imam Khomeini's speeches, messages, interviews, decrees, religious permissions, and letters] (Vol. 20). Tehran, Iran: The Institute for Compilation and Publication of Imam Khomeini's Works.

Khomeini, S. R. (2010c). *Sahifeh Imam: Majmoe asar Imam Khomeini bayanat, payamha, mosahebeha, ahkam, ejazat sharei va nameha* [Sahifeh-Ye Imam: An anthology of Imam Khomeini's speeches, messages, interviews, decrees, religious permissions, and letters] (Vol. 8). Tehran, Iran: The Institute for Compilation and Publication of Imam Khomeini's Works.

Khomeini, S. R. (2010d). *Sahifeh Imam: Majmoe asar Imam Khomeini bayanat, payamha, mosahebeha, ahkam, ejazat sharei va nameha* [Sahifeh-Ye Imam: An anthology of Imam Khomeini's speeches, messages, interviews, decrees, religious permissions, and letters] (Vol. 21). Tehran, Iran: The Institute for Compilation and Publication of Imam Khomeini's Works.

Mesbah Yazdi, M. T. (2010a). *Porshesha va Pasokhha* [Questions and Answers] (Vol. 2). Qom, Iran: Entesharat Moasesh Amozeshi va Pazhoheshi Imam Khomeini.

Mesbah Yazdi, M. T. (2010b). *Porshesha va Pasokhha* [Questions and Answers] (Vol. 1). Qom, Iran: Entesharat Moasesh Amozeshi va Pazhoheshi Imam Khomeini.

Mesbah Yazdi, M. T. (2011). *Negahi Gozara be Nazariyeh Velayat-e Faghih* [A glance at the Theory of the Guardianship of Jurisconsult]. Qom, Iran: Entesharat Moasesh Amozeshi va Pazhoheshi Imam Khomeini.

Moin, B. (2000). *Khomeini: Life of the Ayatollah*. New York, NY: Thomas Dunne Books.

Momen, M. (1995). Velayate Elahi va Hokomat Islami (1) [Divine Guardianship and Islamic State (1)]. *Majaleh Fiqh Ahl Biyt Elahemosalam, 47*, 13–49.

Momen, M. (1999). Beiat (1) Adlei Beiat dar Quran [Allegiance (1) the Evidence of allegiance on the Quran]. *Majaleh Fiqh Ahl Biyt Elahemosalam, 51*, 34–61.

Momen, M. (2000). Din va Mosharekat Sisasi [Religion and Political Participation]. *Faslnameh Olom Sisasi, 7*, 12–19.

Momen, M. (2007). Maliyat dar Hokomat Islami [Tax in the Islamic State]. *Majaleh Fiqh Ahl Biyt Elahemosalam, 45*, 3–26.

Momen, M. (2009a). Ekhtiyar Valy-e Amr dar Ghanongozari [The Authority of Stewardship about legislation]. *Majaleh Fiqh Ahl Biyt Elahemosalam, 55*, 80–91.

Momen, M. (2009b). Ghavanin Sabet va Motoghayer [Static and Dynamic Rules]. *Majaleh Fiqh Ahl Biyt Elahemosalam, 56*, 60–81.

Montazeri, H. A. (2001a). *Khaterat* [Memoirs] (Vol. 2): Author.

Montazeri, H. A. (2001b). *Mabani Fiqhi Hokomat Islami* [The Juridical Foundations of Islamic State] (M. Salvati, Trans., Vol. 2). Tehran, Iran: Entesharat Saraei.

Montazeri, H. A. (2009a). *Enteghad az Khod* [Self Criticism]: Author.

Montazeri, H. A. (2009b). *Hokomat Dini va Hoghogh Ensan* [Theocracy and Human rights]. Tehran, Iran: Entesharat Saraei.

Papan-Matin, F. (2014). The Constitution of the Islamic Republic of Iran (1989 edition). *Iranian Studies, 47*(1), 159–200.

Salehi Najafabadi, N. (1985). *Velayat_e Faghih: Hokomat Salehan* [The Guardianship of Jurisconsult: The Righteous Government]. Qom, Iran: Moaseseh Khadamat Farhangi Rasa.

Yusuf Ali, A. (2016). *Quran* [English translation]. Retrieved from http://tanzil.net/#trans/en.yusufali/1:1

CHAPTER 10

Conclusion

This chapter reviews the material by comparing the three selected views according to the main question and research theory predicated on the methodology outlined earlier in this book.

Human beings have a cognitive proclivity to build their own dogmatic ethical systems and then affect to expand them into a vanity that challenges the transcendent. True political commentators and thinkers understand instinctively that there is more to Politics than following and demonstrating the precise letter of the law with regard to common or popular aspirations, conventions, desires and skills—not from a disrespect for the rules per se (that is a necessary precondition for mental and physical self-discipline). The rules surrounding politics often conflict or are paradoxical, and they do not always apply. So, there must be an ethic underlying such rules. Genuine political thinkers intuitively believe there should be more respect for the ethic than the rules, and that individual politicians should be strictly honest and orientate themselves towards the good rather than obsessing over the correct forms and styles. Truth and honesty should generate—or regenerate—this ethic.

In Chap. 1, an explanation of the research, the significance of the topic and also the relevant methodology of the book was provided. Chapter 2 explored the key concepts covered by the topic, focusing on an explanation of Political Islam and ideology and extrapolating the three main different political viewpoints of Islam based on the philosophies and corpus of Khomeini, Shariati and Bazargan, respectively.

© The Author(s) 2020   193
S. M. Lolaki, *Diverging Approaches of Political Islamic Thought in Iran since the 1960s*,
https://doi.org/10.1007/978-981-15-0478-5_10

In Chaps. 3, 4, 5, 6 and 7, the views of the three important thinkers were analysed. These chapters made comparisons between three Iranian schools of thought as represented by Khomeini, Shariati and Bazargan with special reference to their ideologies, concerns about the West and their advocacy for a return to Shia culture, their views about relations between politics and religion and finally considerations about an Islamic state. The research method was based on the theory that these three Iranian thinkers attempted to transform religion into a political ideology. Accordingly, Chaps. 3, 4, 5, 6 and 7 elaborated on the ideological paradigms of these thinkers with regard to religion in the political realm. These chapters analysed the ideology that emerged from reactions to Western modernity and examined the implications of returning to Shia Islamic culture. Returning to a Shia culture was manifested in two trends: that of the relationship between politics and religion, and the political realities of an idealised Islamic state. Chapter 3 provided a definition of ideology; analysed notion of 'otherness' that arose as a result of Western versions of modernity; and elaborated on the roots of Western modernity. The return to a Shia cultural society was addressed and the expansion of ideas by the three chosen thinkers with regard to the relation between politics, religion and the Islamic state. In the light of this, Chaps. 3, 4, 5, 6 and 7 analysed in more detail the various ideological conceptualisations of Khomeini, Shariati and Bazargan.

Chapters 8, 9 and 10 were devoted to Political Islam. These chapters made comparisons between the three Iranian schools of thought as represented by Khomeini, Shariati and Bazargan. These chapters shed light on the evolution of their thinking and the implications for government in post-revolution Iran with special reference to their ideologies. Chapter 8 investigated the influence of the three Iranian thinkers and their followers on Iran's constitution after the 1979 Islamic Revolution. Chapter 9 examined authority and democracy among two different jurisprudential schools, namely divine legitimacy and the popular legitimacy schools. These two perspectives are both followers of the ideas of Khomeini, though with different interpretations and conclusions. This chapter is devoted to concluding remarks informed by the pertinent theory.

Research Focus

An investigation of Political Islam in Iran from the 1960s until now has been the main focus here, with a concentration on how contemporary political Islamic thought was transformed into a revolutionary ideology and hegemony by Khomeini, Shariati and Bazargan.

The main methodological task of this research has been to explicate how these three important intellectuals played a major role in the Islamic Revolution in 1979 and show how Khomeini, Shariati and Bazargan differed in the way they viewed the role played by religion in the political realm of the state and society. It also examined the way they commonly utilised religion in their political discourses. The core methodological research for my text consisted of critical analysis and discussions of major sources in the writings of Khomeini, Shariati and Bazargan. It sought to combine these three socio-political outlooks into a coherent presentation, a work that has thus far not been addressed in the academic studies of Political Islam. Accordingly, socio-political aspects of the views of each of these political thinkers was studied. In analysing their views, an ideological comparison was made between these views in five key aspects, which revealed how these intellectuals could eventually change the regime (the Pahlavi Dynasty) and incorporate the Islamic ideologies they had developed into the political structure of the new government (the Islamic Republic of Iran). The aspects mentioned earlier included Firstly, explanations of the situation in terms of the subjective and objective views these intellectuals held about the political position of Iranian society over various periods. Secondly, the system of knowledge indicative of a basic reference knowledge presented through the ideas of these three intellectuals. The fact that reference knowledge differed over time, and from one state to another was clarified. For instance, intuitionism, empiricism and philosophy were completely commonplace among the intellectuals of ancient Greece; however, philosophy had an overriding impact. Another example shows that in contemporary Iran, the religious Shia thought proposed by these thinkers mostly ruled out other ideas. Thirdly, the system of norms that defines a number of values including democracy, independence, equality and peace was assessed. What matters is how these elements are prioritised in a society like Iran and, in particular, by the above thinkers. Fourthly, the system of government, which creates the strategies and format of a government, is a factor which determines the system of knowledge and norms. Fifthly, public policy determinations of the administration were elucidated in connection with internal and foreign affairs. The secondary sources were used to discuss the political thoughts of these three intellectuals in an analysis of the differences and similarities, confluences and congruities, between these three schools of Political Islam in Iran.

1—With regard to the explanation of the situation, this research has sought to explain how Political Islam formed in contemporary Iran stem-

ming from the Constitutional Revolution of 1906. The traditional political discourse of Iran (which until then had been based on monarchy and
sharia law) faced a major conflict due to modernity and modernistic ideas
imported from the West. From the perspective of the Iranian thinkers and
people, the authoritarian monarchy was the one most responsible for the
impoverishment of Iranian society. Iranian intellectuals and people thought
that the cause of poverty, famine and injustice was primarily the fault of the
authoritarian monarchy. In this regard, most Iranian thinkers and the people sought to change both the political structure of Iran and bring about
emancipation from the authoritarian regime. At the commencement of
the constitutional Revolution, four principle discourses emerged in Iran.
Firstly, the discourse of secularism where thinkers such as Mirza Malkam
Khan and Mirza Fath-ali Akhundzade supported the constitutional system
and advocated a Western-style separation between religion and state.
Secondly, ideas related to the discourse of an absolutist state found disagreement with the constitutional system as seen in critiques by Mohammad
Rafie Tabatabai and Nezamollmae Tabrizi. Thirdly, a novel discourse was
put forward by jurists, who supported the constitutional system, and
included people like Ayatollah Mohammad Hossein Naini and Ayatollah
Mohammad Kazem Khorasani. Fourthly, the discourse presented by conservative jurists who disagreed with the constitutional system including
jurists Ayatollah Mohammed Kazem Yazdi and Ayatollah Sheikh Fazlollah
Nouri (Ferasatkhah 2009, p. 359).

In the long run, the third and fourth discourses had the greatest impact
on Iranian society. It is noteworthy that Iranian society at that time and
thus the jurists at that time played a major and influential role. Ayatollah
Naini and his followers believed that the system offered by the new constitutional law was sufficient to reduce the overall power of the state and
the absolutist dynasty of the Shah moving society towards a constitutional
monarchy and transferring the main organs of power over to the Iranian
people. He argued that the supervision of parliament by five jurists was
provided for in the new system which could, simultaneously, satisfy the
needs of pious people. In contrast, Ayatollah Sheikh Fazlollah Nouri and
his followers believed that Islam presented a comprehensive package for
both temporal and spiritual matters and any legislation, if called for, must
be undertaken by jurisprudents based on Islamic principles as they alone
possess this right. He concluded that there was no need for constitutional
law and parliament. Also, he believed that as long as the monarchy obeyed
the jurisprudents and Sharia law, there should be no problem with their

rule. (Hosainizadeh 2007, pp. 80–82). Clearly, he and his followers perceived no serious alternative and supported the status quo of Iran without any changes. The differences between constitutionalists, and also the disputes between these two schools, on the one hand, and the interference in Iran by Russia and Britain, on the other hand, caused chaos in Iranian society, and ultimately led to the failure of the Constitutional Revolution. The year 1906 was a turning point when the absolute monarchy was superseded by a constitutional monarchy.

According to the Iranian scholar Hamid Ahmadi, the major constitutionalists sought four important goals during the Constitutional Revolution: Firstly, to advance Iranian society along progressive lines as they believed that compared to the West, Iran had significant internal problems, and it was necessary to reconstruct the country in terms of economics, politics and culture. Secondly, the goal was to establish political stability and security in Iran. At that time Iran was facing significant challenges with regard to its international borders and domestic security. Thirdly, to break the hegemony in Iran of Great Britain and Russia as the two major international players, and to prevent their interference in the internal affairs and agency of Iran. Constitutionalists sought political and economic autonomy for Iran. Fourthly, to realise their dream of establishing a participatory democracy for Iranian society (Ahmadi 2014, pp. 1–3).

The Pahlavi dynasty emerged from turbulence and chaos during the Constitutional Revolution in 1925. Reza Shah and his son, Mohammad Reza Shah, sought to overturn modernisation and modernity through a strong authoritarian orientation. While they pursued the first and second goals of the Constitutional Revolution mentioned earlier, it seems that they sacrificed the third and fourth goals of the thinkers of the Constitutional Revolution. Also, they virtually marginalised all other groups, especially the Islamic and Nationalist groups during their tenure.

In fact, the period of the Pahlavi dynasty, which marginalised political Islamic groups, can be divided into two periods: the first part consisted of the 1920s to the 1950s when some thinkers and groups deemed Islam the best solution to both the temporal and spiritual problems of the society. Among those groups were *Fada'iyan-e Islam* (Devotees of Islam), *Nehzat-e Khodaprastaneh Sosialist* (Movement of God-Worshipping Socialists) and *Hesb Melal Islami* (Islamic Nations Party). The second part comprised the 1960s and the 1970s in which the three thinkers (Khomeini, Shariati and Bazargan) and their followers not only thought of Islam as the best solution to the spiritual and temporal problems but affected to convert the religion into an ideology. The efforts of Khomeini, Shariati and Bazargan and their followers became the main reason for the success of the Islamic Revolution in 1979. In comparison to nationalist, secular, socialist and liberal groups, they played a more important role. After the Revolution and ratification of the constitution of the Islamic Republic of Iran, jurisprudential Islam became dominant. However, after the death of Khomeini, followers of jurisprudential Islam divided into two different schools of thought, namely the divine legitimacy and popular legitimacy schools. Also, it should be noted that the four goals espoused by the constitutionalists were followed by the 1979 Islamic revolutionists. However, the last goal (democracy) has been a subject of controversy between the two jurisprudential schools and also among the wider Iranian populace.

Furthermore, in the subsequent decades (from the 1990s to the present) there has been a slow shift in public sentiment from the dominance of an abstract ideology to an era where people have a greater comprehension of their own role based on their electoral votes. Moreover, some marginalised groups, namely liberal Islamic, secular and nationalist ones such as *Shourai Falan Meli-Mazhabi Iran* (the Council of Nationalist-Religious Activists of Iran), *The National Front of Iran* (Jebhei Meli Iran) virtually supported the popular legitimacy schools during the then controversies and in events like elections. They prefer that Iranian society adopts legal and political reforms that are incremental. However, some minor secular groups such as monarchist groups believe in changing the Islamic Republic through revolution or intervention by foreign countries.

2—With regard to the system of knowledge, the three decades from the 1960s to the 1980s was the period when advocates of Political Islam formed an amalgam of Islamism, nationalism and modernism. Religion, however, gradually became more important than the other aspects, considerations and dimensions. These thinkers believed that a *Maktab-e Vaseteh-e Islam* (school of median Islam) system would take the middle way as some kind of organic continuum between Marxism and Capitalism. Despite these external influences, these three all believed that sociopolitical terms and concepts should be based on Iranian-Islamic values.

When the individual thinkers looked at social and political phenomena using differing methods and references to jurisprudence, history and the interpretation of the Qur'an, they unsurprisingly produced contrasting criticisms about the views of one another.

The ideas of Khomeini centred on both collectivism and individualism, but as far as political ideas were concerned, he leaned towards collectivism. He thought that all Prophets and Imams came to the public sphere to sacrifice themselves for society. However, as far as economics is concerned, he was an advocate of the free market economy and the right of private ownership.

Shariati appeared to draw inspiration from Marxism and Existentialism (Vahdat 2002, p. 132) in order to validate his statement that Iran needed intellectuals similar to Calvin and Luther to trigger an Islamic Protestantism (Boroujerdi 1996, pp. 114–115), while advocating for a new Islam lacking the attendance of conservative clergies. Naturally, this rebuttal attracted some criticism from the clergy who accused Shariati of representing Sunni Islam and Communist ideas (Keddie and Richard 1981, p. 223). Moreover, Shariati, although interested in Western socialism, generally criticised many liberal and democratic ideas of the West (Soroush 2005, pp. 183–184). Indeed, his corpus demonstrated an interest in European philosophy and a tendency towards communitarian ideas.

Bazargan had been impressed by the discipline, technology, workplace ethics, sense of duty, freedom, democracy and human rights in the West. Also, he was affected by analytical philosophy and presented some of his ideas on this during the 1950s. Bazargan was interested in positivistic ideas and sought to introduce into Islamic thought some scientific ideas based on empiricism. According to him, one could observe prosperity, honesty and hygiene in the routine life of people in European countries even though they do not believe in the Qur'an and are not true Christians. In fact, he believed that in those countries, people had accidentally assumed the way determined for humans by the prophets (including prosperity, honesty and hygiene). He asserted that those priests in the West who disagreed with scientific findings in the Middle Ages were not real followers of divine ideas. Thus, he attempted his own interpretation to establish ties between scientific matters and Islam. In this way, he sought to strip religion of the trivial superstitions upheld by some people (Pedram 2004, pp. 110–112).

Overall, Bazargan was an optimistic democrat who over time shifted his emphasis from Political Islam to Social Islam. Within the framework of Social Islam, Islamist groups and thinkers sought to undertake social changes and reforms, and then assume control of government through democratic channels (Feirahi 2015). Bazargan's theory, particularly in his later life, displayed a tendency towards social liberalism.

In summary, Khomeini and Shariati inclined towards ideas revolving around a prompt emancipation for the common people; in contrast, Bazargan prioritised the development of democratic culture and an appreciation of freedom amongst the masses. Khomeini aimed to revive Islam, as he understood it, whilst Shariati expected or intended to reconstruct it in some manner; however, both wished for Islamic civilisation to become as powerful as it had been in the past. Both Khomeini and Shariati adhered to relatively revolutionary ideas, whereas Bazargan articulated reformist ideals. Khomeini sought to prove Islam was a complete package for the temporal and spiritual matters; Bazargan followed this line initially until 1979 shifted his focus to more spiritual matters. In contrast, Shariati believed the same but his ideas about Islamic Protestantism focused more on the temporal affairs of Islam. As the founder of religious intellectualism in Iran, Bazargan attempted to defend Islam from Marxist ideas using the scientific methods of the 1950s. During that time, Marxist thinkers such as Taqi Arani defended Marxist ideology using the scientific language of dialectics. Despite this fact, Shariati continued the way of Bazargan in religious intellectualism. In the 1960s, Marxist ideas, in general, focused on emancipation, but, Shariati, showed Islam as an emancipating religion with his ideas, while at the same time appealing to Iranian society, Marxist groups and Bazargan as well (Aghajari 2003, pp. 79–80). For, Khomeini and his followers, Bazargan and Shariati were seen as coming under the influence of foreign ideologies and as such they broke sharia laws (Table 10.1).

3—With regard to the system of norms, it is important to note that the 1979 Revolution espoused several ideas and slogans, which were popularised and inspired by these thinkers and the Iranian people. But two of them were more important than others. The first was the slogan: independence, freedom and the Islamic Republic, while the second was related to 'Neither the East nor the West, the Republic of Islam'. All of these thinkers disagreed with the West and East hegemony and supported the Non-Aligned Movement based around freedom, justice and independence (and the breaking of any hegemonic ties with both West and East).

The 1960s through to the 1980s turned out to be a very important era, in that some nativism and ideas on the independence movement emerged simultaneously in Latin American, Asia and Africa. Our three Iranian thinkers pursued some of these ideas for Iran, elucidating the establishment of new concepts and norms. Terms such as a return to the Islamic-Iranian self, Iranian nativism, Iranian existence and Iranian original identity emerged. By creating new meaning for some traditional concepts

Table 10.1 The system of knowledge

A definitive comparison and contrast between Khomeini, Shariati and Bazargan

Similarities	These thinkers believed that a **Maktab-e Vaseteh-e Islam** (school of median Islam) system would: Take the middle way as some kind of organic continuum between Marxism and capitalism during the 1960s to the 1970s
	These three commentators all believed that socio-political terms and concepts should be based on **Iranian-Islamic values**
Differences	There is a subtle difference between these thinkers in terms of their **reference** to Islam Khomeini focused on **jurisprudentialism** Shariati focused on the **history of Islam** Bazargan focused on **the Qur'an** That is, their ideas about religion were similar, but their basic approaches, **methods and references** were different
	Khomeini and Shariati leaned towards **emancipation for the masses** Bazargan worked to instal **freedom and votes for the people**
	Khomeini sought the **revitalisation** of Islam, whereas Shariati pursued the **reconstruction** of it
	Khomeini and Shariati both wanted **Islamic civilisation** to become powerful again as it had been in the past Khomeini and Shariati followed **revolutionary ideas** Bazargan leaned towards gradual **reformist ideals**

and terminology, they sought to establish new norms in the context of Iran and to encourage Iranian folk to participate in the public discourse.

By introducing new norms into the Iranian society, the broad characteristics of an ideal Islamic state were defined. Khomeini cited characteristics such as support for oppressed people, governments of justice, freedom and independence.

Following the death of Khomeini in 1989, two competing schools of thought emerged—namely the divine legitimacy and the popular legitimacy schools—revealing different expectations and norms. Advocates and thinkers of the divine legitimacy school prioritised the duties of the common people and stressed terminology such as obedience, followership, raison d'état and the public well-being in an ideal Islamic society. However, voices in the popular legitimacy school championed both duties and rights for the ordinary Iranian people, and emphasised ideas such as freedom, democracy, the right to self-determination and the role of national interest. In general, it is clear that these thinkers all focused on freedom, justice, independence and egalitarian ideals for contemporary Iran suggesting these extant qualities be expanded.

Khomeini focused mostly on the territorial independence and sovereignty of Iran. Form his perspective, foreign hegemony was more catastrophic to the people than domestic tyranny. In contrast, for Bazargan, state despotism was worse than foreign hegemony, and personal freedom was paramount compared to the relative independence of the state. Furthermore, whilst Khomeini and Shariati supported and followed emancipatory ideals, Bazargan focused on the freedom of society as a fundamental human right. Also, it should be recalled that the language Khomeini used to communicate with the common folk was very simple and effective: Ordinary people liked terms such as justice for the poor and national independence for Iran. Giving verbal expression to oppression was very pertinent to the Iranian people (Foran 1993, pp. 389–390). Abrahamian, an Iranian scholar, believes that Khomeini had a greater effect on the religious middle class, while Shariati mostly influenced the modern middle class. Also, more importantly, although both Khomeini and Shariati gave new meanings to some Shia concepts, Shariati was more successful in bridging the gap between the two classes (Abrahamian 1982, pp. 533–535). Abrahamian states that although Shariati showed many anticlerical attitudes in his work, his followers believed that Khomeini was an especially charismatic leader who could make the revolution successful and establish a monotheistic order as a special spiritual leader (Abrahamian 1982, pp. 534–535). Abrahamian asserted that the revolutionary interpretations by these three thinkers of some key Islamic terms and the redefinition of some Shia concepts (such as the oppressed, jihad and Imamate) helped the oppressed masses struggle for the liberation of society from the Shah, whilst upholding the idea of charismatic leadership. In fact, he believed that these intellectuals had indeed transformed Islamic thought into a political ideology which, in the West, was referred to as Political Islam or fundamental Islam (Abrahamian 2008, pp. 144–145).

Moreover, the observations by Khomeini on the historic role of jurists and the religious-minded people in the Tobacco movement (1891), the 1906 Constitutional Revolution, the establishment of a seminary at Qom (the 1920s) and the uprising on 15th of Khordad (5 June 1963) found popular resonance. However, to him, the latter date[1] was the most important one and also the main pillar of the 1979 Islamic Revolution (Khomeini 2010a, p. 407). In contrast, Bazargan thought the 1951 nationalisation of Iran's oil industry movement ignited the 1979 Islamic Revolution; he was interested in the ideas of Mohammad Mosaddegh's regarding the freedom of the people and national independence of Iran. Besides, Bazargan was a prominent member of the National Front of Iran against the Shah Dynasty, and nine years after the coup, in 1963, he and some of his companions formed the Freedom Movement of Iran (as a political party) based on Islamic ideology. They accompanied other nationalist and secular groups in the National Front of Iran. It is necessary to mention that the National Front of Iran was formed by some influential people and important political parties which were part of the opposition against Shah at that time (Jahanbakhsh 2001, pp. 91–94). In addition, Bazargan was more interested in the progressive discourse espoused by some Constitutional Revolution thinkers including Ayatollah Mohammad Hossein Naini (Jahanbakhsh 2001, p. 93) with a subtle difference though: while Ayatollah Mohammad Hossein Naini and Ayatollah Mohammad Kazem Khorasani, using jurisprudence, attempted to open a liberal way for the participation of people in managing Iranian society, Bazargan sought to do the same task in the framework of his interpretation of the Qur'an. Shariati's attitude towards Mohammad Mosaddegh was similar to that of Bazargan though with the difference that unlike Bazargan, Shariati was not an organisational figure (e.g. he was not associated with any party); also, Shariati sought to pave the road for people's participation with reference to the early history of Islam.

It appears that Khomeini was worried about the difference between the two jurisprudential Islam discourses during the Constitutional Revolution and thus sought to reconcile these two schools using his model of *Velayat-e Faqhih* (the guardianship of jurisconsult). Also, the experience of the 1951

---

[1] The demonstrations of 5 June 1963 and 6 June 1963 in Iran were against the arrestment of Ayatollah Khomeini after a speech delivered by him during which he had condemned the king and Israel at the same time. The Shah's regime was taken by surprise by some rallies which albeit were suppressed shortly by police and armed forces, indicated the significance and power of (Shia) religious opposition to Shah, and Khomeini as a prominent political and religious leader. Fifteen years later, Khomeini headed the Iranian Revolution which overthrew Shah and his regime and established the Islamic Republic of Iran.

nationalisation of the Iran oil industry episode led Khomeini and his followers to attempt to dominate liberal and secular groups in the Revolution
to prevent a repetition of history. In fact, in the course of the nationalisation of the Iran oil industry, some jurists such as Ayatollah Seyyed Abol-
Ghasem Mostafavi Kashani and some Islamic groups such as *Fada'iyan-e*
Islam (Devotees of Islam) had virtually accepted the leadership role of
Prime Minister Mohammad Mosddegh though they had some differences
with Mossdegh and secular nationalist groups. To complicate matters further the movement finally failed as a result of the coup against Prime
Minister Mohammad Mosaddegh in 1953 launched by Mohammad Reza
Shah with the help of the US and UK governments, where apparently,
Khomeini and his followers believed that liberal and secular groups could
not overthrow the Pahlavi dynasty and, more importantly, break completely the influence that foreign powers had over Iran.

After the 1979 Islamic Revolution, the followers of Political Islam
always made a separation between themselves and followers of the other
schools. In fact, they deemed other groups secular and thus outsiders were
under the effect of Eastern and Western ideas. Consequently, they gradually eliminated other groups by pushing them out of the public sphere in
Iran. This happened for the first time in the course of the election of the
Assembly of Experts for the Constitution in 1979 during which political
groups such as the liberals and socialists (communists), who were averse to
the Islamic Republic and the principle of guardianship of jurisconsult,
failed to garner a sufficient number of votes to be admitted to the Assembly.
The next stage was during the first few years after the victory of the Islamic
revolution when a similar situation happened between the advocates of
jurisprudential Islam and followers of liberal Islam who were in general
averse to the principle of guardianship of the jurisconsult. Similar differences exist today between the followers of the two schools of jurisprudential Islam, namely divine legitimacy and the popular legitimacy schools
with the former believing that the latter have become secular and liberal
(Table 10.2).

4—Regarding the system of government, the three thinkers suggested
different models. Shariati suggested two theories: first, a revolutionary
government based on the Ummah and the Imamate and second,
'Mysticism, Equality and Liberty' although his untimely death meant he
did not fully articulate and explain this idea. However, his corpus had a
great impact on the formation of the 1979 constitution.

Table 10.2   The system of norms

A definitive comparison and contrast between Khomeini, Shariati and Bazargan

Similarities	The 1979 Revolution espoused two **slogans** which were massively popularised: 'Independence, freedom and the Islamic Republic' 'Neither the east nor the west, the republic of Islam' All three thinkers believed that the messages within these collective slogans, especially the themes of the first one, were the reason that the 1979 revolution was necessary. This is what created an urgency for change within the mood of the common people and encouraged the masses to stand up for the 1979 revolution
	All of these thinkers **disagreed** with: The west and east hegemony (US vs. USSR)
	They all **supported**: The non-aligned movement based around freedom, justice and independence
Differences	Khomeini focused largely on the **independence** of Iran because from his standpoint foreign hegemony was more catastrophic than internal despotism For Bazargan, state **despotism** was more disastrous than foreign hegemony, and freedom was more important than the independence of the country Khomeini and Shariati upheld and pursued general **emancipatory ideal**. Bazargan focused on the **freedom of society** as a basic human right.
	For Khomeini **the uprising on 15th of Khordad** (5 June 1963) was the main pillar of the 1979 Islamic Revolution. Bazargan thought **the 1951 nationalisation of Iran's oil industry movement** ignited the 1979 Islamic revolution.
	Thinkers of the school of divine legitimacy focused only on **the duties** of the common people and emphasised terms such as obedience, followership, raison d'état and public well-being in an Islamic society. However, thinkers in the school of popular legitimacy believed in both **duties and rights** for the Iranian people, and stressed terms such as freedom, democracy, the right to self-determination and the role of national interests in Islamic society.
	The followers of Bazargan, Shariati and the school of popular legitimacy, all believe that although the people and state reached some kind of independence through the revolution, there was a failure to completely follow through on the freedom and justice aspects.

Shariati's first theory, Ummah and Imamate, is seen as one of the most important and controversial theories. Shariati believed that the Ummah refers to a people who have a common ideology and goals, and who move forward to achieve those goals (Shariati 2011, p. 360). Also, he asserted that, from an Islamic political perspective, the Imamate refers to political leadership that seeks to move people forward and guide the society. He believed that this is in contrast with Western political leadership which just seeks merely to manage a society (Shariati 2011, pp. 361–362). The opponents of Shariati believed that the democratic model he proposed and the revolutionary leadership he placed in it had provided a broader opportunity for the clergy to become more powerful and had unintentionally become a reason for accepting the principle of guardianship of jurisconsult, particularly among the youth (Jahanbakhsh 2001, p. 174). In fact, although Shariati objected to the rulership of the clergies (jurisprudents) in an Islamic society (during the absence of Imam Mahdi), by proposing his theory, he bridged the gap between the clergies and intelligentsia and paved the road for the leadership of Khomeini (Foran 1993, pp. 370–371). Moreover, this model of Shariati's could be thought of as a recast of Marxist-Leninist ideas in the framework of Shia beliefs, since Shariati believed that the theory of Ummah and Imamate relates especially to the revolutionary transition period, and that once the society develops and matures in its thinking, democracy becomes a good model for it. However, the nature and model of his democracy was Shura and allegiance. Shariati believed a leader can be elected by the people but cannot be deposed by them. According to Shariati, democracy has two approaches: (a) the public representative should be elected by the people; (b) the duration of the elected term must be extensive. Further, for Shariati, political leadership is synonymous with the Imamate (Shariati 1980, p. 232).

Shariati used the form of Lenin's ideas such as a democratic centralism[2] and its complementary concept of the councils (the soviet government) for the revolutionary transitional period. Then, he recast this form into the framework of Shia ideas and terminology. In addition, with this theory, he sought to justify the difference between Sunni and Shia perspectives concerning successors of Prophet Mohammad. Also, he sought to justify the Imamate of the 12 Shia Imams based on the fact that Shia Muslims believe that Prophet Mohammad appointed Imam Ali as the first Imam on his testament and this succession was continued by Imam Ali for appointing the Imam after him. Historically, during the Imamate period of the Shia

---

[2] A combination of centralism and democracy within a revolutionary party. The communist party sought to use this concept to centralise the leadership of the party and motivate obedience among the members in a manner that in addition to have the feeling of freedom they dynamically involve in execution of the orders of their leader.

Imams, the Muslim society was deemed unprepared for an election to find a successor to Prophet Mohammad. However, during the absence of Imam Mahdi, the Muslim society became sufficiently mature enough to elect a council for temporal leadership. From a Sunni perspective, the Shura system became effective following the death of Prophet Mohammad in terms of choosing the first Caliph (Abu Bakr). Thus, Shariati sought to explain these theological differences from a sociological point of view between Sunni and Shia perspectives as well (Sadra 2012, p. 306). Furthermore, although Shariati rejected both liberal democratic or social-ist systems (wherein hegemony was manifested by the wealthy few or that of a one-party state), his own theoretical model was very similar to a one-party system but one that was predicated upon an Islamic ideology (Keddie and Richard 1981, pp. 221–222). In contrast, advocates of Shariati's model believe that it is a genuine Shura-based democratic model which made a significant contribution in further democratisation processes as seen in the 1979 constitution (Aghajari 2003, pp. 123–124). It is note-worthy that Shariati believed in an Islam devoid of clergies and that he thought that the existence of clergies was a historical phenomenon (Aghajari 2003, p. 39). Also, Shariati with his theory, simultaneously rejected imported ideologies of Marxism and liberalism and equally the rulership of the clerics (Ahmadi 2004, p. 114).

Shariati's second model was 'Mysticism, Equality and Liberty'. This model was generally supported by Neo-Shariati or the Left School that follow Shariati's ideas. Neo-Shariatism are followers of Social Islam today. Shariati proposed his first model when he was delivering a speech in Hussainieh-e-Ershad around 1970, whereas he presented his second theory in 1977. For some neo-Shariatists Shariati's second theory was pro-posed when he was more experienced and his thoughts fully fledged. According to this interpretation, the outcome of the ideas of Shariati today are revealed in social democracy and mysticism (Nasim Bidari 2015, p. 1). Also, some neo-Shariatists believe that his second model supports a liberating theology for contemporary Iran (Manoochehri 2011, pp. 34–36). Thus, they have sought to extend these views in modern Iran.

On the other hand, Khomeini chose an Islamic Republic system, which was based upon *Velayat-e Faqhih* (the guardianship of jurisconsult). As founder of the Islamic Republic of Iran, he employed both modernity and tradition in this system. On the one hand he used duty, guardianship and expediency; on the other hand, he paid attention to rights, freedom and

law. These two sets of concepts form a political order in the Iranian context and are expressed through *fiqh* (Islamic jurisprudence).
Based on the constitution of the Fifth Republic of France,[3] the constitutional law of the Islamic Republic of Iran eventually turned out to be an
amalgamation of the ideas of Bazargan and the principle of *Velayat-e
Faqhih* (the guardianship of jurisconsult), divine law, human rights,
democracy, theocracy, *fiqh*'s (jurisprudent's) authority and popular sovereignty (Abrahamian 2008, pp. 163–164).

Bazargan, on the other hand, had sought an Islamic Democratic
Republic identified by two different types of government: Dictatorship
and democracy. According to him, Islam had grounds to support the democratic model of government (Bazargan 2014, pp. 419–420). Around
1964, when he was in prison as a political activist during the reign of Shah
Mohammad Reza Pahlavi, Bazargan came to the view that the Islamic
state has a special ideology superior to other ideologies such as communism and socialism. He thus sought to propose an ideological model for
an Islamic state. However, he criticised himself for this theory after the
Islamic Revolution in 1979 (Bazargan 2014, pp. 421–422). Around and
after the 1979 Islamic Revolution, Bazargan believed in an Islamic
Democratic Republic of Iran. However, in terms of content, he revised his
position from Political Islam to Social Islam believing in a government
based on the consent of the people in respect to both form and management. Bazargan's Islamic model (Islamic Democratic Republic) took its
credibility from Qur'anic inspiration and interpretation as opposed to
imported ideologies from the West or East. Later, he relied mostly on
normative values to prove the validity of his model claiming the aim of the
prophets was to promote belief in God and the eternal world.

Unlike Bazargan and Shariati, who, in general, disagreed with a government ruled by Jurisconsults and Jurisprudentialists, Khomeini believed
in a system of government ruled by one just jurist. For Bazargan, the role
of institutions were major players in Iranian civil society where he was
allied to the Freedom Movement of Iran (as a political party) in 1961 and
the Human Rights Organisation in 1978 (Jahanbakhsh 2001, pp. 82–84).
Shariati was among the founders of the Foreign Branch of Freedom
Movement of Iran. He involved himself in this job especially when he was
a PhD student in France. Nonetheless, he was, in general, an intellectual
not associated with any party. In contrast, Khomeini, in general, placed

---

[3] Fifth Republic is the system of government in France since 1958 onwards.

Table 10.3   The system of government

A definitive comparison and contrast between Khomeini, Shariati and Bazargan

Similarities	At first, more or less every Islamic school attempted to reform and resist the **constitutional monarchy**
	However, after the actions of the Shah and his followers they started to work towards a **regime change** with revolutionary ideological ideas
Differences	All three thinkers suggested different **systems of government** Shariati suggested two theories: Firstly, a revolutionary government based on the **Ummah and the imamate** Secondly, **'mysticism, equality and liberty'** For Khomeini, an Islamic Republic system based upon *Velayat-e Faqih* (the guardianship of jurisconsult) was chosen Bazargan, on the other hand, proposed an **Islamic Democratic Republic** Bazargan and Shariati disagreed with a **government** ruled by Jurisconsults and Jurisprudentialists
	Khomeini believed in a system of **government** ruled by one just jurist Advocates and thinkers in the school of divine legitimacy believed that the genuine authority of a fully qualified jurist derived from God and the Imam Mahdi. Thus, the ideal Islamic **government** is formed from the **top-down** However, thinkers in the school of popular legitimacy believe that the authority of a fully qualified jurist is granted by the Iranian people through elections and that an Islamic **government** is formed from the **bottom-up**, within the framework of Islamic law

more emphasis on an organisation of clerics and encouraged the clergy to conduct political activities in the mosques both before and after the Revolution. As a consequence, mosques have played the role of political parties and as a faction of institutions in the civil society in contemporary Iran. In general, in post-revolutionary Iran, the role that should be played by political parties has always been a matter of controversy among the revolutionist community which nowadays comprises followers of divine legitimacy and popular legitimacy schools (Table 10.3).

5—In terms of public policy, Khomeini disagreed with any armed insurrection in his revolutionary fight against the Pahlavi dynasty. Even when he was in exile in Najaf city, some close companions requested he advocate for *The People's Mujahidin of Iran* (Mojahedin-e-Khalq Iran), a religious and militant organisation. He refused to do so. Khomeini stated that *The People's Mujahidin of Iran*, referring to Qur'an and Nahj al-Balagha,[4] had sought to convince him to opt for an armed movement against the Shah

---

[4] The most famous corpus attributed to Imam Ali.

but he had refrained from that since he thought this group did not have a robust commitment to Islam (Khomeini 2010d, pp. 143–145). Likewise, Shariati disagreed with the use of force against the dynasty. In fact, he espoused an informative, gradualist and emancipative movement (Shariati 2016, p. 1). Shariati disagreed with the rulership of jurisprudents, some of the groups who were interested in his views—for example, the *Forqan* Group—resorted to terror to achieve their goals after 1979. They assassinated some eminent jurists and followers of jurisprudential Islam, including but not limited to Ayatollah Morteza Motahhari and Ayatollah Mofatteh (Hosainizadeh 2007, pp. 276–278). These two jurists, especially Ayatollah Motahhari, were close companions of Khomeini. It is necessary to reiterate that the 1953 coup against Prime Minister Mohammad Mosaddegh was an important historical event and had a profound impact on the political situation of Iran. First, it caused the Shah to suspend his relations with political opposition activists, and focus security on the intelligence agency (SAVAK). In addition, it led opposition groups, especially political Islamic groups, towards the idea of changing the political regime from that of the Pahlavi Dynasty to something entirely different. Some Islamic groups supported the use of force against the Shah regime overtly or covertly and Bazargan backed the use of force by *The People's Mujahidin of Iran* (Mojahedin-e-Khalq Iran) between 1965 and 1975, given the founders had views close to his own and Ayatollah Mahmoud Taleghani. The latter was a close companion of Bazargan and also a major founder of the Freedom Movement of Iran (as a political party) (Shariati 2016, p. 1). However, after 1979, he disagreed with any kind of armed movement. It is noteworthy that from 1965 to 1975 when the founders of *The People's Mujahidin of Iran* were arrested and executed or imprisoned by Shah's regime, in general, all political religious groups and important figures, except Khomeini, were among their supporters. After this period, some of the members who were out of prison changed their minds and tended towards to communism and socialist ideas forming a new organisation called *Peykar* (Battle) where they lost the support of political religious groups and other important figures. Despite imprisonment some of the members kept their radical Islamic ideas and once released from prison they revived *The People's Mujahidin of Iran*. Some also disagreed with the new constitution and the government, which was to be ruled by Jurists and Jurisprudentialists, and within a short time of their release, they resumed their armed activity but, this time, against the government of the Islamic Republic (Hosainizadeh 2007, pp. 347–349). After 1979, based on the new constitutional law and the dominance of jurisprudential Islam, all other political groups were either gradually pushed out or totally removed from the political scene by more powerful jurisprudential Islamic groups. This trend began with the imprisonment and execution of a small number of supporters of the Shah who could not exit the country (Abrahamian 2008, p. 181). Also, some of the supporters of the armed conflict, for example, *The People's Mujahidin of Iran*, were arrested and sentenced to death or imprisoned. It is important to mention that these groups assassinated some important figures in the body of the Islamic Republic government, for instance in 1981 president Mohammad Ali Rajai and Prime Minister Mohammad Javad Bahonar (Abrahamian 2008, p. 181). Furthermore, some secessionist groups such as *Komoleh party of Iranian Kurdistan* and the *Democratic party of Iranian Kurdistan* were destroyed in the course of the war in Iran's Kurdistan. The remaining members of both secessionist and armed groups left Iran and resided in Iraq receiving support from Saddam Hussein, the then leader of Iraq during the Iran-Iraq War. Moreover, some other parties and groups, especially those with views close to communism and socialism and in line with supporters of jurisprudential Islam in terms of anti-American ideas such as *Tudeh Party of Iran* (Hezb Tudeh Iran) and *The Organisation of self-sacrificers of the people of Iran* (majority) (Fedayan-e Khalq Aksariat) were destroyed as well, since the revolutionists believed that they were followers of Western or Eastern ideas (Hosainizadeh 2007, pp. 350–355).

The National Front of Iran (Jebhehi Meli Iran) disagreed with the parliamentary bill containing lex talionis and also the compulsory wearing of the Hijab for women in the public sphere, and were pushed out of the scene by advocates of jurisprudential Islam (Hosainizadeh 2007, p. 279). The same thing happened to Abolhassan Banisadr, the first president of the Islamic Republic of Iran, who was against the hegemony of Jurists, Jurisprudentialists and the clergies in all affairs of the state and disagreed with the new revolutionary institutions as well. He was finally deposed by parliament and this resolution was confirmed by Khomeini because of the serious conflicts that Banisadr had with adherents of jurisprudential Islam (Hosainizadeh 2007, pp. 338–349).

Likewise, the grand Ayatollah Sayyed Mohammad Kazem Shariatmadari (1905–1986) was accused of plotting against Khomeini. A prominent Marja-e-Taqlid (the source of emulations) who was known as the spiritual father of *The Muslim Republican People's Party* (Hezb-e Jomhurikhah-e Khalq-e Musulman), he held politically liberal Islamic views (Hosainizadeh 2007, pp. 320–321) and was placed under house arrest for the rest of his life. Also, Sadegh Ghotbzadeh who was a close assistant of Khomeini during his exile in France in 1978, and was Iran's foreign minister from 30 November 1979 to August 1980, during the Iran hostage crisis, was executed in 1982 for allegedly plotting the assassination of Ayatollah Khomeini and the overthrow of the Islamic Republic (Esposito and Voll 1996, p. 66). He confessed to inciting a coup against Khomeini with the cooperation of people including Ayatollah Sayyed Mohammad Kazem Shariatmadari. Likewise, Ebrahim Yazdi who was a close companion of Khomeini during his exile in France in 1978 and served after the Islamic Revolution as deputy prime minister and minister of foreign affairs in the interim government of Bazargan resigned in protest at the Iran hostage crisis in November 1979 and his resignation caused him to be marginalised. Since the death of Bazargan in 1995 hitherto, Yazdi had led the Freedom Movement of Iran. It is noteworthy that the marginalisation of Bazargan occurred in 1982 at the end of his first parliamentary term.

In terms of domestic policy, followers of jurisprudential Islam under Khomeini's leadership took a number of actions in relation to the Iranian hostage crisis.[5] The followers of Khomeini called the event a Second Revolution and Bazargan and his members of the interim government resigned in protest over this and other issues on 6 November 1979. However, Khomeini supported intervention since he and supporters of jurisprudential Islam believed that America was to launch another coup in Iran similar to that of 1953 (Abrahamian 2008, p. 168). Khomeini also supported the Cultural Revolution in Iran between 1980 and 1983, which involved the closing of universities and the removal of academics and students who supported ideas and trends from the East and the West. The Cultural Revolution was called the Third Revolution by its supporters

---

[5] An event during which 52 American diplomats and citizens were taken as hostage for 444 days (from November 4, 1979 to January 20, 1981). It happened when a group of Iranian students belonging to the Muslim Student Followers of the Imam's Line who supported the Iranian Revolution stormed the US Embassy in Tehran.

(Abrahamian 2008, p. 177). In addition, the role of the judicial system based on sharia law was given more importance than common law (Abrahamian 2008, pp. 176–177) and new military-related and religious organisations such as Revolutionary Guards emerged. In terms of foreign policy, Khomeini supported exporting revolutionary ideas. Khomeini, in a post-revolution speech, asserted that the Iranian-Islamic Republic is a good role model for other countries to follow, because Iran was an autonomous country and the Islamic Republic was devoted to breaking the hegemonic agendas of the superpowers (Khomeini 2010b, p. 336). In addition, during Khomeini's leadership anti-Western sentiment erupted after the hostage crisis. Also, the issuance of a fatwa ordering the execution of Salman Rushdie, author of *The Satanic Verses* (1988) a book that sparked a wave of protest within Islamic countries (Esposito and Voll 1996, p. 71). Issuance of that fatwa caused a rapid deterioration in the relations between Iran and some Western countries to the extent that they recalled their ambassadors. Likewise, the Iran-Iraq War between September 1980 and August 1988 caused more conflict with several Muslim Arab countries such as Saudi Arabia supporting the Iraqi government and especially president Saddam Hussein during the war. More conflicts erupted also between Sunni and Shia and Arabs and Persians in the region (Esposito and Voll 1996, p. 69).

Although, Khomeini was more interested in a free market based on rational economics, trade and the rights of private ownership (Vahdat 2002, p. 167), in general, he tended towards political and economic collectivism during his leadership. This was partly due to conflict associated with domestic and foreign policies adopted by him and the followers of jurisprudential Islam, as mentioned above. Another reason for empowering collectivistic ideas during the leadership of Khomeini was Mir-Hossien Mousavi the Prime Minister (1981–1989) of Iran who was interested in a command economy. It is noteworthy that prior to the amendment of constitutional law in 1989, the prime minister had more power than the president. After the amendment, however, the position of prime minster was totally removed thus the presidential position became the second highest position after the supreme leadership. Furthermore, two decades out from the 1979 revolution Mir-Hossien Mousavi changed his mind markedly and became interested in further opening up to political, economic and cultural spaces in Iran. In 2009, when he stood as a candidate in the presidential election, he protested against the result because he believed that the voting had been rigged. His protest was supported by a movement called the Green Movement, which, in the beginning, was led by him and his wife, Mrs. Zahra Rahnavard and the other presidential candidate, Mehdi Karroubi. Since February 2011, they have all been under house arrest.

Since Khomeini's death in 1989, two different schools of jurisprudential Islam (namely divine legitimacy and popular legitimacy schools) have evolved as the two major political players in Iran. The interpretation that they yield of Khomeini's actions and the constitution differ from each other. In general, advocates of the divine legitimacy school have sought to stress the collective nature of Khomeini's ideas. The popular legitimacy school, on the other hand, have put greater emphasis on the individualistic side of his ideas. For instance, the domestic public policy adopted by Hojatolieslam wal-muslemin Akbar Hashemi Rafsanjani (1989–1997) during his eight years of presidency was targeted at providing more space for a free market economy (Abrahamian 2008, p. 183). In terms of foreign policy, he sought to establish good relations with the Western countries as well as Muslim countries. In general, he oscillated between the two jurisprudential schools, namely divine legitimacy and popular legitimacy schools. However, in his later life he was one of the supporters of the popular legitimacy school.

As far as domestic policy is concerned, during the tenure of President Hojatoleslam wal-muslemin Seyed Mohammad Khatami (1997–2005), the emphasis was placed on the rule of law, civil society, political pluralism and women's rights, while he also advocated for the provision of wider cultural, economic and political activities. With regard to foreign policy, he was a supporter of good relations with the East, the West and Muslim countries. Furthermore, when delivering a speech in the UN, in 1998, he proposed, for the first time, the notion of dialogue between civilisations, which was in strong contrast to the concept of the clash of civilisations that had been proposed previously (Abrahamian 2008, pp. 185–193). Interestingly, the UN named 2001 as the year of dialogue between civilisations.

Khatami could be thought of as a reformist and supporter of the popular legitimacy schools. It is noteworthy that around the end of his presidency, Iran and the US cooperated to remove Taliban fighters from the government of Afghanistan. This situation continued up to the time the US president, George W. Bush, described Iran and North Korea as an axis of evil and promised retaliation (Abrahamian 2008, pp. 192–193). President Khatami sought to reduce the tension with US through his foreign policy; however, the followers of divine legitimacy school denounced him for approaching the US stating that it was not a trustworthy state with which one could collaborate or negotiate.

In contrast, the next president, Mahmoud Ahmadinejad (2005–2013) had ideas that were closer to those of the divine legitimacy school, particularly in his first six years of presidency. However, during his last two years, he came into periodic and serious conflict with other Iranian government officials (namely the supreme leader, the judiciary and the parliament). This ultimately led to his excommunication by the followers of the divine legitimacy school. In general, he supported collectivist ideas in the realm of politics and the free market in the realm of economics.

A radical and populist figure, Ahmadinejad promised an improvement in social justice services for the masses, a reduction in government corruption and a campaign against poverty and unemployment, in his election campaign (Abrahamian 2008, pp. 193–194). However, he had little success due to his mismanagement and the incompetence of his cabinet. These were exacerbated by the impact of international sanctions imposed on due to Iran's nuclear activities. As far as foreign policy was concerned, Ahmadinejad generated much tension between Iran and the Western counties.

Hojatoleslam wal-muslemin Hassan Rouhani, the President of Iran from 2013 has swayed between the divine legitimacy and popular legitimacy schools with a tendency towards the latter. He is a pragmatic character who managed to make a deal with six powerful countries over Iran's nuclear programme and with the support of the current supreme leader of Iran. Additionally, since Rouhani became president strict sanctions imposed by the US have eased and the economic situation of Iran has improved. With regard to foreign policy, he seeks good relations with Western, Eastern and Muslim countries. After the second round of presidential election in 2017, he was once again re-elected by the Iranian people. However, the new president of the United States of America Donald Trump pulled out from the international nuclear deal and implemented catastrophic sanctions on Iran again. Due to these sanctions, Iran has been faced with some important problems especially with regard to the livelihoods and living standards of the ordinary folk of Iran.

Since 1989, Ayatollah Sayyed Ali Hosseini Khamenei has served as the supreme leader of Iran. This makes him the most powerful person in the Iranian government based on the constitutional law. His perspectives also move between the popular legitimacy and divine legitimacy schools (Tables 10.4 and 10.5).

Table 10.4   Domestic public policy

A definitive comparison and contrast between Khomeini, Shariati and Bazargan	
Similarities	The crises of water resources, environmental issues, the pension fund, the state budget, the banking system and unemployment are six of the **major challenges** the Iranian economy is facing
	The current growing crisis faced by Iran is the **brain drain crisis**. In which some gifted and talented intellectuals emigrate to other countries for a better life
	Iran is presently facing serious **social issues** such as increasing drug addiction, growth in divorce rates, increased poverty and an unprecedented rise in the number of prison inmates
	Currently, the economy is highly dependent on **petroleum**. The number of exports is very little beyond the petroleum industry. On top of this the Iranian **taxation system** is flawed
	There is also a small and poorly resourced **private sector**, meaning that most of the economy is that of the **public sector** giving the government excessive control
Differences	**The relationship between religion and state** The followers of Bazargan, Shariati and the popular legitimacy school, defend a religious government which looks to theology or guidance The divine legitimacy school however support an interconnected and theologically based government, where religion and state are one and the same
	The role of women in society The followers of Bazargan, Shariati and the popular legitimacy school support the presence of a greater number of women in government roles In contrast the divine legitimacy school supports the idea that women are better suited for conducting and looking after family affairs
	The role of humanities and social sciences The followers of Bazargan, Shariati and the popular legitimacy school believed the humanities and social sciences are universal although in some cases are subject to nativism. However, the divine legitimacy school believed that the basis of Western humanities was materialistic which was not consistent with religious principles, as it was based upon non-monotheistic beliefs, which were not compatible with Islamic principles. The humanities and social sciences would only then be the correct, useful and an educator of human integrity, when based on divine thought and divine vision

(continued)

Table 10.4 (continued)

A definitive comparison and contrast between Khomeini, Shariati and Bazargan

Revolutionary and reformist ideas
The followers of Bazargan, Shariati and the popular legitimacy school support a both revolutionary and reformist Iran though leaning predominantly towards reformist ideas
However, the divine legitimacy school solely support the revolutionary ideas for contemporary Iran

Authority and democracy
The followers of Bazargan, Shariati and the popular legitimacy school believe in representative policies and support the open space for economic, cultural, social and political atmospheres in Iran
However, the divine legitimacy school believe in policies that compressively centralise the organs of power, especially for the supreme leader of Iran

The role of secularism in government
The popular legitimacy school support a mixture of secularism and religion in the Iranian government
The divine legitimacy school repudiate all aspects of secularism for Iran, as they believe that religion should rule the state
However, Bazargan and Shariati's followers support the political secularism for Iran and disagree with the rule of Jurisconsults and Jurisprudentialists. They support a change of constitution in Iran with gradual reformation

The role of military forces within politics
The followers of Bazargan, Shariati and the popular legitimacy school disagree with the involvement of military institutions in economics and politics especially the Islamic revolutionary guard corps; however, they are opposed to their reduction and labelling them as terrorists the way the US has

Table 10.5   Foreign public policy

A definitive comparison and contrast between Khomeini, Shariati and Bazargan

Similarities	**Expansion of ties** with the eastern and neighbouring countries of Iran and some European countries too
	Iran is a powerful country and should maintain an effective role in the **Middle East region**
Differences	Khomeini and Shariati tended towards a **global Islamic civilisation** Bazargan leaned towards **Islamic liberal nationalism**
	The divine legitimacy supports the **Axis of Resistance** (referring to an anti-American, anti-Saudi Arabian and anti-Israeli alliance between Iran, Syria, the Houthi movement in Yemen, the Lebanese militant group Hezbollah and the Iraqi Popular Mobilization Forces). Interestingly, a very small minority of Shia jurists support the **initiative jihad**. They say that during the Iran–Iraq (1980–1988) war the conflict was within our borders and that cannot happen again and so therefore the wars and/or our military forces must remain near their borders now The popular legitimacy school also support the balance of power in the Middle East area and support **defensive jihad**
	Followers of the popular legitimacy school of Bazargan and Shariati support the **Iran nuclear deal** and would like for this arrangement to **reduce tensions** within the Middle East region and lead to a de-escalation of the current conflicts with the US. Iran should adapt itself to evolving **global realities** Most of the divine legitimacy school do not believe in **negotiations** in the Middle East and claim that the **US** has pulled out of this agreement in the past, repeatedly. They believe therefore that the Americans are not to be trusted
	The divine legitimacy school prefers and has a tendency to form relationships with **eastern nations**, especially Russia and China, however the popular legitimacy school prefers and has a tendency to form relationships with **Western nations**, especially European countries

REFERENCES

Abrahamian, E. (1982). *Iran between two revolutions*. Princeton, NJ: Princeton University Press.

Abrahamian, E. (2008). *A history of modern Iran*. New York, NY: Cambridge University Press.

Aghajari, S. H. (2003). *Shariati Motofaker Farda* [Shariati a thinker of the future]. Tehran, Iran: Moase nashr va tahghighat zekr.

Ahmadi, H. (2004). *Az Frasoyeh Marzha* [Beyond Overseas]. Tehran, Iran: Entesharat Ghasidehsra.

Ahmadi, H. (2014). *Armanhayeh enghelab mashroteh* [The ideals of the constitutional revolution]. Retrieved from http://www.azariha.org/?lang=fa&muid =38&item=263

Bazargan, M. (2014). *Padideh Pyambari* [Phenomenon of Prophecy] (Vol. 27). Tehran, Iran: Sherkat Shami Enteshar.

Boroujerdi, M. (1996). *Iranian Intellectuals and the West: The Tormented Triumph of Nativism*: Syracuse University Press.

Esposito, J. L., & Voll, J. O. (1996). *Islam and democracy*. Oxford, England: Oxford University Press.

Feirahi, D. (2015). *Islam siasi va Tahavolat Khavar Miyanh (Evolution of political Islam in the Middle East)* Retrieved from http://www.feirahi.ir/?article=252

Ferasatkhah, M. (2009). *Saraghaz Noandishi Moaser* [The beginning of contemporary modernity]. Tehran, Iran: Sherkat sahami enteshar.

Foran, J. (1993). *Fragile resistance: Social transformation in Iran from 1500 to the revolution*. Boulder, CO: Westview Press.

Hosainizadeh, S. M. A. (2007). *Islam siasi dar Iran* [Political Islam in Iran]. Qom, Iran: Mofid University.

Jahanbakhsh, F. (2001). *Islam, democracy and religious modernism in Iran, 1953–2000: From Bāzargān to Soroush*. Leiden, The Netherlands: Brill.

Keddie, N. R., & Richard, Y. (1981). *Roots of revolution: An interpretive history of modern Iran*. New Haven, CT: Yale University Press.

Khomeini, S. R. (2010a). *Sahifeh Imam: Majmoe asar Imam Khomeini bayanat, payamha, mosahebeha, ahkam, ejazat sharei va nameha* [Sahifeh-Ye Imam: An anthology of Imam Khomeini's speeches, messages, interviews, decrees, religious permissions, and letters] (Vol. 5). Tehran, Iran: Institute for Compilation and Publication of Imam Khomeini's Works.

Khomeini, S. R. (2010b). *Sahifeh Imam: Majmoe asar Imam Khomeini bayanat, payamha, mosahebeha, ahkam, ejazat sharei va nameha* [Sahifeh-Ye Imam: An anthology of Imam Khomeini's speeches, messages, interviews, decrees, religious permissions, and letters] (Vol. 11). Tehran: Institute for Compilation and Publication of Imam Khomeini's Works.

Khomeini, S. R. (2010c). *Sahifeh Imam: Majmoe asar Imam Khomeini bayanat, payamha, mosahebeha, ahkam, ejazat sharei va nameha* [Sahifeh-Ye Imam: An anthology of Imam Khomeini's speeches, messages, interviews, decrees, religious permissions, and letters] (Vol. 7). Tehran, Iran: Institute for Compilation and Publication of Imam Khomeini's Works.

Khomeini, S. R. (2010d). *Sahifeh Imam: Majmoe asar Imam Khomeini bayanat, payamha, mosahebeha, ahkam, ejazat sharei va nameha* [Sahifeh-Ye Imam: An anthology of Imam Khomeini's speeches, messages, interviews, decrees, religious permissions, and letters] (Vol. 8). Tehran, Iran: The Institute for Compilation and Publication of Imam Khomeini's Works.

Manoochehri, A. (2011). *Nazariyehai Enghelab* [Theories of Revolution]. Tehran, Iran: Entesharat Samt.

Nasim Bidari. (2015, July 10). Shabcheragh [Night Lights]. Interview with Ehsan Shariati. *Nasim Bidari.* Retrieved from http://www.yazdfarda.com/news/1395/03/107294.html

Pedram, M. (2004). *Theologians and modern intellectuals in post-Iranian revolution.* Tehran, Iran: Gaam-e Naw Press.

Sadra, M. (2012). *Barasi taamol rohaniyat va andishehai chap dar doreh moaser (The interaction of the clergies and left ideas in the contemporary era).* Baqir al-Olum, Qom, Iran.

Shariati, A. (1980). *Tarikh tamadon* [History of civilization] (Vol. 12). Tehran, Iran: Daftare Tanzim va Nashre Asar Shariati.

Shariati, A. (2011). *Ali* (Vol. 26). Tehran, Iran: Nashr Amon.

Shariati, E. (2016). Modafe Pedar [The Defender of Father]. In M. Tohidi & A. Shamlo (Eds.). Tehran, Iran: Shargh Newspaper.

Soroush, A. (2005). *Az Shariati* [From Shariati]. Tehran, Iran: Moasesh Farhangi Serat.

Vahdat, F. (2002). *God and juggernaut: Iran's intellectual encounter with modernity.* Syracuse, NY: Syracuse University Press.

REFERENCES

Abrahamian, E. (1982). *Iran between two revolutions*. Princeton, NJ: Princeton University Press.

Abrahamian, E. (2008). *A history of modern Iran*. New York, NY: Cambridge University Press.

Aghajari, S. H. (2003). *Shariati Motofaker Farda* [Shariati a thinker of the future]. Tehran, Iran: Moase nashr va tahghighat zekr.

Ahmadi, H. (2004). *Az Frasoyeh Marzha* [Beyond Overseas]. Tehran, Iran: Entesharat Ghasidehsra.

Ahmadi, H. (2014). *Armanhayeh enghelab mashroteh* [The ideals of the constitutional revolution]. Retrieved from http://www.azariha.org/?lang=fa&muid=38&item=263

Amirahmadi, H., & Parvin, M. (1988). *Post-Revolutionary Iran*. Boulder, CO: Westview Press.

Arjomand, S. A. (2009). *After Khomeini: Iran Under His Successors*. New York, NY: Oxford University Press.

Ayubi, N. N. (1991). *Political Islam: Religion and politics in the Arab world*. London, England: Routledge.

Bashiriyeh, H. (2002). *An introduction to the political sociology of Iran: The era of the Islamic republic*. Tehran, Iran: Negah-e Moaser Press.

Bashiriyeh, H. (2012). *Tarikh Andishehai Sisasi dar Gharn Bistom* [History of political thought in the twentieth century] (Vol. 1). Tehran, Iran: Nashr Nay.

Bazargan, M. (1963). *Marz bin din va sisasat* [The frontier between religion and policy]. Tehran, Iran: Bina.

© The Author(s) 2020
S. M. Lolaki, *Diverging Approaches of Political Islamic Thought in Iran since the 1960s*,
https://doi.org/10.1007/978-981-15-0478-5

Bazargan, M. (1985). *Bazyabi arzeshha* [Regaining values]. Tehran, Iran: Enteshrate Nehzate Azadi.

Bazargan, M. (1998). *Besat* [Prophetic mission] (Vol. 1–22). Tehran, Iran: Bonyad Bazargan.

Bazargan, M. (1999). *Mabahes elmi ejtemae Islami* [Scientific, social, Islamic controversy] (Vol. 8). Tehran, Iran: Sherkat Sahami Enteshar.

Bazargan, M. (2005). *Mabahes Eteghadi va Ejtemaei* [Theological and Social issues] (Vol. 11). Tehran, Iran: Sherkat Sahami Enteshar.

Bazargan, M. (2006). *Modafeat* [Court Defenses] (Vol. 6). Tehran, Iran: Sherkat Shami Enteshar.

Bazargan, M. (2007). *Mghalat Eteghdi va Ejtemaei* [Articles Believe and Social] (Vol. 16). Tehran, Iran: Sherkat Shami Enteshar.

Bazargan, M. (2008). *Koba, Hendostan, Iran* [Cuba, India, Iran] (Vol. 15). Tehran, Iran: Sherkat Shami Enteshar.

Bazargan, M. (2009a). *Bazgast be Quran (1)* [Returning to the Quran (1)] (Vol. 18). Tehran, Iran: Sherkat Sahami Enteshar.

Bazargan, M. (2009b). *Besat* [Prophetic mission] (Vol. 2). Tehran, Iran: Glam.

Bazargan, M. (2009c). *Besat (2)* [Prophetic mission (2)] (Vol. 17). Tehran, Iran: Sherkat Shami Enteshar.

Bazargan, M. (2009d). *Enghelab Eslami Iran (1)* [Islamic Revolution in Iran (1)] (Vol. 22). Tehran, Iran: Sherkat Shami Enteshar.

Bazargan, M. (2009e). *Mbahes Bonyadin* [Fundamental Topics] (Vol. 1). Tehran, Iran: Entesharat Ghlam.

Bazargan, M. (2010a). *Bazyabi Arzesha* [Recovery values] (Vol. 26). Tehran, Iran: Sherkat Shami Enteshar.

Bazargan, M. (2010b). *Bazyabi Arzesha (1)* [Recovery values (1)] (Vol. 25). Tehran, Iran: Sherkat Shami Enteshar.

Bazargan, M. (2011). *Maghalat Ejtemaei va Fani* [Social and Technical Articles] (Vol. 4). Tehran, Iran: Sherkat Shami Enteshar.

Bazargan, M. (2012). *Enghelab Eslami Iran (3)* [Islamic Revolution in Iran (3)] (Vol. 24). Tehran, Iran: Sherkat Shami Enteshar.

Bazargan, M. (2014). *Padideh Pyambari* [Phenomenon of Prophecy] (Vol. 27). Tehran, Iran: Sherkat Shami Enteshar.

Beinin, J., & Stork, J. (1997). *Political Islam: Essays from Middle East report.* Berkeley, CA: University of California Press.

Boroujerdi, M. (1996). *Iranian Intellectuals and the West: The Tormented Triumph of Nativism*: Syracuse University Press.

Byaniyeh Ayatollah Golpayagani dabreh Pishnevis Ghanon Asasi [The statement of Grand Ayatollah Golpayagani about the draft of constitutional law]. (1979, July 22). *Jomhori Islami*, p. 4.

Byaniyeh Jonbesh Mosalmanan Mobarez darbreh Pishnevis Ghanon Asasi [The statement of militant Muslims movement about the draft constitutional law]. (1979, August 8). *Omat*, p. 7.

Dabashi, H. (2006). *Theology of discontent: The ideological foundation of the Islamic revolution in Iran.* New Brunswick, NJ: Transaction Publishers.

Didgahhai Enteghadi darbreh Pishnevis Ghanon Asasi [The critical views to the draft of constitutional law]. (1979, August 6). *Nashriyeh Mojahed,* p. 6.

Edareh Kol Omor Farhangi Va Rvabet Omomi Majles Shorai Islami. (1985a). *Sorat Mashroh Mozakerat Majles Baresi Nhaei Ghanon Asasi Jomhori Islami* [The Final Review of Constitutional Law of Islamic Republic] (Vol. 2). Tehran, Iran: Edareh Kol Omor Farhangi Va Rvabet Omomi Majles Shorai Islami.

Edareh Kol Omor Farhangi Va Rvabet Omomi Majles Shorai Islami. (1985b). *Sorat Mashroh Mozakerat Majles Baresi Nhaei Ghanon Asasi Jomhori Islami* [The Final Review of Constitutional Law of Islamic Republic] (Vol. 1). Tehran, Iran: Edareh Kol Omor Farhangi Va Rvabet Omomi Majles Shorai Islami.

Edareh Kol Omor Farhangi Va Rvabet Omomi Majles Shorai Islami. (1985c). *Sorat Mashroh Mozakerat Majles Baresi Nhaei Ghanon Asasi Jomhori Islami* [The Final Review of Constitutional Law of Islamic Republic] (Vol. 4). Tehran, Iran: Edareh Kol Omor Farhangi Va Rvabet Omomi Majles Shorai Islami.

Edareh Kol Omor Farhangi Va Rvabet Omomi Majles Shorai Islami. (1990). *Sorat Mashroh Mozakerat Shuorai Baznegari Ghanon Asasi* [The Revision of the Constitutional Law]. Tehran, Iran: Edareh Kol Omor Farhangi Va Rvabet Omomi Majles Shorai Islami.

Esposito, J. L., & Voll, J. O. (1996). *Islam and democracy.* Oxford, England: Oxford University Press.

Feirahi, D. (2010). *Din va Dolat dar Asr Modern (2)* [Religion and State in Modern Age (2)] (Vol. 2). Tehran, Iran: Rokhdad No.

Feirahi, D. (2012). *Nezam Sisasi va Dolat dar Islam* [Political System and State in Islam]. Tehran, Iran: Enteshrat Samt.

Feirahi, D. (2014). *Fiqh va Siyasat dar Iran Moaser* [Jurisprudence and politics in contemporary of Iran] (Vol. 2). Tehran, Iran: Nashr Nei.

Feirahi, D. (2015). *Islam siasi va Tahavolat Khavar Miyanh (Evolution of political Islam in the Middle East)* Retrieved from http://www.feirahi.ir/?article=252

Ferasatkhah, M. (2009). *Saraghaz Noandishi Moaser* [The beginning of contemporary modernity]. Tehran, Iran: Sherkat sahami enteshar.

Foran, J. (1993). *Fragile resistance: Social transformation in Iran from 1500 to the revolution.* Boulder, CO: Westview Press.

Fuller, G. E. (2003). *The future of political Islam.* New York, NY: Palgrave.

Gellner, E. (1992). *Postmodernism, reason and religion.* London, England: Routledge.

Ghazi Shariat Panahi, S. A. (2005). *Bayestehai Ghanon Asasi* [Necessary for the Constitutional Law]. Tehran, Iran: Mizan.

Gilles, K. (2002). *Jihad: The trail of political Islam.* Cambridge, MA: Harvard University Press.

Grousset, R., & Deniker, G. (1955). *La face de l'Asie.* Paris: Payot.

Hashemi, S. M. (1995). *Hoghogh Asasi Jomhori Islami Iran* [The fundamental rights of the Islamic Republic of Iran] (Vol. 1). Tehran, Iran: Daneshgah Shahid Beheshti.

Heywood, A. (1998). *Political ideologies: An introduction* (2nd ed.). New York, NY: Palgrave.

Heywood, A. (2012). *Political ideologies: An introduction* (5th ed.). New York, NY: Palgrave Macmillan.

Hosainizadeh, S. M. A. (2007). *Islam siasi dar Iran* [Political Islam in Iran]. Qom, Iran: Mofid University.

Hosseini Beheshti, S. M. (2012). *Mabani Nazari Ghanon Asasi* [The Theoretical Foundations of Constitutional Law] (Vol. 3). Tehran, Iran: Entesharat Bogheh.

Hosseini Beheshti, S. M. (2013). *Hezb Jomhori Eslami (Goftarha, Goftegoha va Neveshtarha)* [Islamic Republican Party (Speeches, Talks and Texts)]. Tehran, Iran: Entesharat Rozaneh.

Jahanbakhsh, F. (2001). *Islam, democracy and religious modernism in Iran, 1953–2000: From Bāzargān to Soroush.* Leiden, The Netherlands: Brill.

Javadi Amoli, A. (2012). *Velayat-e Faghih Velayat-e Feghahat va Edalat* [The Guardianship of Jurisconsult the Guardianship of Jurisprudence and Justice]. Qom, Iran: Nashre Asrae.

Johnson, P. (2013). *The Renaissance: A short history.* London, England: Phoenix.

Kadivar, M. (2001). *Hokomat Velaei* [Theocratic State]. Tehran, Iran: Nashr Nay.

Kadivar, M. (2012, 2016). *Seir Tahavol Andisheh Ayatollah Montazeri ghesmat chaharom [The Evolution of Thought Ayatollah Montazeri Part 4]* Retrieved from http://mkadivar.wpengine.com/?p=4013

Katoziyan, N. (2001). *Gami besoye Edalat* [A step toward Justice] (Vol. 1). Tehran, Iran: Entesharat Daneshgah Tehran.

Keddie, N. R., & Richard, Y. (1981). *Roots of revolution: An interpretive history of modern Iran.* New Haven, CT: Yale University Press.

Khomeini, S. R. (1998). *Resaleh Ejtehad va Taghlid* [Ijtihad and imitation paper]. Tehran, Iran: The Institute for Compilation and Publication of Imam Khomeini's Works.

Khomeini, S. R. (2000). *Velayt Faghih* [Islamic Government: Governance of the Jurist]. Tehran, Iran: Institute for Compilation and Publication of Imam Khomeini's Works.

Khomeini, S. R. (2010a). *Sahifeh Imam: Majmoe asar Imam Khomeini bayanat, payamha, mosahebeha, ahkam, ejazat sharei va nameha* [Sahifeh-Ye Imam: An anthology of Imam Khomeini's speeches, messages, interviews, decrees, religious permissions, and letters] (Vol. 1). Tehran, Iran: The Institute for Compilation and Publication of Imam Khomeini's Works.

Khomeini, S. R. (2010b). *Sahifeh Imam: Majmoe asar Imam Khomeini bayanat, payamha, mosahebeha, ahkam, ejazat sharei va nameha* [Sahifeh-Ye Imam: An anthology of Imam Khomeini's speeches, messages, interviews, decrees, religious permissions, and letters] (Vol. 16). Tehran, Iran: The Institute for Compilation and Publication of Imam Khomeini's Works.

Khomeini, S. R. (2010c). *Sahifeh Imam: Majmoe asar Imam Khomeini bayanat, payamha, mosahebeha, ahkam, ejazat sharei va nameha* [Sahifeh-Ye Imam: An anthology of Imam Khomeini's speeches, messages, interviews, decrees, religious permissions, and letters] (Vol. 17). Tehran, Iran: The Institute for Compilation and Publication of Imam Khomeini's Works.

Khomeini, S. R. (2010d). *Sahifeh Imam: Majmoe asar Imam Khomeini bayanat, payamha, mosahebeha, ahkam, ejazat sharei va nameha* [Sahifeh-Ye Imam: An anthology of Imam Khomeini's speeches, messages, interviews, decrees, religious permissions, and letters] (Vol. 19). Tehran, Iran: The Institute for Compilation and Publication of Imam Khomeini's Works.

Khomeini, S. R. (2010e). *Sahifeh Imam: Majmoe asar Imam Khomeini bayanat, payamha, mosahebeha, ahkam, ejazat sharei va nameha* [Sahifeh-Ye Imam: An anthology of Imam Khomeini's speeches, messages, interviews, decrees, religious permissions, and letters] (Vol. 5). Tehran, Iran: Institute for Compilation and Publication of Imam Khomeini's Works.

Khomeini, S. R. (2010f). *Sahifeh Imam: Majmoe asar Imam Khomeini bayanat, payamha, mosahebeha, ahkam, ejazat sharei va nameha* [Sahifeh-Ye Imam: An anthology of Imam Khomeini's speeches, messages, interviews, decrees, religious permissions, and letters] (Vol. 11). Tehran: Institute for Compilation and Publication of Imam Khomeini's Works.

Khomeini, S. R. (2010g). *Sahifeh Imam: Majmoe asar Imam Khomeini bayanat, payamha, mosahebeha, ahkam, ejazat sharei va nameha* [Sahifeh-Ye Imam: An anthology of Imam Khomeini's speeches, messages, interviews, decrees, religious permissions, and letters] (Vol. 12). Tehran, Iran: The Institute for Compilation and Publication of Imam Khomeini's Works.

Khomeini, S. R. (2010h). *Sahifeh Imam: Majmoe asar Imam Khomeini bayanat, payamha, mosahebeha, ahkam, ejazat sharei va nameha* [Sahifeh-Ye Imam: An anthology of Imam Khomeini's speeches, messages, interviews, decrees, religious permissions, and letters] (Vol. 18). Tehran, Iran: The Institute for Compilation and Publication of Imam Khomeini's Works.

Khomeini, S. R. (2010i). *Sahifeh Imam: Majmoe asar imam Khomeini bayanat, payamha, mosahebeha, ahkam, ejazat sharei va nameha* [Sahifeh-Ye Imam: An anthology of Imam Khomeini's speeches, messages, interviews, decrees, religious permissions, and letters] (Vol. 13). Tehran, Iran: The Institute for Compilation and Publication of Imam Khomeini's Works.

Khomeini, S. R. (2010j). *Sahifeh Imam: Majmoe asar Imam Khomeini bayanat, payamha, mosahebeha, ahkam, ejazat sharei va nameha* [Sahifeh-Ye Imam: An anthology of Imam Khomeini's speeches, messages, interviews, decrees, religious permissions, and letters] (Vol. 15). Tehran, Iran: The Institute for Compilation and Publication of Imam Khomeini's Works.

Khomeini, S. R. (2010k). *Sahifeh Imam: Majmoe asar Imam Khomeini bayanat, payamha, mosahebeha, ahkam, ejazat sharei va nameha* [Sahifeh-Ye Imam: An anthology of Imam Khomeini's speeches, messages, interviews, decrees, religious permissions, and letters] (Vol. 20). Tehran, Iran: The Institute for Compilation and Publication of Imam Khomeini's Works.

Khomeini, S. R. (2010l). *Sahifeh Imam: Majmoe asar Imam Khomeini bayanat, payamha, mosahebeha, ahkam, ejazat sharei va nameha* [Sahifeh-Ye Imam: An anthology of Imam Khomeini's speeches, messages, interviews, decrees, religious permissions, and letters] (Vol. 2). Tehran, Iran: The Institute for Compilation and Publication of Imam Khomeini's Works.

Khomeini, S. R. (2010m). *Sahifeh Imam: Majmoe asar Imam Khomeini bayanat, payamha, mosahebeha, ahkam, ejazat sharei va nameha* [Sahifeh-Ye Imam: An anthology of Imam Khomeini's speeches, messages, interviews, decrees, religious permissions, and letters] (Vol. 3). Tehran, Iran: The Institute for Compilation and Publication of Imam Khomeini's Works.

Khomeini, S. R. (2010n). *Sahifeh Imam: Majmoe asar Imam Khomeini bayanat, payamha, mosahebeha, ahkam, ejazat sharei va nameha* [Sahifeh-Ye Imam: An anthology of Imam Khomeini's speeches, messages, interviews, decrees, religious permissions, and letters] (Vol. 4). Tehran, Iran: The Institute for Compilation and Publication of Imam Khomeini's Works.

Khomeini, S. R. (2010o). *Sahifeh Imam: Majmoe asar Imam Khomeini bayanat, payamha, mosahebeha, ahkam, ejazat sharei va nameha* [Sahifeh-Ye Imam: An anthology of Imam Khomeini's speeches, messages, interviews, decrees, religious permissions, and letters] (Vol. 6). Tehran, Iran: The Institute for Compilation and Publication of Imam Khomeini's Works.

Khomeini, S. R. (2010p). *Sahifeh Imam: Majmoe asar Imam Khomeini bayanat, payamha, mosahebeha, ahkam, ejazat sharei va nameha* [Sahifeh-Ye Imam: An anthology of Imam Khomeini's speeches, messages, interviews, decrees, religious permissions, and letters] (Vol. 7). Tehran, Iran: Institute for Compilation and Publication of Imam Khomeini's Works.

Khomeini, S. R. (2010q). *Sahifeh Imam: Majmoe asar imam Khomeini bayanat, payamha, mosahebeha, ahkam, ejazat sharei va nameha* [Sahifeh-Ye Imam: An anthology of Imam Khomeini's speeches, messages, interviews, decrees, religious permissions, and letters] (Vol. 10). Tehran, Iran: The Institute for Compilation and Publication of Imam Khomeini's Works.

Khomeini, S. R. (2010r). *Sahifeh Imam: Majmoe asar Imam Khomeini bayanat, payamha, mosahebeha, ahkam, ejazat sharei va nameha* [Sahifeh-Ye Imam: An anthology of Imam Khomeini's speeches, messages, interviews, decrees, religious permissions, and letters] (Vol. 14). Tehran, Iran: The Institute for Compilation and Publication of Imam Khomeini's Works.

Khomeini, S. R. (2010s). *Sahifeh Imam: Majmoe asar Imam Khomeini bayanat, payamha, mosahebeha, ahkam, ejazat sharei va nameha* [Sahifeh-Ye Imam: An anthology of Imam Khomeini's speeches, messages, interviews, decrees, religious permissions, and letters] (Vol. 8). Tehran, Iran: The Institute for Compilation and Publication of Imam Khomeini's Works.

Khomeini, S. R. (2010t). *Sahifeh Imam: Majmoe asar Imam Khomeini bayanat, payamha, mosahebeha, ahkam, ejazat sharei va nameha* [Sahifeh-Ye Imam: An anthology of Imam Khomeini's speeches, messages, interviews, decrees, religious permissions, and letters] (Vol. 21). Tehran, Iran: The Institute for Compilation and Publication of Imam Khomeini's Works.

Khomeini, S. R. (2010u). *Sahifeh Imam: Majmoe asar imam Khomeini bayanat, payamha, mosahebeha, ahkam, ejazat sharei va nameha* [Sahifeh-Ye Imam: An anthology of Imam Khomeini's speeches, messages, interviews, decrees, religious permissions, and letters] (Vol. 9). Tehran, Iran: The Institute for Compilation and Publication of Imam Khomeini's Works.

Khomeini, S. R. M. M. (1942). *Kashf al asrar* [Key to the secrets]. Qom, Iran: Bita.

Khomeini, S. R. M. M. (1965a). *Ketab baie* [Book of social dealings] (Vol. 2). Qom, Iran: Bita.

Khomeini, S. R. M. M. (1965b). *Ketab baie* [Book of social dealings] (Vol. 1). Qom, Iran: Bita.

Khomeini, S. R. M. M. (1965c). *Tahrir al-vasileh* [Commentary on the vehicle] (Vol. 1). Qom, Iran: Bita.

Khomeini, S. R. M. M. (1996a). *Sahife- ye- Noor* [The lighting page] (Vol. 4). Tehran, Iran: Ministry of Culture and Islamic Guidance.

Khomeini, S. R. M. M. (1996b). *Sahife- ye- Noor* [The lighting page] (Vol. 3). Tehran, Iran: Ministry of Culture and Islamic Guidance.

Khomeini, S. R. M. M. (1996c). *Sahife- ye- Noor* [The lighting page] (Vol. 16). Tehran, Iran: Ministry of Culture and Islamic Guidance.

Manoochehri, A. (2011). *Nazariyehai Enghelab* [Theories of Revolution]. Tehran, Iran: Entesharat Samt.

McLellan, D. (1986). *Ideology*. Milton Keynes: Open University Press.

Mesbah Yazdi, M. T. (2010a). *Porshesha va Pasokhha* [Questions and Answers] (Vol. 2). Qom, Iran: Entesharat Moasesh Amozeshi va Pazhoheshi Imam Khomeini.

Mesbah Yazdi, M. T. (2010b). *Porshesha va Pasokhha* [Questions and Answers] (Vol. 1). Qom, Iran: Entesharat Moasesh Amozeshi va Pazhoheshi Imam Khomeini.

Mesbah Yazdi, M. T. (2011). *Negahi Gozara be Nazariyeh Velayat-e Faghih* [A glance at the Theory of the Guardianship of Jurisconsult]. Qom, Iran: Entesharat Moasesh Amozeshi va Pazhoheshi Imam Khomeini.

Milani, M. M. (1994). *The making of Iran's Islamic revolution: From monarchy to Islamic republic*. Boulder, CO: Westview Press.

Mirsepassi, A. (2000). *Intellectual discourse and the politics of modernization: Negotiating modernity in Iran*. Cambridge, MA: Cambridge University Press.

Moin, B. (2000). *Khomeini: Life of the Ayatollah.* New York, NY: Thomas Dunne Books.

Momen, M. (1995). Velayate Elahi va Hokomat Islami (1) [Divine Guardianship and Islamic State (1)]. *Majaleh Fiqh Ahl Biyt Elahemosalam, 47,* 13–49.

Momen, M. (1999). Beiat (1) Adlei Beiat dar Quran [Allegiance (1) the Evidence of allegiance on the Quran]. *Majaleh Fiqh Ahl Biyt Elahemosalam, 51,* 34–61.

Momen, M. (2000). Din va Mosharekat Sisasi [Religion and Political Participation]. *Faslnameh Olom Sisasi, 7,* 12–19.

Momen, M. (2007). Maliyat dar Hokomat Islami [Tax in the Islamic State]. *Majaleh Fiqh Ahl Biyt Elahemosalam, 45,* 3–26.

Momen, M. (2009a). Ekhtiyar Valy-e Amr dar Ghanongozari [The Authority of Stewardship about legislation]. *Majaleh Fiqh Ahl Biyt Elahemosalam, 55,* 80–91.

Momen, M. (2009b). Ghavanin Sabet va Motoghayer [Static and Dynamic Rules]. *Majaleh Fiqh Ahl Biyt Elahemosalam, 56,* 60–81.

Montazeri, H. A. (2001a). *Khaterat* [Memoirs] (Vol. 2): Author.

Montazeri, H. A. (2001b). *Mabani Fiqhi Hokomat Islami* [The Juridical Foundations of Islamic State] (M. Salvati, Trans., Vol. 2). Tehran, Iran: Entesharat Saraei.

Montazeri, H. A. (2009a). *Enteghad az Khod* [Self Criticism]: Author.

Montazeri, H. A. (2009b). *Hokomat Dini va Hoghogh Ensan* [Theocracy and Human rights]. Tehran, Iran: Entesharat Saraei.

Mosahebeh ba Ayatollah Shariatmadari darbreh Pishnevish Ghanon Asasi [The interview about the draft of constitutional law with Grand Ayatollah Shariatmadari]. (1979, July 31). *Bamdad,* p. 9.

Mosahebeh darbreh Pishnevis Ghanon Asasi ba Yadollah Sahabi [Yadollah Sahabi interview about the draft of constitutional law]. (1979, June 16). *Kayhan,* p. 9.

Mujahidin of Islamic Revolution Organization. (1979). *Byaniyeh Shomareh 14 [The Political Party Statement 14].* Tehran, Iran: Mujahidin of Islamic Revolution Organization.

Naghdhai Ayatollah Marashi Najafi darbareh Pishnevis Ghanon Asasi [The comments of Ayatollah Marashi Najafi on the draft of constitutional law]. (1979, July 22). *Jomhori Islami,* pp. 1–2.

Naghdhai Jebhei Meli Iran darbreh Pishnevish Ghanon Asasi [The comments of The National Front of Iran on the draft of constitutional law]. (1979, July 18). *Bamdad,* pp. 1–3.

Nasim Bidari. (2015, July 10). Shabcheragh [Night Lights]. Interview with Ehsan Shariati. *Nasim Bidari.* Retrieved from http://www.yazdfarda.com/news/1395/03/107294.html

Papan-Matin, F. (2014). The Constitution of the Islamic Republic of Iran (1989 edition). *Iranian Studies, 47*(1), 159–200.

Pedram, M. (2004). *Theologians and modern intellectuals in post-Iranian revolution.* Tehran, Iran: Gaam-e Naw Press.

Plamenatz, J. (1970). *Ideology*. New York, NY: Praeger.

Possamai, A. (2009). *Sociology of religion for generations X and Y*. London, England: Equinox.

Pratt, D. (2006). Terrorism and religious fundamentalism: Prospects for a predictive paradigm. *Marburg Journal of Religion, 11* (1), 1–15. Retrieved from http://www.uni-marburg.de/fb03/ivk/mjr/pdfs/2006/articles/pratt2006.pdf

Rahnema, A. (1998). *An Islamic utopian: A political biography of Ali Shariati*. London, England: I.B. Tauris.

Rajaee, F. (2007). *Islamism and modernism: The changing discourse in Iran*. Austin, TX: University of Texas Press.

Roy, O. (1994). *The failure of political Islam*. Cambridge, MA: Harvard University Press.

Sadra, M. (2012). *Barasi taamol rohaniyat va andishehai chap dar doreh moaser (The interaction of the clergies and left ideas in the contemporary era)*. Baqir al-Olum, Qom, Iran.

Saeli Koredh Deh, M. (2005). *Shuorai Enghelab Islami Iran* [The Council of the Islamic Revolution of Iran]. Tehran, Iran: Markaz Asnad Enghelab Islami.

Sahabi, E. (2004). *Nagoftehai Enghelab va Mabahes Bonyadi Meli* [Untold Revolution and National foundamental Topics]. Tehran, Iran: Game Noe.

Salehi Najafabadi, N. (1985). *Velayat_e Faghih: Hokomat Salehan* [The Guardianship of Jurisconsult: The Righteous Government]. Qom, Iran: Moaseseh Khadamat Farhangi Rasa.

Shariati, A. (1980a). *Tarikh tamadon* [History of civilization] (Vol. 12). Tehran, Iran: Daftare Tanzim va Nashre Asar Shariati.

Shariati, A. (1980b). *Tarikh va shenakht adiyan* [History and knowledge of religion] (Vol. 15). Tehran, Iran: Bina.

Shariati, A. (1981a). *Hosein varese Adam* [Hosein Adam's heir] (Vol. 19). Tehran, Iran: Ghalam.

Shariati, A. (1981b). *Islam shenasi* [Islamology] (Vol. 16). Tehran, Iran: Ghalam.

Shariati, A. (1981c). *Omat va Imamat* [Nation and Imamate] (Vol. 26). Tehran, Iran: Ghalam.

Shariati, A. (1989). *Islam shenasi* [Islamology] (Vol. 30). Tehran, Iran: Chapakhsh.

Shariati, A. (1995). *Shie* [Shiite] (Vol. 7). Qom, Iran: Bita.

Shariati, A. (2002). *Mazhab alihe mazhab* [Religion versus religion] (Vol. 22). Tehran, Iran: Chapakhsh.

Shariati, A. (2006). *Ma va Iqbal* [We and Iqbal] (Vol. 5). Tehran, Iran: Entesharat Elham.

Shariati, A. (2007). *Khodsazi Enghelabi* [Revolutionary Self monitoring] (Vol. 2). Tehran, Iran: Enteshrat Elham.

Shariati, A. (2008a). *Ba Mokhatabhai Ashena* [With Familiar Audiences] (Vol. 1). Tehran, Iran: Enteshrat Chappakhsh va Bonyad Farhangi Doctor Ali Shariati.

Shariati, A. (2008b). *Bazgasht* [Return] (Vol. 4). Tehran, Iran: Entesharat Elham.

Shariati, A. (2008c). *Islamshenasi (3)* [Islamology (3)] (Vol. 18). Tehran, Iran: Entesharat Elham.

Shariati, A. (2009a). *Bazshenasi Hoviyat Irani Islami* [Recognition of Iranian and Islamic identity.] (Vol. 27). Tehran, Iran: Entesharat Elham.

Shariati, A. (2009b). *Miad ba Ebrahim* [The Vow with Abraham] (Vol. 29). Tehran, Iran: Enteshrat Agah.

Shariati, A. (2009c). *Shie* [Shiite] (Vol. 7). Tehran, Iran: Entesharat Elham.

Shariati, A. (2009d). *Tarikh va Shenakht Adiyan (1)* [History and Understand Religions (1)] (Vol. 14). Tehran, Iran: Sherkat Shami Enteshar.

Shariati, A. (2010a). *Hosein Varese Adam* [Hosein Adam's heir] (Vol. 19). Tehran, Iran: Entesharat Ghalam.

Shariati, A. (2010b). *Islamshenasi Mashhad* [Mashhad Islamology] (Vol. 30). Tehran: Chappakhsh.

Shariati, A. (2010c). *Jahanbini va Ideology* [Worldview and ideology] (Vol. 23). Tehran, Iran: Sherkat Shami Enteshar.

Shariati, A. (2010d). *Mazhab Alihe Mazhab* [Religion versus religion] (Vol. 22). Tehran, Iran Entesharat Chappakhsh.

Shariati, A. (2010e). *Tarikh Tamadon (1)* [History of Civilization (1)] (Vol. 11). Tehran, Iran: Entesharat Ghalam.

Shariati, A. (2010f). *Tarikh Tamadon (2)* [History of Civilization (2)] (Vol. 12). Tehran, Iran: Entesharat Ghalam.

Shariati, A. (2011a). *Ali* (Vol. 26). Tehran, Iran: Nashr Amon.

Shariati, A. (2011b). *Asar Gonagon (1)* [Various Works (1)] (Vol. 35). Tehran, Iran: Nashr Didar.

Shariati, A. (2011c). *Islamshenasi (1)* [Islamology (1)] (Vol. 16). Tehran, Iran: Glam.

Shariati, A. (2011d). *Islamshenasi (2)* [Islamology (2)] (Vol. 17). Tehran, Iran: Entesharat Ghalam.

Shariati, A. (2011e). *Jahatgiri Tabghati Islam* [The Class Orientation of Islam] (Vol. 10). Tehran, Iran: Entesharat Ghalam.

Shariati, A. (2011f). *Niyayesh* [Invocation] (Vol. 8). Tehran, Iran: Entesharat Elham.

Shariati, A. (2011g). *Tashyoe Alawi va Tashyoe Safavi* [Alawi Shiite and Safavid Shiite] (Vol. 9). Tehran, Iran: Entesharat Chappakhsh.

Shariati, A. (2011h). *Vizhehgihai Ghoron Jadid* [New Features Century] (Vol. 31). Tehran, Iran: Chappakhsh.

Shariati, A. (2011i). *Zan* [Woman] (Vol. 21). Tehran, Iran: Enteshrat Chapakhsh.

Shariati, A. (2012a). *Che Bayad Kard?* [What Must Do?] (Vol. 20). Tehran, Iran: Enteshrat Ghlam.

Shariati, A. (2012b). *Ensan* [Man] (Vol. 24). Tehran, Iran: Entesharat Elham.

Shariati, E. (2016). Modafe Pedar [The Defender of Father]. In M. Tohidi & A. Shamlo (Eds.). Tehran, Iran: Shargh Newspaper.

Soroush, A. (2005). *Az Shariati* [From Shariati]. Tehran, Iran: Moasesh Farhangi Serat.

Tabatabaei, S. (2009). *Khaterat sisasi ejtemaei doctor Sadeq Tabatabaei* [Social and Political memoirs doctor Sadeq Tabatabaei] (Vol. 3). Tehran, Iran: Nashr Oroj.

The Party of Diligent people of Iran's Nation. (1979). *Noghteh Nazrat darbreh Pishnevis Ghanon Asasi [The views on the draft of Constitutional Law]*. Tehran, Iran: The Party of Diligent people of Iran's Nation.

Tudeh Party of Iran. (1979). *Majmoeh Byanieha va Etelaeihai Hezb Tudeh Iran* [The collection of Statements and Notifications of Tudeh Party of Iran]. Tehran, Iran: Hezb Tudeh Iran.

Vahdat, F. (2002). *God and juggernaut: Iran's intellectual encounter with modernity*. Syracuse, NY: Syracuse University Press.

Vincent, A. (2010). *Modern political ideologies* (3rd ed.). Chichester, England: Wiley-Blackwell.

Yosefi Ashkevari, H. (1997). *Shariati va naghd sonnat* [Shariati and criticism of tradition]. Tehran, Iran: Yad Avaran.

Yusuf Ali, A. (2016). *Quran* [English translation]. Retrieved from http://tanzil.net/#trans/en.yusufali/1:1

INDEX

© The Author(s) 2020   233
S. M. Lolaki, *Diverging Approaches of Political Islamic Thought in
Iran since the 1960s*,
https://doi.org/10.1007/978-981-15-0478-5